Reading the Symptom

Modern American Literature
New Approaches

Yoshinobu Hakutani
General Editor

Vol. 15

PETER LANG
New York • Washington, D.C./Baltimore • Boston
Bern • Frankfurt am Main • Berlin • Vienna • Paris

Mohamed Zayani

Reading the Symptom

Frank Norris, Theodore Dreiser, and the Dynamics of Capitalism

Preface by Jean-Joseph Goux

PETER LANG
New York • Washington, D.C./Baltimore • Boston
Bern • Frankfurt am Main • Berlin • Vienna • Paris

Library of Congress Cataloging-in-Publication Data

Zayani, Mohamed.
Reading the symptom: Frank Norris, Theodore Dreiser, and the dynamics
of capitalism / Mohamed Zayani.
p. cm. — (Modern American literature: new approaches; v. 15)
Includes bibliographical references.
1. American fiction—History and criticism. 2. Naturalism in literature.
3. Capitalism and literature—United States—History. 4. Norris, Frank,
1870–1902. Vandover and the brute. 5. Dreiser, Theodore, 1871–1945.
Sister Carrie. 6. Norris, Frank, 1870–1902. McTeague. I. Title. II. Series:
Modern American literature (New York, N.Y.); vol. 15.
PS374.N29Z39   813'.40912—DC21   97-27273
ISBN 0-8204-3910-X
ISSN 1078-0521

Die Deutsche Bibliothek-CIP-Einheitsaufnahme

Zayani, Mohamed:
Reading the symptom: Frank Norris, Theodore Dreiser, and the dynamics of
capitalism / Mohamed Zayani. –New York; Washington, D.C./Baltimore;
Boston; Bern; Frankfurt am Main; Berlin; Vienna; Paris: Lang.
(Modern American literature; Vol. 15)
ISBN 0-8204-3910-X

The paper in this book meets the guidelines for permanence and durability
of the Committee on Production Guidelines for Book Longevity
of the Council of Library Resources.

© 1999 Peter Lang Publishing, Inc., New York

Printed in the United States of America.

For S. Sahraoui

ACKNOWLEDGEMENTS

I would like to thank Jonathan Elmer and Cary Wolfe for their genuine interest in this project, their invaluable suggestions, and their unfailing support. I would like also to extend my thanks to Patrick Brantlinger, Eugene Eoyang, Salah El-Moncef, and Chad Tew who shared much of their time and insights.

An earlier version of the penultimate section of chapter three appeared as "Syntactic Involutions and Negative Precipitations in Frank Norris' *McTeague*," *Language and Literature* 20 (1995): 11-18, and is reprinted here with permission. Likewise, material from chapter five appeared as a review of Paul Civello's *American Literary Naturalism and its Twentieth-Century Transformations, American Literary Realism* 29.1 (1996): 91-92, and is reprinted with permission.

TABLE OF CONTENTS

PREFACE

by Jean-Joseph Goux

The tight historical solidarity between the genre of the novel and the development of capitalism has long been recognized. Some tentative approaches, with varying degrees of depth and sophistication, have already been proposed to account for such a solidarity. At the heart of this on-going debate are several pointed questions: What new status of the individual, in his relation to society and its values, does the bourgeois world of capitalism establish, which can explain the biographical quest of the novelistic hero? How does a particular perception of the world, such as the one we find in the realism of Stendhal, Balzac, and Flaubert, or more expressly in the naturalism of Zola, become the most significant mode of representation during the nineteenth century? What pre-bourgeois literary tradition needs to be contested before this new mode of representation can establish itself and assert its legitimacy? Can one retrace and construe the changes that the novel has undergone simply by examining the history and development of capitalism over the past two centuries? Can such a pursuit shed additional light on more recent developments in the novel with regard to narration, character, plot, linear progression of time, and the like? Is it safe to assume that to each major phase in the history of capitalism corresponds a single hegemonic vision, or is it more sensible to conceive of history as a ceaseless struggle between competing visions and antagonistic articulations? It is these and other important questions which do not cease to stimulate our interest and even shake our certitude that Mohamed Zayani engages. His project addresses, head on, issues with not only aesthetic, but also ethical, political, philosophical, and sociological implications.

The methodological and analytical framework that the author meticulously develops enables him to revisit, with an informed precision, the works of two prominent figures in American literary naturalism, Frank Norris and Theodore Dreiser, who at the turn of the nineteenth century have driven the exigencies of this new vision to its limit. The central question that informs the author's project pertains to the possibility of reinscribing the logic of naturalism within the historical specificity of capitalism without necessarily falling into an economism, which confines the analysis to the explicit economic themes which pervade the naturalist novel (whether it be the fascination with gold, the demon of speculation, or the lure of the commodity).

One cannot but appreciate the degree of clarity and conceptual coherence with which the author avoids the shortcomings that have shackled even the most vigorous accounts of the period, namely the recourse to an explanatory model which embraces an economic perspective but which presents the economy as a closed system, i.e., as a category that is void of any contradiction, struggle, or negation. Distancing himself from those views that conceive of capitalism as a purely economic category, Mohamed Zayani argues that capitalism provides the socio-symbolic or the structuring whole within which naturalism is produced and from which it cannot be dissociated. At the same time, he insists that this totality, with its dynamic structure, its contradictions, and its non-economic articulations (for which the economy is nonetheless the pointed manifestation), is both more open and more complex than many critics are willing to admit.

Reading the Symptom is certainly a book that deserves attention, if for nothing else, at least for its vigorous attempt to restitute the critical force that American literary naturalism incarnates.

Jean-Joseph Goux
Lawrence Favrot Professor of French Studies at Rice University

CHAPTER ONE

American Literary Naturalism
and the Limits of Revisionism

The critical reconstruction of American literary naturalism over the past decade or so has not only refined our understanding of this movement but also broadened its historical significance. At the forefront of this ongoing revision are two provocative studies: June Howard's *Form and History in American Literary Naturalism* and Walter Benn Michaels' *The Gold Standard and the Logic of Naturalism*.[1] The juxtaposition of these two readings of naturalism is instructive because they share some fundamental assumptions. Both critics attempt to move beyond the question of reference, representation, and verisimilitude; both of them examine naturalism not for what it signifies but for what it reveals about signification itself; both of them abandon a heuristic approach in favor of a theory of literary production that situates naturalism within a certain phase in the history of capitalism. As will become clear, however, Howard's and Michaels' readings of naturalism are of particular interest not only because they share some critical perspectives but also because they epitomize, each in its own way, the limits of revisionism in its most vigorous moments. Understanding the nature of these limits can provide the basis for a more sustained reading of naturalism.

In *Form and History in American Literary Naturalism*, Howard focuses on the ways in which naturalists generated narrative out of the historical and cultural materials available to them. More specifically, she examines how certain conceptions of character, plot, and

organizational strategies in naturalism came to constitute a
development in the ideology of form that bears the mark of its
specific historical reality at the end of the nineteenth century.
Focusing on a number of issues that shaped the era (such as new
economic forces, class warfare, immigration, populism, nativism,
determinism, sensationalism, and reformism), Howard turns the
inquiry from theme to thematic—that is, from "the sheer content of a
novel" to "the organization of its semantic field that establishes its
possibilities for meaning" (40). Her argument rests on the
assumption that there is an essential connectedness between genre
criticism and historical analysis: "Literary history can be seen as the
history of forms, as the study of the continual remaking of the
possibilities of literary discourse in concrete historical circumstances
rather than the tradition of a self-contained procession of great writers
or literary movements" (9). For Howard, the explanatory power of
genre stems from its ability to mediate between the individual text or
specific features in the text and the conditions of its production.
Genre, as she puts it, is a concept that is "uniquely capable of
revealing interrelations of ideological discourses, cultural practices,
and social institutions" (10).

Howard's generic approach is largely indebted to Fredric
Jameson's Marxist cultural analysis, and more specifically to the
allegorical method adumbrated in *The Political Unconscious*.
Jameson's project probes anew the relationship between literary texts
and modes of social and economic experience. For him, a cultural
object can be satisfactorily grasped neither within the exclusivity of
the text nor within the parameters of its context but, instead, through
an examination of its subtext. Jameson's underlying premise is that
history is grounded in material reality but this reality is accessible
only through "an immanent analysis of the text" (*Political* 23). This
proposition enables him to restructure the problematic of ideology
around the all-informing process of narrative. By grasping the text as
a symbolic act, the organizing unity of which lies within the dominant
mode of production, Jameson moves from ideology *per se* to the
ideology of form: "ideology is not something that informs or invests
symbolic production; rather the aesthetic act is itself ideological, and
the production of aesthetic or narrative form is to be seen as an
ideological act in its own right, with the function of inventing
imaginary or formal 'solutions' to unresolvable social
contradictions" (*Political* 79). Far from being a retreat from social
and historical questions, the attention to the ideology of form is an
attempt to approach history through its effects: "it would seem

necessary to invent a new, historically reflexive, way of using categories, such as those of genre, which are so clearly implicated in the literary history and the formal reproduction they were traditionally supposed to classify and neutrally describe" (Jameson, *Political* 107).

Howard's attention to the ideology of form both echoes and extends Jameson's proposition: "My contention will not be that naturalism has an ideology or reflects an ideology, but that the form itself *is* an immanent ideology. It is a way of imagining the world and the relation of the self to the world, a way of making sense ... out of the comforts and discomforts of the historical moment" (ix). Setting herself apart from those critics who insist tactlessly upon a relation between literature and reality, Howard argues that the structures of representation are more complex than mere reflection. In her view, a reflexive approach can only produce a naive understanding of naturalism because it posits a direct connection between the text and the world it represents. Instead of setting literary texts against reality, she proposes to examine the ways in which "naturalism is shaped by and imaginatively reshapes a historical experience that, although it exists outside representation and narrative, we necessarily approach through texts" (70). Howard, then, rejects an empiricist theory of literary reflection in favor of a theory of literary production: "The object we know is produced by the operations of knowledge; it is the object of knowledge, which is always distinct from the real object" (27). For Howard, literary forms do not exist as essences but as effects of historically specific circumstances which in turn act as limiting conditions for literary production: "Naturalism does not provide a window into reality. Rather it reveals history indirectly in revealing *itself*—in the significant absences silouhetted by the narratives, in the ideology invoked by the very program that proclaims a transparent access to the real, in its transmutation of content into form and form into content. The search for the real must give way to the search for the historical" (29).

The non-reflexive approach that informs Howard's *Form and History in American Literary Naturalism* is also at the heart of Michaels' *The Gold Standard and the Logic of Naturalism*.[2] In order to avoid the *cul-de-sac* that has marked the critical conception of naturalism, Michaels cagily moves away from the spurious question of referentiality: "I use the term *naturalism* rather than the more general term *realism* not to help breathe new life into the old debate over what naturalism is and how it differs from realism; indeed, I hope to avoid that debate entirely... Insofar as naturalism has been continually (and plausibly) defined as a variant of realism, it has been caught up in endless theorizing about the nature and very possibility of realistic representation" (*Gold Standard* 26–27). By taking issue with the conception of literature as a direct reflection of social conditions, Michaels not only renders the question of representation irrelevant but also calls for a redefinition of the terms of the debate beyond the signifier/signified dyad. His ostensible purpose is not to identify a specific relation between literature and the real but instead to map out the reality in which certain literature finds its place. Wresting naturalism from the legacy of referentiality, he resituates it squarely within a culture of commodification. In his view, turn-of-the-century American literature is characterized above all by an unceasing and over-arching market expansion—what he calls "unrestrained capitalism" (*Gold Standard* 18)—which pervades all aspects of vital activities. To talk about the logic of naturalism is also necessarily to talk about the logic of the market.

What motivates Michaels' project, in part, are the theoretical limitations that characterize oppositional criticism. *The Gold Standard and the Logic of Naturalism* is, in many ways, a response to such cultural critics as T. J. Jackson Lears and Richard Wightman Fox, whose attempts to imagine alternative views of America posit a culture that is influenced by the needs and ideals of the powerful. Their conception of cultural hegemony in particular and social history in general rests heavily on the study of dominant elites: "accredited experts set out to manage not only the economic arena, but the rest of the social order as well" (Fox xii). The influence of this group, however, is not limited to enhancing the ethos of capitalism; the cultural elite have also attempted to mitigate its adverse effects. This is the thrust of Lears' elaborate cultural history of the period, *No Place of Grace*. Faced with a "crisis of cultural authority" and in need of revitalization through "authentic experience," turn-of-the-century American society experienced an increasing "nostalgia for the past" (Lears, *No Place* 57, 65, 102). At least among certain factions, there was a "fascination with primal, aggressive impulse" (Lears, *No Place* 137) which found its most visible outlet in the growing interest in exploring the joys and terrors of Medieval and Oriental beliefs. Over time, however, these anti-modernist trends did little more than reinforce the strains they set out to oppose. These strategies of resistance ended up not challenging capitalism but working within its fold. What started as a reaction against modernization, rationalization, and overcivilization in the waning decades of the nineteenth century gradually turned into a "therapeutic assimilation" to the culture of commodification in the early decades of the twentieth century (Lears, *No Place* 89).

From the vantage point of *The Gold Standard and the Logic of Naturalism*, Lears' emphasis on an anti-modernist strain (thwarted as it may be) is not only dubious but also misguided. It rests on the assumption that "the value of American cultural productions is understood to consist in what Lears calls their 'subversive' potential, their attempt to resist 'incorporation in the dominant culture'" (Michaels, *Gold Standard* 15). According to Michaels, Lears' argument drags behind it the cortege of a long tradition that privileges art and endows it with an oppositional value. A succinct account of the nature and origin of this traditional view can be found in Daniel Bell's *The Cultural Contradictions of Capitalism*. For Bell, one of the central contradictions of capitalism is a disjunction between the economic realm (with its principle of functional rationality) and the cultural realm (with its enfranchised ethos). Interestingly enough, although these two realms are not related to each other as cause and effect they have been intimately connected during their formative years. Concomitant with the rise of bourgeois entrepreneurship, which introduced a radical *laissez-faire* individualism into economics, is the rise of independent art, which introduced a radical experimentation in culture. Both trends were motivated by the same guiding principles, namely a repudiation of institutions and a search for independence, autonomy, and self-determination. The coming of age of capitalism, however, led to a disjunction—even an inimical relationship—between the economic and cultural realms:

> Both impulses, historically, were aspects of the same sociological surge of modernity. Together they opened up the Western world in a radical way. Yet the extraordinary paradox is that each impulse then became highly conscious of the other, feared the other and sought to destroy it. Radical in economics, the bourgeoisie became conservative in moral and cultural taste. The bourgeois economic impulse was organized into a highly restrictive character structure whose energies were channeled into the production of goods and into a set of attitudes towards work that feared instinct, spontaneity, and vagrant impulse. In the extreme Puritanism of America, laws were passed to constrain intemperate behavior, while in painting and literature, bourgeois taste ran to the heroic and banal. (Bell 17)

One of the intriguing outcomes of this disjunction is the quintessentially urban figure of the *flâneur*. In the *flâneur*'s idleness and resignation one can sense not only a suspicious attitude towards

capitalism but also an indictment of the bourgeois ethos. Walter
Benjamin has well captured this anti-bourgeois attitude. In his view,
the *flâneur*'s "leisurely appearance as a personality is his protest
against the division of labour which makes people into specialists. It
is also his protest against their industriousness.... The more conscious
he becomes of his mode of existence, the more he polarizes himself,
the more he will be gripped by the chill of the commodity economy
and the less he will feel like empathizing with commodities"
(*Baudelaire* 54–58). In the art of strolling, Benjamin sees the vigilant
consciousness of a *flâneur* whose fascination with the spectacle is
never so strong as to blind him to the horrible reality of capitalism.

An approach akin to Michaels', however, would argue that while
in appearance the *flâneur*'s nonchalance seems to oppose capitalism,
in reality it exemplifies the very passivity of the consumer in front of
the spectacle and the acquiescence of the individual in front of the
commodity. In *The Gold Standard and the Logic of Naturalism*, the
assumption that there can be a critical relationship between the artist
and his or her culture is not only put into question but reversed
altogether. The naturalist novelist cannot transcend the culture of
commodification; naturalism is not oppositional to the culture of
market-place consumption but an integral part of it. This line of
analysis leads Michaels to refute the view that Charlotte Perkins
Gilman's "The Yellow Wallpaper," for instance, has a subversive
potential. Gilman, he argues, neither criticizes nor repudiates the
culture of consumption: "Gilman's texts ... resist consumer culture
only in ways allowed by their radical acceptance of a logic of
consumption.... From this perspective, it seems much more plausible
to describe 'The Yellow Wallpaper' as an endorsement of consumer
capitalism than a critique of it" (*Gold Standard* 17). The same
observation can be extended to Dreiser's *Sister Carrie*. According to
Michaels, the claim that the novel is either an indictment or
endorsement of the market rests on a skewed premise: "What exactly
did it mean to think of Dreiser as approving (or disapproving)
consumer culture? Although transcending your origins in order to
evaluate them had been the opening move in cultural criticism ... it is
surely a mistake to take this move at face value: not so much because
you can't really transcend your culture but because, if you could, you
wouldn't have any terms of evaluation left" (*Gold Standard* 18). To
ascribe a critical value to the text or endow its author with an
oppositional stance is to posit a privileged—even utopian—space
outside culture. The question as to whether naturalist texts reflect or
criticize reality seems "to posit a space outside the culture in order

then to interrogate the relations between that space and the culture" (Michaels, *Gold Standard* 26–27).   In Michaels' account, then, naturalism is neither a progressive force motivated by what may be termed, after Richard Hofstadter, "a passion for getting the inside story" (*Age* 197) nor a "post-progressive critique of consumption" (Michaels, *Gold Standard* 17) as the work of Lears and Fox suggests; it is simply the exemplification of the logic of capitalism.

Interestingly enough, what Michaels argues at the level of culture, Howard vindicates at the level of form.   For the latter, naturalism stands out less by the position that the author takes *vis-à-vis* the issues and controversies that confront his or her society than by the proclivity of form to reproduce these issues.   The naturalist text, as Howard puts it, "preserves" (121) the contradictions that characterize the period. What is worked out at the thematic level is undone by the form's tendency to wholly shape ideological possibilities of meaning: "For Norris as for others of his period hereditary determinism offers a satisfying way of understanding individual destiny in terms of biology, social problems in terms of the evolution of species—in short, the historical as the natural. But its consequences as worked out in the narratives themselves often reinscribe the disturbing social contradictions that the abstract theories claim to resolve" (Howard 93).   Seen from this perspective, Norris' *The Octopus*, for instance, becomes important not as an unequivocal reform novel that denounces the Southern Pacific trusts but as the articulation of an anxiety—largely attributed to class dynamics—that was widely felt at the time. In *The Octopus*, the threat of social unrest which the naturalists attempted to resolve (namely the threat of the soulless corporations) is reinscribed through a reappropriation of the theme of the savage (which takes the form of the insurrectionary mob).

For Howard, the issues that absorbed naturalists do not just figure in the philosophy that their novels adumbrate; they are "inescapably implied" (117) either through a register of characterization or a pressure on plot. Although naturalist characters are often portrayed as victims who inevitably succumb to forces beyond their control, this victimization does not necessarily make them less threatening: "Whatever form it may take, whatever effort may be made to capture and control it in webs of causality or plot, the brutal Other signifies danger" (Howard 103). The vulnerability of the characters intimates a sense of insecurity which throws the reader into moments of doubt as to whether anyone can ever be safe. It is true that the reader acquires a privileged perspective, but this advantage also leaves him or her in a precarious position. This effect is particularly salient in *Sister*

Carrie. Here, Dreiser "gives us an outcast with whom we must empathize, and as we follow Hurstwood down into his abyss the distinction between self and other seems fearfully precarious.... The exemption from determinism thus itself becomes a disturbing confinement; the barrier that separates the privileged spectator from the helpless actor seems to imprison both" (Howard 101–26). As the novel unfolds, the disjunction between the realm of freedom and the realm of force becomes even more noticeable. After losing his job, Hurstwood becomes a detached character content with reading the newspapers and watching the world go by. The privileged perspective he acquires, however, is inconsequential in the sense that it leads to little or no action. Even though Hurstwood becomes gradually involved with the web of events that entangle the city, and is eventually caught up in a violent strike, the gap between contemplation and action remains, for the most part, unbridged. Exhausted and dispirited by the rough world outside, Hurstwood goes back to his apartment with a new sense of understanding but little promise for further action: "The characters who represent the understanding of the narrator and the reader inevitably find that somehow when they enter the terrain of choices and consequences, they are no longer themselves; they can never put the suggestion of their understanding into effect" (Howard 111). The threat of paralysis and immobility that haunts Hurstwood suggests that the denial of human agency in naturalism is imposed by the plot of decline that is inherent in the form itself. From this vantage point, it becomes hardly surprising to find a discrepancy between what the author writes and what appears in his or her fiction. The narrative may, in fact, reveal an immanent ideology that may not be necessarily on a par with what the writer would claim.

Underlying this proposition is a subtle distinction between the manifest content of the novel and its political unconscious, to borrow Jameson's terminology. By arguing that naturalism is bound to reproduce the very ideological conflicts and tensions it purports to resolve, Howard re-articulates Jameson's more elaborate formulation of the dynamic possibilities of the text. For the author of *The Political Unconscious*, "the literary structure, far from being completely realized on any one of its levels tilts powerfully into the underside or *impensé* or *non-dit*, in short, into the very political unconscious, of the text, such that the latter's dispersed semes ... direct us to the informing power of forces or contradictions which the text seeks in vain wholly to control" (49). This line of argument not only puts into question the critical value of the literary text, but also calls for a reconsideration of the function of literary criticism. For Jameson, as for Howard, the task of analysis does not consist in delineating the position that an author takes, but in mapping out the historical possibilities of the text or, better yet, constructing the complex structures of representation upon which the work rests: "my own analysis ... does not affirm or negate the project of naturalism but is oblique to it, as I rewrite the assertions and antinomies of naturalism in terms of historical contradictions and reconstruct its historical conditions of possibility and its intervention in those conditions" (Howard 126). The implications of this position highlight, once again, the commonality between the projects of Howard and Michaels. For both critics, reading does not consist in uncovering but constructing the meaning of history. Howard's contention that "it does not do justice to the full significance of genre to diagnose forms as progressive or reactionary, as truthful or mendacious" (Howard 22) is, in many ways, a reiteration of Michaels' claim that the spaces that literature makes available to the reader "are all very much within the culture, and so the project of interrogating them makes no sense; the only relation literature as such has to culture is that it is part of it" (*Gold Standard* 26–27).

In spite of these affinities, however, it would be misleading to suggest that *The Gold Standard and the Logic of Naturalism* and *Form and History in American Literary Naturalism* are fully compatible. Although Michaels and Howard reach a similar conclusion about naturalism—namely that naturalism is an accomplice with the society it seeks to change—they come to this conclusion from different perspectives and with different theoretical assumptions. Much like Michaels, Howard regrounds naturalism within socio-economic developments at the end of the nineteenth century. Where they differ drastically, however, is in their understanding of the vicissitudes of political economy. While Michaels focuses on the logic of capitalism as such, Howard emphasizes certain developments in the history of capitalism which she deems unescapable. She even takes pain to distinguish her version of capitalism from Michaels': "I find Michaels's analysis provocative and frequently persuasive, but his conclusions are undermined by an excessively abstract use of 'capitalism'" (190, n. 20). To avoid these shortcomings, Howard provides a historical survey of the socio-economic changes which affected the United States in the second half of the nineteenth century. Ensuing from these complex transformations are tensions which were inscribed in the very form of the novel: "when Americans of the late nineteenth and early twentieth centuries voiced their thoughts for contemporaries or recorded them for posterity they often repeated that they felt themselves living in a time of change and uncertainty.... To immerse oneself in the documents of the period is gradually to come to recognize the depth of [the naturalists'] sense of confusion and danger and to respect the historical specificity of their repeated discomfort" (Howard ix–xi). Although Howard emphasizes "the decisive dominance in economic and social life of market relations" (71) as an inescapable aspect of existence in late nineteenth-century America, she does not go very far in explaining the theoretical implications of this historical development in the way Michaels does. The conceptual basis upon which the latter's argument rests privileges the logico-historical over the facto-historical, which is to say that capitalism in *The Gold Standard and the Logic of Naturalism* does not function as an interpretative model, but as a structuring principle. The market stands out as much for its formal production as it does for its material production. In its twin economico-textual manifestation, the market encompasses everything—the production of desire, subjectivity, the commodity, the money economy, speculation, representation, writing, and above all the production of the self. What ties these different forms of production together is a unified field—or what I will refer to as a totality—that is not particularly emphasized in Howard's project.

The second nodal point around which Howard's understanding of naturalism revolves is class struggle. The sense of unrest she identifies is due in part to "the presence of class struggle in a nation with a constantly increasing, largely immigrant urban proletariat that was both very vulnerable to the recurrent economic depressions and relatively visible to other classes" (71–72). It is in this sense, for example, that Howard finds the theme of atavism particularly revealing. The naturalists' preoccupation with the brute constantly reminds us of a world in which action and meaning are tightly connected with class warfare. Atavism seems to offer the naturalists a compelling way of representing the disruptive forces that emanated out of labor unrest and class domination: "the proletarian's very vulnerability in the labor market is ideologically represented as an act of aggression.... We encounter the brute in its far-flung manifestation as a creature perpetually outcast, yet perpetually to be cast out as it inevitably reappears within self and within society. The terror of the brute includes, certainly, the fear of revolution and chaos" (87–95). Underlying this proposition is a specific view of history. Howard, in fact, subscribes to a version of Marxism that conceives of class struggle as the impetus of history. This leads her, almost inevitably, to fall back on ideology as a mediating concept between the authors' purposeful actions and thoughts, on the one hand, and the historical moment that shapes these actions and thoughts, on the other hand. Howard, it must be said, does not equate ideology with illusion or mystifying false consciousness. The version of ideology she offers is far from being a facile or narrow one. Invoking Althusser's caveat not to treat ideology as a simple relation but a relation between relations, a second degree relation, Howard rejects the reflexive theory of ideology for a more complex one. At the same time, however, her appropriation of the concept of ideology is problematic. It is so not because occasionally she refers to ideology as a "collective fantasy" (79) or because she fails to specify whose ideology is under consideration (the working class ideology or the ruling ideology),[3] but primarily because the concept of ideology as such posits an understanding of dominance that is bound up with the notion of subjectivity. From the perspective of *The Gold Standard and the Logic of Naturalism*, an ideology-based criticism (even in its revitalized form) is inadequate as a theoretical framework for thinking through the dynamics of history outside the question of agency. Michaels overtly rejects the notion of the subject, whether it be individual agent or class subject. In his view, to reflect on the subject's position *vis-à-vis* culture is to obscure the fact that the subject is constituted by that very culture—in short, that the subject is not an agent but an effect.

The key to Michaels' proposition to do away with ideology is, of course, Michel Foucault. In a much quoted passage, Foucault rejects the concept of ideology for three main reasons. To the extent that ideology implies mystification, it is always implicated in claims about truth; it "stands in virtual opposition to something else which is supposed to count as truth" (Foucault, *Power* 118). For Foucault, the claim for a hypostatized horizon of truth rests on an epistemological assertion that is open to scrutiny. Tightly connected with this position is a suspicion towards the viability of talking about economic determinism: "ideology stands in a secondary position relative to something which functions as its infrastructure" (Foucault, *Power* 118). Foucault's reformulation of the concept of power on the basis of strategies rather than agencies is one such attempt to work outside the problem of determinism. Power hardly operates through the use of ideology: "The exercise of power is not simply a relationship between partners, individuals or collective; it is a way in which certain activities modify others. Which is to say, of course, that something called Power, with or without a capital letter, does not exist. Power exists only when it is put into action" (Foucault, "Subject" 788). Power is not something that is possessed, but something that circulates; it is not a localized property, but a diffuse strategy. In the words of Deleuze, power can be defined "only by the particular points through which it passes" (*Foucault* 25). Foucault's third and most pertinent objection to the concept of ideology, then, emanates out of his understanding of power as a set of relations that are exercised by society rather than an instrument of class dominance possessed by a privileged group and motivated by economic interest. Underlying Foucault's argument is an adamant objection to a humanist position which both presupposes and privileges the category of the human subject: "the concept of ideology refers, I think necessarily, to something of the order of the subject" (Foucault, *Power* 118). By decentering the subject, Foucault proposes to reconceive of the relationship between one's actions and the consequences of these actions beyond a humanistic perspective in which the human being is considered a subject of history rather than a bearer of structures and, more insistently, beyond the type of causal thinking or economic determinism one finds in classical Marxism. Discarding the view that individuals submit to power because they are either deceived or convinced by ideology, Foucault argues that the subject is discursively constructed where discourse refers to "a field of regularity for various positions of subjectivity" rather than "a phenomenon of expression" (*Archeology* 55). In Foucault's formulations, "discourse is not the majestically unfolding manifestation of a thinking, knowing, speaking subject, but, on the contrary, a totality, in which the dispersion of the subject and his discontinuity with himself may be determined. It is a space of exteriority in which a network of distinct sites is deployed" (*Archeology* 55). The discourse, then, is not something appropriated by a given subject; rather the opposite is true—the subject is a discursive formation.[4]

Foucault's proposition to conceive of the subject as constituted rather than given is strongly echoed in Michaels' project: "the economy really is man-made, and yet it is still not a person" (*Gold Standard* 179). The logic of naturalism transcends personal or group interests; it lies within the interest of the money economy as such. Turning away from the troublesome question of agency, Michaels calls for a new category that can seize the logic of naturalism in its full complexity—belief. In his view, the subject does not have a stable existence prior to the cultural field he or she negotiates. More specifically, Michaels claims that the referent, and by extension meaning, is not filtered through what the subject believes but is rather constituted by that very belief, which in turn is constituted by Foucaultian discursive structures imposed by the logic of the market. This line of analysis enables Michaels to stitch together, not without grace, the structures of belief and the dynamics of desire. The subject of naturalism, as he put it, "consists only in the beliefs and desires made available by the naturalist logic—which is not produced by the naturalist subject but rather is the condition of his existence" (*Gold Standard* 177). Naturalism, then, does not reflect a certain reality about the market; the market is indeed all we get: "it becomes, of course, impossible to keep capitalism out—not only because capitalism provides the objects of fear and desire but because it provides the subjects as well.... [T]he logic of capitalism produces objects of desire only insofar as it produces subjects, since what makes the objects desirable is only the constitutive trace of subjectivity those objects bear" (Michaels, *Gold Standard* 20). Seen from this vantage point, naturalism can no longer be linked to the postulate of transparency. The social involvement of these texts, as Michaels puts it, depends not on their "direct representation of the money controversies" but on their "indirect representation of the conditions that the money controversies themselves articulated" (*Gold Standard* 175).

Although Michaels is engaged here to provide a critique of Howard, a close examination of some of the assumptions upon which his own argument is founded suggests that, in spite of its critical sophistication, *The Gold Standard and the Logic of Naturalism* is not void of theoretical problems. Although Michaels offers a materialist reading of naturalism that goes beyond the limits of a reflexive account and an ideology-based criticism, the reader soon realizes that his proposition to conceive of late nineteenth-century American literature as unrestrained capitalism rests on a questionable claim. It must be said at the outset, however, that the most insistent problem is not that Michaels fails to see that the economics of the naturalist novel has an indisputable biological basis—although one has to admit, along with Jameson, that Michaels' economically grounded argument ignores "(perhaps prematurely) all those traditional readings of naturalism (including those of the naturalists themselves) in terms of instinct, atavism, archaic libido, and obsession (the great human rages that seize on characters of Zola or Norris and shake them by the neck like forces of Nature)" (*Postmodernism* 196). Nor is the problem, as Donald Pizer for instance has argued, that Michaels falls into "the absolutism of the economic argument" (*Theory* 205). According to Pizer, Michaels adopts an interpretative strategy that reduces everything to an economic perspective which is not only attractive in and of itself but also appealing because it "can be readily adopted to discussions of power and sexuality in life and art" (*Theory* 205). Such a critique, it seems to me, does not do justice to the complexity of Michaels' argument. Part of the excitement one draws from *The Gold Standard and the Logic of Naturalism* comes precisely out of Michaels' formulation of a materialist reading which breaks away with the reflexive account of base and superstructure with which many critics seem to be content.[5] As I see it, the limits of Michaels project are not polemical but methodological. The problematic aspect of *The Gold Standard and the Logic of Naturalism* does not consist in economic determination *per se* but in the absence of relative determination. The historical model upon which Michaels' argument rests has a teleological bent that is hard to ignore. It can neither recognize the unevenness of social formations nor account for the contingency of history.

The first thing one notices about the model Michaels proposes is its cynical dynamism. Michaels' version of capitalism rests on a vision of the market that is caught up in endless circulation, a system that has no inside or outside, a model that argues against any possibility of the subject ever transcending the system but, at the same time, presents this system as a transcendental category above and beyond change. Although the market is not void of moments of disfunctionality, these are always already neutralized because the disruptive element, Michaels contends, is "not subversive of the capitalist economy, but constitutive of its power" (*Gold Standard* 48). Although the market generates dynamic relations, these are always recouped within a position that inflexibly emphasizes determination and totality. The rigidity of these two categories renders Michaels' model suspect because even in Marx's original formulations, as the late Althusser points out, determination and totality "are subject to other concepts that define *the limits of their validity*: the concepts of process, contradiction, tendency, and limit" (*Éléments* 63). By over-emphasizing the omnipotence of the market, Michaels reverts back to an old theoretical position—determinism. It seems that he has foregone the classical view of naturalism as a biological determinism only to embrace a peculiar type of economic determinism.

From this vantage point, Michaels' argument has more affinities with the claims of Lears and Fox than one is initially led to believe. They both are caught in one form of reduction or another that fails to recognize the full complexity of the market. Mark Seltzer's comment on current strains in cultural materialism adequately captures the superficial differences between these two positions:

> On the one side, there is what we might call an *agoraphobic* account (the
> insistence on an essential opposition between the market and the self and
> its wants); on the other, an *agoraphilic* account (the identification of the
> self and its wants with an inevitable and ineluctable market). If the first or
> "oppositional" account acknowledges the power of the market to determine
> internal and affective states but opposes or dislikes it, the second or "post-
> oppositional" account posits an identity between the market and internal or
> affective states that makes opposition, or liking or disliking, simply
> irrelevant, since both likes and dislikes are themselves "products" of the
> market within. (*Bodies* 127)

It thus seems that what Lears argues at the level of the subject,
Michaels reiterates at the level of the system. If for the former
opposition or resistance is always coopted by the system, for the latter
it is systematically reified because it is part of the system's internal
strategies. Both Lears and Michaels struggle with what may be
termed, after Jameson, "the dilemma of getting out of the system"
(*Postmodernism* 204), only to affirm the futility of such an endeavor.
What is missing is the theoretical necessity to account for those
moments, trends, or impulses that escape reification.[6] What this
means, in part, is that a viable account of the logic of the system
cannot leave unaddressed the question of change and mutation. In
sacrificing diachrony for synchrony, Michaels' formulation of the
specificity of naturalism fails to account for the dynamic character of
history. The system Michaels proposes is reductive and ultimately
untenable because the unevenness of a specific socio-historical
formation and the heterogeneity of historical developments prevent its
reduction to a closed system.[7] In *The Gold Standard and the Logic of
Naturalism*, there is no *dépassement*, only fulfillment; there is no
transformation, only endless repetition and ceaseless expansion
impelled by an *apriori* theoretical necessity—the necessity to
reproduce which gives the market an indefinite character. Naturalism
is simply capitalism unfailingly at work, i.e., capitalism with a
predictable equilibrium and an unproductive evenness. The
contingency of history is such that one cannot content oneself with an
analysis of the logic of the system, as Michaels does in homology
after homology. It is important to map out the law that governs the
dominant practices, but it is also necessary to point out the historical
transience of these realities and to indicate the dynamics of their
development and transition. In the words of Marx, it is important not

only to analyze the "law of the phenomena" but also to examine the "law of their variation" (*Capital* 100). Historical structures are viable only when considered as tendencies rather than stable entities.

In the final analysis, it becomes clear that *The Gold Standard and the Logic of Naturalism* assumes a theoretical position that is profoundly conservative. At the same time, however, the questions that Michaels has raised are certainly not to be rejected; rather, they call for a more adequate theorization of the market. The real value of Michaels' project, then, does not lie in the claims he has advanced—since these have only partially dislocated traditional critical assumptions—but in the interpretative possibilities he has opened up and the critical territories he has marked. Michaels has laid the groundwork, so to speak, for rethinking naturalism. His book gives us a measure of what has to be eschewed and what remains to be addressed. If one is to avoid the shortcomings that accompany the conception of naturalism as an all-encompassing totality or a closed system, it becomes indispensable to enact a symptomatological reading that depicts the incremental elements and emergent impulses that work towards complicating the historical unfolding of the period. It is important to account for hard facts and regnant trends, but it is equally important to accentuate unevenness, difference, discordance, and heterogeneity. A viable historical perspective has to seize the period in question in its continuity and discontinuity, in its structuration and destructuration, in its formation and transformation. My account of naturalism, then, reiterates the correlation between the logic of naturalism and the logic of capitalism but emphasizes the need to recognize and elucidate the unstable and untotalizing nature of the system within which naturalism operates. Naturalism, I argue, articulates and reproduces the convulsive character of capitalism; it is characterized by a disposition towards transgression that is symptomatic of the dynamically unstable nature of capitalism.

Before proceeding with the specific textual analyses, a few observations are in order. Given the emphasis on the correlation between the logic of naturalism and the logic of capitalism, the focus on Dreiser and Norris seems to be an obvious choice. Together, these two authors provide a resonant portrayal of some of the most insistent economic forces and unescapable trends that have shaped the period. *Sister Carrie* and *McTeague*, above all others, have been considered as textual sites on which the economic theme is played out in naturalism. For many critics, Sister Carrie's undiminishing lust for the commodity, much like Trina's insatiable desire for gold, embodies the spirit of capitalism. For my purpose, however, these novels are of renewed interest not so much because they deal, most compulsively and conspicuously, with economic themes but because they do so in ways that exceed the field of political economy *tout court*. It is a basic assumption of this project that naturalism is structured around an economic principle but cannot be reduced to it. The logic of capitalism is pervasive precisely because of its capacity to infiltrate the different enclaves of the social totality. Capitalism functions in extended structures; it entails not only material production but also formal reproduction. To talk about capitalism is to talk about the extensive deployment of a prodigious and complex system. Whence the need to trace the economic in the non-economic—to map out those territories or registers where the process of production and exchange is not strictly, visibly, or ostensibly economic.

To pursue the example of *Sister Carrie*, the logic of capitalism in this novel is not limited to money, nor is it confined to material production. It is at the heart of all that which is repetitive and rhythmic. The rhythms that pervade the novel epitomize the very motion of capitalism in its relentless generation of surplus value. It is interesting that one of the first things Carrie notices about Chicago is a certain cadence: "The sound of the hammer engaged upon the erection of new structures was everywhere heard" (ii 14). The city stands out less as a setting than as a movement: "The large plates of window glass, now so common ... gave the floor offices a distinguished and prosperous look. The casual wanderer could see as he passed a polished array of office fixtures, much frosted glass, clerks hard at work. She walked bravely forward, led by an honest desire to find employment and delayed at every step by the interest of the unfolding scene, and a sense of helplessness amid so much evidence of power and force which she did not understand" (ii 14). Even when certain aspects of the city are meticulously described the thrust of these depictions lies less in what the scenes themselves represent than in the motion they convey. All we get are glimpses of people who are entangled in action, presented from the perspective of a character who is constantly on the move. The passage where Dreiser describes Chicago deserves to be quoted at length because it conveys a compulsion to repeat that is crucial to understanding the rhythm within which the novel unfolds:

In 1889 Chicago had the peculiar qualifications of growth which made such adventurous pilgrimages even on the part of the young girls plausible. Its many growing commercial opportunities gave it widespread fame, which made of it a giant magnet, drawing to itself, from all quarters, the hopeful and the hopeless.... Great industries were moving in. The huge railroad corporations which had long before recognized the prospects of the place had seized upon vast tracts of land for transfer and shipping purposes. Street-car lines had been extended far out into the open country in anticipation of rapid growth. The city had laid miles and miles of streets and sewers through regions where, perhaps, one solitary house stood out alone—a pioneer of the populous ways to be. There were regions open to the sweeping winds and rain, which were yet lighted throughout the night with long, blinking lines of gas-lamps, fluttering in the wind. Narrow board walks extended out, passing here a house, and there a store, at far intervals, eventually ending on the open prairie. (ii 13–14)

Chicago stands out less as a space of being than a space of becoming. It is characterized first and foremost by its potential growth and its endless possibilities. The long lines of lamps that fill in the uninhabited territories and the board walks that stretch in the open prairie convey a city that is almost caught up in a hysterical labor. The numerous images of renewal, investment, development, and expansion are impelled by the law of value; they are driven by the need to reinvest at the heart of capitalism.

The character of the city is all the more imposing because it anticipates the character of the protagonist herself. The energy that is associated with Chicago is, in fact, crucial to understanding Sister Carrie: "The city has its cunning wiles, no less than the infinitely smaller and more human tempter" (i 1). There is an intriguing correlation between the expanding metropolis with its "vast buildings" (ii 15) and the restless imagination of a "desireful" (x 88) character who is constantly "drifting, until she was on a borderless sea of speculation" (xxi 187). Chicago, writes Dreiser, is full of promises and possibilities: "Its population was not so much thriving upon established commerce as upon the industries which prepared for the arrival of others" (ii 14). At times, the city's never ending expansion is indistinguishable from Carrie's incessant longing: "Almost invariably she would carry the vivid imagination away with her and brood over them the next day alone. She lived as much in these things as in the realities which made up her daily life" (xxxii 287). The dynamic character of the city and the protean character of Carrie become two sides of the same coin. Chicago can even be said to be a gigantic mirror-image of Sister Carrie herself. Much like "the vast city which stretched for miles and miles in every direction" (ii 10), Carrie's desire is unmeasurable: "She was too full of wonder and desire to be greedy. She still looked about her upon the great maze of the city without understanding" (xiii 115). The sense of movement and flux that characterizes the city reinforces the sense of restlessness and longing that defines Dreiser's heroine. They both are defined by a certain rhythm which in turn is impelled by the compulsion to repeat that is at the heart of capitalism. From this vantage point, the study of rhythm in the novel becomes a study of the tautology of capitalism in its most insidious effects.

It must not be concluded too hastily, however, that capitalism, and by extension naturalism, are structured around a movement that repeats itself indefinitely and unfailingly. An analysis of the ludic element in Norris' *Vandover and the Brute*, for instance, enables us to complicate the foregoing analysis. Vandover's addiction to gambling in particular reveals a creative impulse, the implications of which are worth pursuing. Seen from one perspective, gambling is the example *par excellence* of the compulsion to repeat. For Walter Benjamin, the mechanic movements and reflex actions reflected in gambling both reproduce and extend the drudgery and monotony that the worker experiences in the work place: the gambler "does not lack the futility, the emptiness, the inability to complete something which is inherent in the activity of a wage slave in a factory. Gambling even contains the workmen's gesture that is produced by the automatic operation, for there can be no game without the quick movement of the hand by which the stake is put down or a card is picked up. The jolt in the movement of a machine is like the so-called *coup* in a game of chance. The manipulation of the worker at the machine has no connection with the preceding operation for the very reason that it is its exact repetition" (*Baudelaire* 134–35). The compulsion to repeat, which Benjamin identifies here, is at the heart of Vandover's ludic experience, particularly after the death of the Old Gentleman. It is obvious that Vandover's reckless behavior is not motivated by the desire to win: "It was not with any hope of winning that he gambled" (xvi 289). In fact, the pleasure Vandover draws from the game not only precludes winning but also makes satisfaction inconceivable, which is tantamount to saying that the pleasure of gambling is a pleasure of endless repetition: "Night and day he sat over the cards, the passion growing upon him as he continued to lose" (xvi 289). Gradually, however, the game of money entangles Vandover in a bizarre experience, thus creating a curious interplay in the novel between that which is determinate, repetitive, and predictable, on the one hand, and that which is stochastic, aleatory, and fortuitous, on the other hand. Norris takes pain to convey a growing irrationality in Vandover's behavior, made even more grotesque by the influence of the disease he had contracted: "Little by little the fifteen thousand in the bank dwindled. It is not all of it in cards. Certain habits of extravagance grew upon Vandover, the natural outcome of his persistent gambling, the desire of winning easily being balanced by the impulses to spend quickly. He took a certain hysterical delight in flinging money with both hands" (xvi 290). The habit of gambling grows on him in such a way that he can stop neither when he is winning nor when he is losing: "It was a veritable mania, a wild blind frenzy that knew no limit" (xvi 289).

The intensity that this pecuniary experience engenders becomes even more amplified in *McTeague*. The unpredictable developments that befall Vandover also entangle Trina, except that her passion is not for flinging money away but hoarding it. Both characters are seized by an irresistible, inexplicable, and even hysterical impulse. Norris uses the same terms to describe the intensity of Trina's hoarding instinct after McTeague has stolen the money she took pains to save over the years: "Trina had begun to save again, but now it was with an eagerness that amounted at times to a veritable frenzy" (xix 355). Later in the novel, Trina becomes even more restless and starts to withdraw some of the lottery money she entrusted with Uncle Oelbermann: "Trina began to draw steadily upon her capital, a little at a time. It was a passion with her, a mania, a veritable mental disease" (xix 357). The hysteric dimension that Trina's desire assumes introduces an element of indeterminacy in the novel which goes radically against the sense of regularity and repetitiveness that marks her hoarding instinct. Sporadic as they may be, the moments of intensity that accompany Trina's pecuniary desire suggest that capitalism cannot be reduced to a stable movement. With the deployment of capitalism comes the possibility that contradictions develop which lead to moments of unpredictable resolution. Capitalism is characterized not only by its tautology but also by its uneven constitution, inherent contradictions, and creative impulses. Recognizing the interplay of these creative impulses or moments of intensity is crucial in grasping naturalism in its full complexity.

CHAPTER TWO

Ludic Naturalism: Determinacy and Indeterminacy in *Vandover and the Brute*

In an early and perceptive study on naturalism, Donald Pizer has pointed out an interesting hybridity in Norris' fiction. Throughout his writings, Norris combines two strains: the extraordinary and excessive in human nature, which he derives from Le Conte; and the local and the contemporary, which he adapts from Zola. Much of the aesthetic effect in Norris' naturalism, as Pizer sees it, stems from an experience that is "both commonplace and extraordinary, both familiar and strange, both simple and complex" (*Realism* 12). This contrariety has gained even a deeper resonance in the context of current critical debates in which the emphasis is no longer on the unity of the text but its heterogenous constitution.[1] The attention to discordance, discontinuity, and difference which fuels much of literary and critical theory today seems to offer a viable theoretical framework capable of unfurling unsuspected dimensions in Norris' naturalistic vision. Drawing on Bakhtin's concept of heteroglossia, for instance, Leonard Cassuto points out an "aesthetic ambiguity" (47) in Norris' writings that extends beyond hard determinism. *McTeague*, he argues, stands out less for its unity than for its widely diverse topography. Far from enacting a simple determined inevitability, the novel is a concatenation of contrasting ingredients. Likewise, in a recent article, Jonathan Cullick draws attention to a defining tension in Norris' fiction between a repetition of routine and a disruption of unexpected events: "Repetition of events, and the opposite circumstance of unexpected events, are devices in Norris' narrative.... In Norris' world, there are only extremes. Instead of stability, there is only routine, repetition, and predictability. Instead of adventure, there is only disruption, transgression, and surprise" (38).

This interplay between determinacy and indeterminacy in Norris' fiction points to a ludic dimension at work even in a novel as deterministic as *Vandover and the Brute*. Hardly any account of the fate of Vandover—a genteel promising artist—is complete without a reference to the evolutionary theme at the core of this novel. Subject to the unsolicited promptings of instinct and victim of the animal within him, Vandover succumbs to the forces of evil. He squanders his money, loses his artistic talent, and is ultimately reduced to an impoverished brute. Vandover's sensuality, indulgence, and recklessness dramatize his fall from virtue and innocence to sin and corruption and, in doing so, gives the novel an allegorical valence that extends its relentless determinism. To over-emphasize these deterministic and allegorical strains, however, is to overlook an important dimension in the novel—its ludic dimension. Without discounting these allegorical overtones and evolutionary implications, I would like to pursue a more complex understanding of the novel beyond the notion of flat realism (i.e., rendering a pre-given text) or hard determinism (i.e., following a causally motivated thinking). Although *Vandover and the Brute* deals with some of the major themes and motifs that run through naturalism, it does so in ways that complicate these themes and motifs rather than reproduce them. Indeed, the novel includes spaces of play and reversibility the implications of which are worth exploring.

Nowhere is this ludic dimension more acute than in the episode of the elusive painting in which Vandover experiences a curious effect of presence and absence. Immersed in his art, where he has found a momentary refuge from his grief over the death of his father, Vandover encounters a mysterious and strenuous resistance from the work itself: "The outlines grew faint, just perceptible enough to guide them in the second more detailed drawing" (xiv 224). In front of his canvas, Vandover experiences an unexpected sense of estrangement, and is soon overcome by a feeling of disorientation: "he began but could not recall how the lines should run" (xiv 224). In his hand, the forms that make the painting resist materialization: "in his imagination he saw just how the outlines should be, but somehow he could not make his hand interpret what was in his head" (xiv 244). The inarticulateness of Vandover's artistic sensibility points even to the absence of a coordinating element: "Some third medium which the one used to act upon the other was sluggish, dull; worse than that, it seemed to be absent" (xiv 224). Vandover is neither able to draw his painting nor with-draw from it.

Vandover's relentless effort to overcome this momentary inertia bespeaks more than a simple defiance; it hides a deep fear which leads the reader to suspect that the vanishing picture is tinged with a more insistent significance. A partial clue to the disorientation that Vandover experiences in front of his canvas can be pointed out in the sporadic references to a feminine element in the novel: "Any feminine influence would have been well for him at this time: that of an older sister, even that of a hired governess.... There was no feminine influence about Vandover at this critical time to help him see the world in the right light and to gauge things correctly, and he might have been totally corrupted while in his earliest teens had it not been for another side of his character that begun to develop about the same time. This was his artistic side" (i 8–11). The passage presents Vandover's recourse to his art as a substitute for a feminine influence. The correlation becomes even more insistent in the episode of the vanishing painting. Following the nimble, and yet disorderly, movement of Vandover's uncertain fingers one can discern a ludic element behind which stands a libidinal investment. The uncanny artistic experience that makes the hand willing but the form resistant is intimately connected to the figure of the mother. The novel opens with a recollection of an indelible memory of the sick mother in the train station during the migration of the family from Boston to San Francisco. Although a remote memory, the scene of the death of the mother has an enduring impact on Vandover. There is, in fact, an intriguing tenacity between his commitment to his art and his attachment to his mother. One may even speak of a congeniality between an artistic block and a psychic inhibition.

The reflection/refraction that ensues from Vandover's crisis in front of his canvas is very much akin to the presence/absence pattern that Freud has identified in the child's play. The dynamics of the uncanny playful representation that entices Vandover has a structural affinity with the dynamics involved in the child's attempt to cope with the absence of the mother. For Freud, the "postponement" (18:10) or "flight from satisfaction" (18:42) associated with the pursuit of pleasure is crucial to an understanding of a partial displacement that accompanies the child's playful activity—what Freud calls "a yield of pleasure of another sort" (18:16). The child's preoccupation with his game does not reveal an attachment to the mother but an indifference. This is not to say, however, that the child renounces his mother completely. He allows her to disappear without protest only to stage a game of disappearance and return himself. In such an activity, the child is not induced by the object itself—since he does the same thing with "any small object he could get hold of" (Freud 18:14)—but by the ability to stage the disappearance of the object in order to rediscover it. It would be safe to assume, then, that the child's play is not just a form of compensation for the absence of the mother but also a form of "down-play" (Lyotard, *Discours* 354), the purpose of which is to overcome the anxiety that ensues from the threat of separation. In playing the *fort/da* game, the child down-plays the absence of the mother by making himself "master" (Freud 18:16). In this sense, the repetitive appeal of the *fort/da* game becomes both a precaution against absence and a mechanism that enables the "overpowered" child (Freud 18:16) to pass from a passive experience (the disappearance of the mother) to a more active experience (staging the disappearance of the mother). The reproduction of separation enables him to become the agent who exercises the separation rather than the subject who undergoes it: "children can master a powerful impression far more thoroughly by being active than they could by merely experiencing it passively. Each fresh repetition seems to strengthen the mastery they are in search of" (Freud 18:35). Through this voluntary play, the child gains control over his object of desire and in so doing both wards off the influence of the mother and masters her absence. In this sense, staging the disappearance of the spool, as Winnicott has observed, becomes "the unconscious backcloth for love of a real object; that is, an object outside the area of the subject's omnipotent control" (94).

The foregoing analysis enables us to emphasize a dimension that is equally important in Freud's analysis of the experience of the child and Norris' depiction of the experience of the young Vandover—the eminence of representation over presence. It is interesting to note that what Vandover remembers is not so much the figure of the mother but her disappearance: "This scene of her death was the only thing that Vandover could remember of his mother" (i 5). Vandover's recollection of his mother is simply that of an evanescent presence. Likewise, the child's game, as Freud conceives it, points not so much to the presence of the mother but the presence of her absence—what may be termed, after Moustafa Safouan, "the fleeting quality of her presence" (53). This apparent paradox is central in Freud's analysis of the mirror stage. The child's play in front of the mirror is an assurance that the mother's absence is an illusion: "during this long period of solitude the child had found a method of making *himself* disappear. He had discovered his reflection in a full length mirror which did not quite reach to the ground, so that by crouching down he could make his mirror-image 'gone'" (Freud 18:15, n. 1). This dimension in the child's play is important because it points to the irreducibility of the object of desire to a mere absence or a mere presence. For the child, the absence of the object of desire is only a quasi-absence because every seeming *fort* entails an inevitable *da*. What the *fort/da* game enables the child to achieve, then, is the capacity to simultaneously isolate and abstract the experience of absence in a way that ensures the permanent and unfailing representation of the mother beyond her real presence: "'to be' is dissociated from 'to be perceived' and becomes synonymous with 'to be thought' instead. Indeed, the child in his game accomplished something more than the acquisition of a particular representation.... It is what one might call *pure representation*" (Safouan 56). The mechanism of transfer which enables the child to master the absence of the mother in the projected surreality of the object of desire is key to understanding Freud's theory of the pleasure principle. Because access to the mother is made unthinkable by the threat of castration, the *fort/da* game becomes a substitution for an unrealizable desire, which is tantamount to saying that the pleasure that the child draws from playing is, in essence, a pleasure of repetition.[2]

Now we are in a better position to apprehend the double bind of Vandover's ludic experience. In the train station, Vandover finds himself caught between two swift moments of appearance and disappearance. The unexpected death of the invalid mother, with which the book opens, is dramatized by the sudden appearance of the train. A sense of futility is conveyed as the migrating family expecting the arrival of the train at any time are, instead, confronted with the sudden death of the mother: "By and by she drew a long sigh, her face became the face of an imbecile, stupid, without expression, her eyes half-closed, her mouth half-open, her head rolled forward as though she were nodding in her sleep, while a long drip of saliva trailed from her lower lip. Vandover's father bent over her quickly, crying out sharply, 'Hallie!—what is it?' All at once the train for which they were waiting charged into the depot, filling the place with a hideous clangor and with the smell of steam and of hot oil" (i 4–5). The vanishing figure of a debilitated mother is intensified by the fleeting presence of a transiting train. This scene of abandonment has an enduring effect. The sudden and disorienting disappearance of the mother remains an enigma for the incomprehensibly abandoned child. Although Vandover can recall only "little of his past" (i 3), he is unable to forget this particular scene.

The simultaneity between the appearance of the locomotive and the disappearance of the mother introduces a curious interplay between presence and absence which points ahead to Vandover's vanishing picture. Indeed, the image of the bewildered painter in front of his canvas reenacts the scene of the bedazzled child in front of his dying mother. Mark Seltzer even describes the painting Vandover is attempting as a "sentimental death scene" (*Bodies* 37). Behind the presence/absence pattern that characterizes Vandover's artistic experience lies an ambivalent wish to see his mother "whom he had always believed to be some kind of angel" (i 11)—a wish he has entertained ever since he became motherless: "He prayed that he might be a good boy and live a long time and go to heaven when he died and see his mother" (i 9). The vanishing picture bespeaks a curious reversal whereby the desire to inscribe on the canvas, the desire to make visible, becomes a substitute for the act of seeing itself. The contemplation of the vanishing image on the space of the canvas is simultaneously a form of evocation and evacuation of the mother. Behind Vandover's lack of execution lies an unwillingness to yield to the force of an attachment that has so far exercised a strong influence on him. His inability to enact the second and more detailed drawing, to follow the sketched lines and elicit them, is an unconscious unwillingness to restage a memory. The impulse to remember compels Vandover to repeat.[3] The canvas becomes a ludic maternal space where Vandover plays an affective game. The whole incident becomes an enactment of the *fort/da* game, although not as pleasant, for Vandover is not exactly enjoying the game: "Vandover nerved himself against it, not daring to give in, fearing to allow himself to see what this really meant" (xiv 225). In the disarticulation of the painting one can sense the articulation of a reticent desire; in the dematerialization of the painting one can read the dematernalization of Vandover. The mother becomes this fleeting and evasive figure that can be encountered only in a "no woman's land," to borrow Philip Berthier's neologism (250).

Such as it is then, the inconclusiveness of representation that corrupts Vandover's art recapitulates the fragmentation of his memory: "Vandover would have to get at his life during his teens, Vandover would have been obliged to collect these scattered memory pictures as best he could, rearrange them in some more orderly sequence, piece out what he could imperfectly recall and fill in the many gaps by mere guesswork and conjecture" (i 5). As the novel unfolds, the loss of art becomes undistinguishable from the experience of death as such: "Vandover had passed this week in an agony of grief over the loss of his art, a grief that seemed even sharper than that which he had felt over the death of his father. For this last calamity was like the death of a child of his, some dear, sweet child, that might have been his companion throughout all his life" (xv 232).⁴ Vandover's loss of his art is inseparable from a more general sense of deprivation. Insofar as it remains vague, indefinite, and inconclusive, Vandover's thwarted experience stimulates a renewed interest in his art that entangles him in a compulsion to repeat: "again and again he would put himself at his easel, only to experience afresh the return of the numbness in his brain, the impotency of his fingers" (xv 232). Every false start announces a new inscription; every disintegration entails a reiteration. Vandover is engaged in an indefinite play that seeks to give articulation to the form. He desperately clings to his object of desire in an act that comes close to idealization.⁵

Although the influence of the mother is enduring, it is not the only one in the novel. The other important influence on Vandover is his old college chum, Charlie Geary. An analysis of the relation between the two characters, after they have graduated from Harvard and returned to San Francisco, can extend the implication of the ludic dimension at work in the novel. Overcoming the reserved attitude and moral uprightness of his college years, Vandover embarks on a more promiscuous life—or to put it in deterministic terms, he succumbs to "the animal in him" (xvii 324). The outcome of this recklessness is the unfortunate affair with Ida Wade. Not long after she has been seduced by Vandover, the girl becomes terrified at the prospect of having an illegitimate child and eventually commits suicide. Ensuing from this incident are two events, the former—which will be addressed later—is the death of the father, the latter is a bizarre litigation in which Vandover finds himself embroiled. Looking listlessly at the morning paper, Vandover suddenly catches sight of the announcement of a suit that Hiram Wade, Ida's father, has brought against him, seeking twenty-five thousand dollars as a settlement for the suicide of his daughter. Pretending to come to Vandover's aid with the aim of swindling him, Geary offers to defend his old friend:

"What am I here for if it isn't to help you? ... Don't you suppose that I can help you more as Wade's lawyer than I could as your lawyer? ... I could get you out of this hole better as Wade's lawyer than as your own.... I had just as soon do it for you, only listen to this: don't you say a word about the case to anybody, not to your lawyer, nor to anybody. If Field should write to

you, tell him you have counsel already.... And there is another thing you
must understand: I'm not your lawyer, of course; you see that I could be
disbarred if I was lawyer for both sides. It's like this, you see: I'm Wade's
lawyer—at least the firm I am with are his lawyer—and of course I'm acting
in Wade's interest." (xv 236–38)

The first thing one notices about this case is that it proceeds according
to atypical rules. Geary acts as a *de jure* lawyer for Wade and a *de
facto* lawyer for Vandover. He voluntarily offers to help his friend
not as his lawyer but as "the counsel for the other side" (xv 235).
The outcome of this "playing back and forth between the two
parties" (xv 237) is intriguing: Geary is and is not Vandover's lawyer,
and inversely Vandover has (il)legal advice without officially having a
lawyer.

It should not escape the reader that the case in question is a
double case.   The dispute between Wade and Vandover can be
juxtaposed with another contention between Geary and Vandover:
"why could he not make the Wade suit a machine with which to force
Vandover into the sale of the property?" (xv 252).   But for these
machinations to succeed, Geary has to play with the law: "in order to
carry out the delicate and complicated affair it was absolutely
necessary to keep Vandover from seeing a lawyer" (xv 254).   Geary
can achieve his gains only by inflicting losses on Vandover.   The
logic that transpires from this zero-sum game is the logic of
accumulation—the multiplication of profits for one player means also
the multiplication of losses for the other.   At the end of the deal,
Vandover "had neither his property nor its equivalent in money" (xv
267) while Geary has both and more: "Geary was swindling his best
friend out of a piece of property valued at twelve thousand six
hundred dollars, and preventing him from reselling the same piece at
a very advanced figure.... Ah, you bet, just think of it, after all, not
only would Vandover believe that Geary was doing him a great
service, but the office would be delighted with him for winning his
first case, they would get a heavy fee from Wade, and he would nearly
double his money invested in the block in the mission" (xv 254–55).

Seen in this light, the coalescence between the ludic and the
judicial elements becomes highly significant; the two registers are
hardly distinguishable in the novel.   At least historically, as Johan
Huizinga reminds us, there has always been a systematic solidarity
between legal justice and play: "The judicial contest is always subject
to a system of restrictive rules which, quite apart from the limitations
of time and place, set the lawsuit firmly and squarely in the domain of

orderly, antithetical play. The active association of law and play, particularly in archaic culture, can be seen from three points of view. The lawsuit can be regarded as a game of chance, a contest, or a verbal battle" (78). In modern times, however, these qualities are often concealed beneath an ethical conception of justice. Although justice has both an ethical and a ludic dimension, the exceeding preoccupation with the former has obfuscated the persistence of the latter. In other words, the emphasis on right and wrong has dwarfed the idea of winning and losing. What is particularly intriguing about *Vandover and the Brute* is the pre-eminence of the ludic dimension over the judicial one.

This is of course not to deny the allegorical dimension of the novel. *Vandover and the Brute* is, in many ways, an allegory about the fall of a virtuous character from innocence to sin, although the moral struggle may not be readily discerned because it is woven into the struggle to survive. The conflict that the novel stages between Vandover's better side and his brutish side, as Charles Walcutt has pointed out, "is a thoroughly moral one. It is a conflict between Vandover's free and responsible spirit and a series of circumstantial influences (the disease is merely one of several) which win out over him largely because of his culpable moral weakness" (119–20). The novel provides ample support for this reading: "the blow he has given his father, he could see that the Old Gentleman crushed under it.... Vandover could not but feel that he had hastened his death, and that in so doing he had destroyed another influence which would have cultivated and fostered his better side" (vii 110–xiv 216). It is true that the devastating effect of Vandover's promiscuity on the Old Gentleman—since he has allegedly died out of grief—infuses the case with a moral dimension, but the litigation itself is less about right and wrong than it is about winning and losing. The outcome of the game is less decided by ethical standards (the pursuit of justice) than it is determined by economic principles (the pursuit of profit). Both the litigant and his lawyer are motivated by the desire to profit from the situation. In the case of Geary, the prospects for a successful career depend largely on his ability to "make a brilliant success of the case" (xv 250), on his ability to make the most out of this opportunity: "Vandover ought to see that with Geary it was a matter of business; he, Geary, was only an instrument of the law; if Geary did not take the case, some other lawyer would. At any rate, whether Van would see it in this light or not, Geary was determined to take the case; it was too good an opportunity to let it slip" (xv 251). For Geary everything comes down to a game of competition; Vandover is his "old college chum" (xv 254) but his adversary and competitor nonetheless. Likewise, the outcome of the case is important for Wade primarily because it enables him to realize his economic prospects: "He also had his ambitions.... [H]e had some scheme that he wanted to go into right away, and that he wants ready money, right on the nail, you know, to carry it through" (xv 250). To that extent, Wade's real motivation is not so much retribution as it is compensation. The economic metaphor that instills his response to Geary's suggestion to settle for eight thousand dollars instead of ten betrays his pecuniary lust: "it would seem like selling my daughter's honour if we should compromise at any less figure" (xv 256).

The litigation culminates in a curious settlement whereby Geary wins over his adversary as well as his client. By establishing two coalitions, whereby Wade and Vandover are involved with each other but isolated, Geary acquires an omniscient viewpoint that ensures his cognizance of anterior moves, tightens his control over the game, and favors him always to win. In this game, Geary's success is guaranteed under all circumstances. What makes Geary the chief player in the novel and the greatest beneficiary of the litigation, however, is neither the cunning game he plays with his client, Wade, nor the roguish coalition he forms with his pseudo-client, Vandover. Behind both games is yet another game of speculation. Geary's stakes are not limited to the case he is handling, but transcend it to a more seductive game with the shoe manufacturers: "there was money in the investment if one could and would give the proper attention to pushing it.... Geary knew that a certain immense boot and shoe concern was after the same piece of property. The houses themselves were nothing to the boot and shoe people; they wanted the land in order to build their manufactory upon it. A siding of the railroad ran down the alley just back of the property, a fact that hurt the lot for residence purposes, but that was indispensable for the boot and shoe people" (xv 251–52). To that extent, the success of the case that Geary handles is not to be measured on the basis of the settlement he has reached with the disputing parties but on the success of the second and more lucrative game. Winning the Wade case is only the gambit for a bigger game—to beat the shoe people to the property in question in order to sell it to them at a higher price: "Geary knew that the heads of the manufactory were determined to buy the lot, and he was sure that if properly handled by clever brokers they could be induced to offer at least one third more than its appraised valuation. It was a chance for a fine speculation, and it was torture to Geary to think that Vandover, or in fact any one besides himself, was going to profit" (xv 252). The interpenetration of the two cases becomes even more explicit at the moment of finalizing the arrangement with Vandover. Thus, when Geary goes over the details of the arrangement in his head one last time, "looking for weak points" (xv 265), his calculations do not bear on the case immediately at hand but on the deal in prospect: "Suppose the boot and shoe people did not buy the lot? He could resell it elsewhere, even below its appraised value and yet make money by the transaction; the lot was cheap at ten thousand; it might bring twelve; even as an ordinary, legitimate speculation it was to be desired at such a figure. Suppose the boot and shoe people backed out entirely, suppose even he could not find another purchaser for the property, why, then, he could hold on to it; the income from the rents was fully 10 per cent of the price he would have paid for it" (xv 265).

The game that Geary plays, then, seems to be marked by an unfailing regularity. His schemes enable him to have a direct influence on the course and outcome of the game. Thus, when Vandover unexpectedly proposes to sell his property, Geary readily accepts the offer. He has thoroughly checked the status of the property and fully studied the possible complications that may arise from the deal, leaving little or no room for chance:

> "Can't we settle the whole matter today?" said Vandover. Right here now. Let's get it done with."
> Geary nearly bounded from his seat. He had been wondering how he might accomplish this very thing. "Alright," he said briskly, "no reason in waiting." He had seen to it that he should be prepared to close the sale the moment that Vandover was willing. Long ago, when he had the idea of buying the block he had spent a day in the offices of the country recorder, the tax collector, and the assessor, assuring himself of the validity of the title, and only two days ago he had gone over the matter again in order to be sure that no encumbrances had been added to the block in the meanwhile. He found nothing; the title was clear. (xv 266)

Nothing seems to happen by chance in the interplay between Geary and his pseudo-client; everything is part of a well designed scheme. Even when Geary encounters few unexpected developments, these do not seem to threaten his machinations. Thus, finding himself in charge of the Wade case, he sees in the litigation a "chance for a 'deal'" (xv 253) and ventures to offer Wade eight thousand dollars in cash instead of the ten thousand he requested as a settlement:

Wade struck his hand to his head. "I tell you, he's brought dishonor upon my gray hairs," he exclaimed.

"Exactly, of course I understand how you feel," replied Geary, "but now about this eight thousand? I tell you what I'll do." He had resolved to stake everything upon one last hazard. "See here, Mr. Wade, there is a difference between eight thousand dollars and ten thousand, but the use of money is worth something, isn't it? And money down, cold hard cash, is worth something, isn't it? Well, now, suppose you got that eight thousand dollars money within three days?" (xv 256)

Chance moves do not seem to vitiate the rational character of the game that Geary plays. While for Vandover the variable is a contingency, for Geary it is a strategy. The deal he presents to Vandover as a chance to be seized is, in fact, a calculated risk: "He wants the ready money; he don't want depreciated real estate. You will have to find a purchaser in the next week if you possibly can in such a short time, and make over the money to Wade. But if you can't sell in that time you will have to dig up ten thousand instead of eight. It is a hard position for you, Van; it's just a chance, you know, but I thought I would give you the benefit of that chance. If you want to give me a power of attorney I'll try and sell it for you" (xv 263). Even in those situations which Geary has not created or predicted, contingency is far from modifying the outcome of the game. The complications that arise while bargaining with Vandover consolidate Geary's schemes:

"You couldn't possibly get more than nine thousand for that block today. You see the railroad hurts it."

"I suppose so," replied Vandover. "I've heard the governor say as much in his time."

"Of course," exclaimed Geary, delighted at this unexpected turn. (xv 262)

This and other instances in the novel warrant a provisional conclusion: Geary's game is not void of chance, but the element of chance is, for the most part, controlled. The outcome of the game is always manipulated or, at least, relatively so.

An examination of the coalescence between the economic and somatic registers in the novel, however, leads us to complicate this provisional conclusion. The representation of the disintegrated body in the novel extends the implication of the economic theme but at the same time introduces new variables into what seems to be a determined course of events. Geary's machinations have not only an economic dimension but also a somatic one which apparently reinforces his control over the game. The prospects for final success or ruin are discretely (re)inscribed on the symptomatology of the body. Norris, in fact, interrupts the story-line of Geary's machinations, putting off the details of how he swindles his old chum, in order to introduce a detailed exposition of the mental and physical state of Geary's victim. Vandover's declaration to Geary that "I'm in a lot of trouble nowadays!" (xv 237), for instance, is a commentary on the frail condition of his health as much as it is a commentary on the shaky state of his financial affairs. His calamity—"Twenty five thousand dollars! It would ruin him" (xv 233)—is dramatized by the threat of disease: "The old touch of unreasoning terror came back, together with a sudden terror of the spirit, a sickening sinking of the heart, a loathing of life, terrible beyond words" (xv 240). Vandover's loss of control over his body reflects his loss of control over his affairs:

> his mind was still busy going over for the hundredth time all the possibilities of Hiram Wade's suit, and he was just wondering whether something in the way of compromise might not be arranged, when with the suddenness of a blow between the eyes the numbness in his head returned, together with the same unreasoning fear, the same depression of spirits, the same fearful sinking of the heart. What! it was coming back again, this strange attack, coming back even when his attention was not concentrated, even when there was no unusual exertion of his brain! (xv 241)

The frailty of Vandover's body discretely extends the uncertainty of his financial prospects; the deterioration of his physical condition is an implicit commentary on the vulnerability of his affairs.

The insidious effect that is equally at work in the somatic and the economic registers is reiterated even more forcefully during an encounter between Geary and Vandover shortly after Wade has brought suit against Vandover. Geary starts the conversation with a comment on his adversary's weakness: "what's the matter with *you*? You look all frazzled out, all pale around the wattles" (xv 257). Geary's observation about Vandover's deteriorating condition is also an intuitive commentary on his arid affairs. The coalescence between the precarious state of the protagonist's body and the inauspicious state of his affairs, between the devastated Vandover and the divested Vandover, is intriguing: "You keep on getting thin like you have for the past few days and I'll have to be calling you Skinny Seldom-fed again, like we used to" (xv 258). Knowing that Geary is working out schemes to strip Vandover of his property, the statement becomes richly ironic.

It should not go unnoticed, though, that Geary's depiction of Vandover's disorderly state betrays his own anxiety about the affairs he is conducting. His representation of a body on the verge of disintegration bespeaks a fear of disruption or, more specifically, a fear of losing the deal. Geary's commentary on Vandover's health is a way of warding off the likelihood of disarray; it provides a pseudo-reassurance against the possibility of his own failure, for illness as Sander Gilman puts it, "is a real loss of control that results in our becoming the Other whom we have feared, whom we have projected onto the world.... Disease, with its seeming randomness, is one aspect of the indeterminable universe that we wish to distance from ourselves. To do so, we must construct boundaries between ourselves and those categories of individuals whom we believe (or hope) to be more at risk than ourselves.... The construction of the image of the patient is thus always a playing out of this desire for a demarcation between ourselves and the chaos represented in culture by disease" (2–4). Seen from this perspective, the representation of disease becomes a form of negative self-definition. In declaring Vandover "frazzled," "gone-in," and "Skinny Seldom-fed" (xv 258), Geary is distancing himself from the degenerated, impoverished, and reckless Vandover and, by the same token, proclaiming himself as healthy, wealthy, and wise. To mark the other as contaminated is to construct a perspective that implicitly excuses oneself from the threat of dysfunctionality: "that's like you," says Geary to Vandover (xv 258). Such a characterization fixes the image of the other in a state of perpetual disarray; Vandover simply does not conform to the norm which Geary supposedly epitomizes. In the outlook that Geary depicts, then, the reference to bodily disease cannot be easily disengaged from the references to financial disaster. The unhealthiness of Vandover adumbrates not only a bodily disruption but also an economic crisis: "you *do* look gone-in this morning, sure... Never saw you looking so bad; you ought to be more careful, Van; there'll be a smash some time" (xv 258). Geary's ambition and determination to gain control over the business deal is projected in reverse as his enemy's loss of control over his body. In order to ward off the risk of his enterprise, Geary has to ward off the threat of disease; his imagining of the healthy body becomes a way of managing his own affairs.

The correlation between the economic and somatic registers is far from being imposed on the novel. In fact, it fits squarely within the naturalist philosophy. An explicit—even aphoristic—rendering of this philosophy can be readily seen in Dreiser's *Sister Carrie*: "A man's fortune or material progress is very much the same as his bodily growth. Either he is growing stronger, healthier, wiser, as the youth approaching manhood, or he is growing weaker, older, less incisive mentally, as the man approaching old age" (xxxiii 300–01). The passage clearly overlays an economic perspective on a natural process. In the naturalist project, everything is subject to the law of nature which favors the strong and weeds out the weak. What is particularly instructive about *Vandover and the Brute* is not so much the fact that Geary's fears of losing control over the course of events are assuaged within the representation of the body, but the way in which the diagnosis of disease functions as an economic prognosis. The depiction of disease in the novel points to an element of indeterminacy that extends the discussion of the economic theme beyond the sphere of repetition, regularity, and predictability. The representation of the disintegrated body introduces a disruptive or negative element into what seems to be a determined course of events. Geary's fear of losing control over the body translates a fear of losing control over the business affairs he is conducting. In spite of Geary's machinations and carefully wrought designs, there are elements that defy his control and threaten to interfere with the success of his game. The negative element metaphorized in the threat of disease suggests that the game of money is far from being within the control of its individual players.

The element of risk associated with the game of money figures even more explicitly with the theme of gambling in the second half of the novel. The story of Vandover after Geary's scam is basically that of a gambler who brings upon himself his own decline and destruction: "All his life Vandover had been sinking slowly lower and lower; this, however, was the beginning of the last plunge. The process of degeneration, though inevitable, had been gradual as long as he indulged generally in all forms of evil; it was only now when a passion for one particular vice absorbed him that he commenced to rush headlong to his ruin" (xvi 290). After the death of his father, Vandover embarks on a life of debauchery and soon becomes addicted to gambling. He gambles away all his money and even loses his bonds in this fashion: "Vandover's only pleasure was gambling. Night and day he sat over the cards, the passion growing upon him as he continued to lose, for his ill luck was extraordinary. It was a veritable mania, a wild blind frenzy that knew no limit" (xvi 289).

Vandover's financial losses are further dramatized by Geary's material gains. While Geary is making a fortune, Vandover is losing his. Such a course of events is hardly surprising given that the two characters are involved in what seem to be two different games. At first glance, the game that embroils the speculating Geary stands in marked distinction to the game that entangles the gambling Vandover. The former corresponds to a game of competition while the latter corresponds to a game of chance. The two games have different ways of determining a winner. In the game of competition, the player counts on himself for winning, while in the game of chance he cannot rely solely on himself. In the former, the player operates within circumstances and situations he has created and on which he has a deliberate control; in the latter, the player is engaged in a game that involves a situation not of his creation and on which he has only partial or no control. Thus, the efficacy and predictability with which Geary carries out his schemes are absent from Vandover's gambling. Gambling, in fact, entangles the player in a world of debacles—a world where chance constantly defies predictability.

This preliminary distinction between games that are logical and certain, on the one hand, and games that are incalculable and uncertain, on the other hand, should not obscure their relatedness. As Roger Caillois has pointed out, games of competition (*agôn*) and games of chance (*alea*) are contradictory but nonetheless complementary:

> Chance is courted because hard work and personal qualifications are powerless to bring such success about.... Under these conditions, *alea* again seems to be a necessary compensation for *agôn*, and its natural complement. Those it dooms are entirely without hope in the future. It provides new experience. Recourse to chance helps people tolerate competition that is unfair or too rigid. At the same time, it leaves hope in the dispossessed that free competition is still possible in the lowly situations in life, which are necessarily more numerous. (114–15)

Although gambling has existed for a long time, it acquires a new relevance under capitalism. The faith in such uncertain gains as gambling might bring is rooted in the belief that gains which cannot be obtained by hard work can be achieved by luck. Norris' most explicit elaboration of this point occurs in his last novel, *The Pit*. Here play, or "Pit gambling" (iv 130) as Norris calls it, is presented as the logical extension of a system where hard work is valued and competition is sanctified: "It's as easy to get into [a speculation on wheat] as going across the street. They make three hundred, five hundred, yes, even a thousand dollars sometimes in a couple of hours, without so much as raising a finger. Think what that means to a boy of twenty-five who's doing clerk work at seventy-five a month. Why it would take him maybe ten years to save a thousand, and here he's made it in a single morning. Think you can keep him out of speculation then?" (iv 130). Seen from this perspective, gambling is not at odds with the logic of capitalism but on a par with it. The prospects for sudden wealth which make gambling alluring provide an escape from reality. Gambling, in fact, neutralizes the effect of competition, or at least makes it more tolerable and, in so doing, contributes to the consolidation of the dominant socio-economic system. Gambling, as Norris points out in *McTeague*, is appealing because it democratizes: "The lottery was a great charity, the friend of the people, a vast beneficent machine that recognized neither rank nor wealth nor station" (vii 114).

There is, yet, another way in which gambling extends the logic of capitalism. Underlying gambling is an empty production that can bring to light an important aspect of the category of value. The sense of purposelessness—even futility—that characterizes Vandover's play points to an element of wastefulness. The pleasure that one derives from gambling, in particular, and playing, in general, as Caillois points out, is inseparable from the experience of waste: "Play is an occasion for pure waste of time, energy, ingenuity, skill and often money" (6). The squandering of money that gambling calls for is governed by the same intense expenditure, the same exceeding energy that motivates the law of value. The destruction of value is not the opposite but the underside of the production of value, which is tantamount to saying that capitalism entails not only production for the sake of production but also destruction for the sake of destruction.6 As the novel proceeds, Vandover "ceased to be economical" (xviii 337) and has become passionately immersed in gambling. Under the spell of this "new craze" (xvi 289), Vandover can stop neither when he is a winner nor when he is a loser: "Vandover won as often as he lost, but the habit of cards grew upon him steadily" (xvi 281). Even after he has lost all his money, he cannot resist the "the temptation that drew him constantly to the gambling-table" (xvi 289). In his ludic ardor, Vandover is no longer in use or exchange value but in "abuse value" (Serres, *Parasite* 80). His addiction to gambling is motivated by a useless expenditure and driven by an indulgence in losing for the sake of losing. Gambling becomes the index for a whole experience of extravagance, waste, and excess: "Certain habits of extravagance grew upon Vandover, the natural outcome of his persisted gambling, the desire of winning easily being balanced by the impulses to spend quickly. He took a certain hysterical delight in flinging away money with both hands.... The fifteen thousand dollars ... he has gambled or flung away in a little less than a year. He never invested it, but ate into it day after day ... moved simply by a reckless desire for spending" (xvi 290).

The third way in which gambling can be related to the logic of capitalism is probably the most intricate one. Gambling is particularly significant in the novel because it introduces an element of contingency at the heart of determinacy. It points to a certain playfulness that is inherent in the logic of capitalism. The implication of this playfulness is most explicitly explored in the last novel of Norris' unfinished trilogy. Much like *Vandover and the Brute*, *The Pit* has an element of contingency at its core. The novel depicts the irresistible temptation of a shrewd character, Curtis Jadwin, to speculate on wheat exchange in the Chicago Board of Trade. Although Jadwin has decided to abandon financial speculation, he cannot resist his ludic instinct for long: "the trouble is, not that I don't want to speculate, but that I *do*—too much" (iii 86). Confident in his success, he engages anew in the perils of a game of money and gradually becomes engrossed in it. Switching from the position of a bear to that of a bull, he decides to corner the market by buying enormous amounts of wheat at a low price in order to increase demand and consequently raise prices. Suddenly, however, he is caught up in the frenzied excitement of the pit. The unexpected influx of large quantities of wheat breaks Jadwin's corner, flooding the market with more supply than he can buy to hold his position. As the game progresses, Jadwin finds himself unable to control the risks he has taken or limit the possibility of disorder he has involuntarily initiated. In spite of his calculation and intuition, Jadwin cannot exercise any control over the course of events, and he loses all his money in the end. Ironically, he finds himself victimized by a situation he had purposefully sought to avoid. It is all the more ironic given his response to the pressures of his assistant, Sam Grety, to seize the opportunity to speculate on a seemingly winning gamble: "Sam, I had sort of made my mind to keep out of speculation since my last little deal. A man gets into this game, and into it, and into it, and before you know it he cannot pull out—and he don't want to. Next he gets his nose scratched, and he hits back to make up for it and just hits into the air and loses his balance—and down he goes" (iii 86). The events that make havoc of Jadwin's fortune bespeak an element of contingency at the heart of the socio-economic system that underlies much of the action of the novel. More specifically, the complications that arise point to what Goux calls "the ludic dimension of capitalism" ("General" 215). The underlying assumption behind this ludic dimension is that the strategy of capitalism is not only cumulative but also innovative.

This ludic dimension is particularly significant because it puts into question the Weberian and neo-Weberian conception of capitalism as a manipulative, rationalizing system. While Adorno and Horkheimer, for instance, saw in capitalism the incarnation of an administrated rationality that extends Max Weber's characterization of modernity as an iron cage of rationality,[7] more recent accounts have drawn attention to the unpredictable nature of capitalism—a critical move which attempts to account for both the structure of capitalism (the logic of its organization) and its metamorphosis (the logic of its evolution). This dual interest can be seen not only in Deleuze's schizoanalytical version of poststructuralism—which argues that capitalism engenders the profusion of flows that drive towards a limit that is never reached because it is continuously displaced[8]—but also in the apologetic discourse of such economists as George Gilder. In Gilder's view, capitalism is not void of chance, but the element of chance invigorates rather than impoverishes capitalism. For Gilder, capitalism is more aptly defined by its uncertainties than its certainties: "Economists who themselves do not believe in the future of capitalism, will tend to ignore the dynamics of chance and faith that largely will determine the future.... Chance is the foundation of change" (266). Pursuing the implications of this ludic dimension in capitalism enables us to have a better understanding of the interplay between determinacy and indeterminacy, which can extend the analysis of the economics of the novel, in particular, and of naturalism, in general, beyond what Walter Benn Michaels calls "unrestrained capitalism" (*Gold Standard* 18)—an even system that reproduces itself unfailingly and indefinitely. Both *Vandover and the Brute* and *The Pit* suggest that capitalism is not a closed or evenly-constituted system but an open configuration that produces fissures and engenders contradictions—in short, a system that is inherently ludic.

An analysis of the relationship between speculation and gambling can provide some further insights on the relationship between the systematic and the asystematic. In the minds of many, speculation is somewhat distinct from gambling. While the outcome of the former is conceived as predictable and scientific, the outcome of the latter is regarded as unpredictable and random. A more careful consideration,

however, may suggest otherwise. As Huizinga has pointed out, the two
practices have more in common than is often admitted:

> The hazy borderline between play and seriousness is illustrated very
> tellingly by the use of the words "playing" or "gambling" for the
> machinations of the stock exchange. The gambler at the roulette table will
> readily concede that he is playing; the stock-jobber will not. He will
> maintain that buying and selling on the off-chance of prices rising or
> falling is part of the serious business of life, at least of business life, and
> that it is an economic function of society. In both cases the operative
> factor is the hope of gain; but whereas in the former the pure fortuitousness
> of the thing is generally admitted (all "systems" not withstanding), in the
> latter the player deludes himself with the fancy that he can calculate the
> future trends of the market. At any rate the difference of mentality is exactly
> small. (52)

What this observation means, in part, is that the distinction between
play (gambling) and non-play (market speculation) is a pseudo-
distinction because in neither case can the player reliably predict or
elicit the outcome. Jadwin's failure, in particular, points to an
irrational or frenetic element that defies control; it suggests that
speculation is open to the paradoxes of hazard in the same way
gambling is subject to the randomness of chance. In *The Pit*, Jadwin
himself equates speculation with gambling: "These fellows
themselves, the gamblers—well, call them speculators, if you like. Oh,
the fine, promising manly young men I've seen wrecked—absolutely
and hopelessly wrecked and ruined by speculation!" (iv 130). Much
like gambling, capitalist investment involves entrusting money or
property and awaiting returns in the uncertain future; one ventures
with neither an assurance of reward nor a shield from uncertainty.

A historical perspective on the correlation between gambling and
speculation can further extend these observations. The relationship
between the uncertainties inherent in gambling and the ludic
dimension associated with capitalism was purposefully repressed
during Norris' own time; in fact, it was even disclaimed. It is
interesting to note, along with Reuven and Gabrielle Brenner, that
bucket shops, which flourished in the second half of the nineteenth
century in the United States, were often condemned by such large
financial institutions as the Chicago Board of Trade because they
made speculation reprehensibly indistinguishable from gambling.
Speculation in these shops involved sums of money which were not
any larger than those spent for gambling: "Bucket shops were

disapproved of by the Chicago Board of Trade (which in 1905 won a
legal battle against them) because of the fear that they would bring
into general disrepute the legitimate exchange, since trade in futures
would be viewed as mere gambling" (Brenner 92).   If this
controversy suggests something, it is the fine line that distinguishes
speculation from gambling.   Investment—however tightly controlled
it may be—is also gambling in the sense that the outcome is neither
reliably predictable nor fixed in advance.   Much like gambling,
speculation is haunted by specters of fluctuation, unpredictability, and
disorder.

The element of contingency that suffuses *The Pit* is not wanting in
Vandover and the Brute.   In the latter novel, contingency extends
even beyond the theme of gambling.   While gambling seems to be the
central repository for the element of indeterminacy in the novel, it is
not the only one.   An analysis of the letter that Vandover receives
from his bank informing him that his account has been overdrawn
enables us to pursue this aspect in the novel from a slightly different
perspective.   Much like the ominous letter that McTeague receives
from City Hall barring him from practicing dentistry, the letter
Vandover receives from the bank highlights an aleatory element at
work in the novel.   It adumbrates a number of unexpected
developments:

> Was it possible that he no longer had any money at the bank? Was his
> fifteen thousand gone?   From time to time his bank-book had been
> balanced, and invariably during the first days of each month his checks had
> come back to him, used and crumpled, covered with strange signatures and
> stamped in blue ink; but after the first few months he had never paid the
> least attention to these.... But it was absurd to think that the money was
> gone. Pshaw! one could not spend fifteen thousand in nine months! It was
> preposterous!   This notice was some technicality that he could not
> understand.... In a second he knew that he was ruined. The true meaning of
> the notice became apparent with the swiftness of a great flush of light. He
> had spent his fifteen thousand dollars! (xvi 296–97)

In this passage, Vandover's indulgent behavior and his failure to hold
his account in check are presented as two sides of the same coin. Not
only does Vandover lose the money he has inherited from the Old
Gentleman, but he does so in the most stunning way. Keeping his
check-book in balance is as mysterious as playing cards. Both
practices are wrought with a certain incomprehensibility that recalls
the incomprehensibly abandoned child during the scene of the death

of the mother.   The connection hardly escapes the reader.
Vandover's indulgence, as Norris observes, is closely associated with
the feminine: "he never kept accounts, having a veritable feminine
horror of figures" (xvi 296–97).
     Considering such moments in the novel, it becomes hardly
surprising that *Vandover and the Brute* grabbed the attention of a
psychoanalyst even before it received serious attention among literary
critics.   In an interesting discussion of the novel, Edmund Bergler
draws attention to the psychoanalytical dimension of Vandover's
ludic experience, connecting the feminine aversion of money that
Vandover experiences to the theme of gambling that dominates the
last chapters of the book.   Bergler even compares the story of
Vandover to an actual clinical case in which the patient exhibits
similar symptoms.   In gambling, Vandover operates under a psychic
masochism which precludes satisfaction.   Gambling is not only an
irresistible passion but a destructive experience: "Vandover's only
pleasure was gambling.   Night and day he sat over the cards, the
passion growing upon him as he continued to lose, for his ill luck was
extraordinary.   It was a veritable mania, a wild blind frenzy that knew
no limit" (xvi 289).   The masochistic behavior Bergler identifies at
the heart of Vandover's passion for the game can further be related to
a compulsive experience behind which stands the absent figure of the
mother.   In Bergler's view, Vandover exemplifies the type of gambler
who "appears to want proof he is loved, just as he apparently wants to
win when he gambles.   But unconsciously he remains unsatisfied
unless he receives his daily 'dose of injustice'" (83).   The gambler is
satisfied neither when he wins nor when he loses: "It was not with any
hope of winning that he gambled" (xvi 289).   Behind Vandover's
addiction to gambling is not a desire to win, but a need for mere
titillation.   Translating this observation to the libidinal context,
Vandover's desire for the mother is, arguably, motivated not by a
search for satisfaction but by a denial of the mother.   Throughout the
novel, Vandover experiences his object of desire as a *beyond*.   Such
an experience involves what may be termed, after Julia Kristeva,
"*jouissance* as nostalgia" (*Tales of Love* 356) where the figure of the
mother is close at hand and yet lost forever, insistent and yet elusive.
Norris' depiction of Vandover in the scene where he relates the death
of the mother further elucidates this ambivalence.   In the train station,
Vandover's unsettling and anxious gaze is minutely described:
"Vandover stood close to his father...   He looked about him
continuously, rolling his big eyes vaguely, watching now the repair-
gang, now a huge white cat dozing on an empty baggage truck" (i 4).

What is intriguing in this scene is the reservedness with which Vandover observes his mother. Although he seems to be observing everything around him except the figure of his mother, this very disinterestedness betrays him. Attracted and yet repulsed, Vandover finds a satisfaction in eyeing the passengers who "were walking up and down the platform staring curiously at the invalid lying back in the steamer chair" (i 4). While in appearance Vandover is indifferent, in reality he is discreetly looking at his mother, imagining her figure in the countenance of the curious passengers.

Seen from this perspective, the novel is not only punctuated with the experience of loss, as Barbara Hochman has observed, it is also suffused with an involuntary memory of the mother.[9] The concluding pages of the novel strike the reader as a reenactment of the opening episode in two essential ways. The novel opens with the figure of an orphan child recalling the death of his debilitated mother and closes with a child eyeing the degenerated Vandover scrubbing the floor of a cottage in an industrial neighborhood. The physiognomy of the mother at the outset of the novel is reproduced even more dramatically at the end in the conspicuous animalistic depiction of Vandover himself. It is as if Vandover reexperiences the death of the mother in his own degeneration. The parallel between the opening episode and the closing scene suggests that the influence of the mother has not ceased with her death but is, instead, repressed.[10] A similar mechanism can also be seen at work in the case of the father, only this time, the implications of repression bear more on political than libidinal economy. As long as the father is alive, the realty business he is involved with is profitable. The father, in fact, manages to hold the system together or, to borrow a psychoanalytical terminology, he manages to repress the disruptive element. With his death, however, the potential disruptive element that accompanies investment becomes more manifest; in the hands of Vandover, things start to fall apart. This dimension suggests that capitalism is also subject to upheavals or internal contradiction which, although not always manifest, are nonetheless operative and—like the return of the repressed—are susceptible to emerge.

The Old Gentleman is a prosperous San Francisco businessman who has made his money in real estate. His business success suggests a skill in management and an intuition for investment: "People spoke of the Old Gentleman as one of the most successful realty owners in the city" (i 7). In more than one way, the father epitomizes stability, predictability, and control. With the death of the father, however, things started to take a new turn. Convening with Mr. Field, the lawyer, to discuss his father's will, Vandover realizes that the realty business he has inherited may not be as prosperous as his father led him to believe that it was. In fact, the income from renting the property Vandover has inherited will not be enough to support him:

> Vandover made another hasty calculation on his cuff, and leaned back in his chair staring at the lawyer, saying:
>   "Why, that leave eighty-four dollars a month, net."
>   "Yes," asserted Field. "I made it that, too."
>   "Why, the Governor used to allow *me* fifty a month," returned Vandover, "just for pocket money."
>   "I'm afraid you mustn't expect anything like that, now, Mr. Vandover," replied Field, smiling. (xi 165)

The anxiety caused by the death of the Old Gentleman provides some insights into the dynamics of the novel. The business undertakings of the father are less stable than they seem. Although the speculations of the Old Gentleman are not as variable as those of Curtis Jadwin in *The Pit*, no balance is sustained either. The father, as Norris notes in the opening chapter, was somehow involved in speculation. He often speculated by having two mortgages on the same piece of property:

> He believed this to be a shrewd business operation, since the rents as they returned to him were equal to the interest on a far larger sum than that which he had originally invested. He said little about the double mortgage on each piece of property "improved" after this fashion and which often represented a full two-thirds of its entire value. The interest on each loan was far more than that covered by the rents; he chose his neighborhoods with great discrimination; real estate was flourishing in the rapidly growing city, and the new houses, although built so cheaply that they were mere shells of lath and plaster, were nevertheless made gray and brave with varnish and cheap mill work. They rented all at first, scarcely a one was ever vacant.... So pleased did he become with the success of his new venture that in course of time all his money was reinvested after this fashion. (i 7–8)

While the capitalist investments of the Old Gentleman may appear to be void of risk, the balance he achieves is in fact contrived. The father, as Mr. Field told Vandover, had to live on an additional income from the law business: "when your father was alive and pursing his profession, he made a comfortable income besides that which he derived from his realty. His law business I consider to have been excellent when you take everything into consideration. He often made five hundred dollars a month at it. Such are the figures the papers show. Handsome allowance while he was alive, but all that is stopped now!" (xi 165). The Old Gentleman, then, is able to survive through a compensatory mechanism—the supplementary income from the law business—and once this mechanism is gone, the disruptive elements—which have so far been repressed—start to gain ground and to undermine the stability of the system.

The ludic dimension inherent in speculation and gambling can be seen at the level of the text itself. *Vandover and the Brute* not only makes use of the theme of play but is arguably a playful novel. I use the term playful to designate a set of narrative strategies, textual maneuvers, and rhetorical moves which, whether consciously or not, complicate the unfolding of the novel. In *Games Authors Play*, Peter Hutchinson draws attention to the role of literary games in structuring the relationship between the reader and the text: "a literary game may be seen as any *playful*, self-conscious and extended means by which an author situates his reader to deduce or speculate, by which he encourages him to see a relationship between different parts of the text, or between the text and something extraneous to it" (14). For Hutchinson playfulness is an integral part of the literary text; it is a means for drawing the reader into an inquiring relationship with the text. Literature can be said to be inherently ludic either because it is fictive and in this sense invites different interpretations or, to borrow Bakhtin's terminology, heteroglossic insofar as it is "multiform in style and variform in speech and voice" (*Dialogic* 261). Every novelistic text, as Nancy Morrow observes, "plays a particular kind of game with the readers: by encouraging them to participate in the play of language and ideas, by making them believe in the imagined world of the text, or even challenging them to solve a particular problem or puzzle" (22). Realism is apparently an exception, because realist representation tends to resist playful tendencies.[11] Playfulness is a feature that realism and naturalism often strive to suppress. At least from the standpoint of its proponents, the realist novel is less associated with fiction than it is with fact; it does not provide a fictional version of reality but reality itself: "Just as the realist must convince readers that the fictional world is factual, she or he must persuade them that the characters are faithful reproductions of 'real' people, typical and exemplary, case studies that illustrate some 'fact' about contemporary life" (Morrow 29–30). The kind of unpredictability that suffuses *Vandover and the Brute*, however, alerts us to a playful dimension at work even in what is often conceived as strict realism. If this ludic dimension warrants further attention it is not merely because the novel conveys the inherent playfulness of fiction but because it is ludic in specific ways. In fact, the causal determinism one expects in such a naturalist novel is continuously deconstructed.

Consider the following sentence, for instance, in which Norris conveys Vandover's anxiety about the Wade case: "He has all the sensations of terror, but without any assignable reason, and this groundless fear became in the end the cause of a new fear" (xv 240). The sentence clearly states that Vandover's fear is groundless; at the same time, this fear cannot be dismissed because it provides the ground for another fear. Norris assures the reader that the fear which has overwhelmed his character is a mere hallucination but is nonetheless worthy of consideration because it engenders a more significant fear: "he was afraid of this fear that was afraid of nothing" (xv 240). This playfulness is far from being incidental. Earlier in the novel, we encounter a similar equivocation. The death of the Old Gentleman leaves Vandover in a state of extreme anguish and agitation. His confusion takes the form of a blurry vision. The uncertainty of his prospects is presented as a lack of clarity: "There was nothing, nothing. He clearly saw the fate towards which he was hurrying" (xiv 219). Out of this unsettling experience emerges an oxymoron which the reader can hardly fail to notice—Vandover clearly saw the indistinctness of his future. What his vision has crystallized is an unsurmountable ambiguity and a prevailing amorphism.

Another example of this literary playfulness is the game that Geary plays on Vandover. The numerous exchanges between the two characters are marked by an ambiguity that purposefully hinders communication. The success of Geary's machinations depends on his ability to develop discursive ploys and recondite arguments. His discourse does not disclose his intentions but is, instead, aimed at misleading his adversary: "Vandover had often wondered at Geary's persistence in the matter, and had often asked him what he could possibly want of the block. But Geary was very vague in his replies, generally telling Vandover that there was money in the investment if one could and would give the proper attention to pushing it" (xv 251). This lack of clarity endows Geary with a degree of protection which increases his chances of winning. The same strategy of incommunicability is reiterated in a curious episode towards the end of the novel, except that the roles are reversed. Hungry, impoverished, and desolate, Vandover, who has gambled away all his money, pays an unexpected visit to Geary to beg for a dollar. The ambiguity of the exchange between the two points to a ludic element; Vandover is, in fact, playing his own game with Geary. To the question "what have you done with your bonds?" (xviii 331), Geary receives neither a definite answer nor a satisfying explanation but is, instead, inundated with a number of perplexing stories:

> "Bonds?" repeated Vandover, dazed and bewildered. "I ain't never had any bonds. What bonds? Oh, yes," he exclaims, suddenly remembering, "yes, I know, *my* bonds, of course; yes, yes—well, I—those—those, I had to sell those bonds—had some debts, you see, my board and my tailor's bill. They got out some sort of paper after me. Yet, I had forgotten about my bonds. I lost every damned one of them playing cards—gambled 'em all away." (xviii 331)

Geary's inquiry is met with a series of claims that do not clarify but further confuse. Vandover's statements are not meant to be lucid but ludic. With every excuse, he concocts a new story that denies the one that precedes it: "Well first I began to pawn things when my money got short—the Old Gentleman's watch that I said I never would part with, then my clothes" (xviii 332). Even when Vandover implicitly admits that he has been bluffing and promises to be sincere, the conversation is soon diffused with another baffling story that seeks to crystallize the truth even while further mystifying it: "'I don't want to run any bunco game. I'm an honest man—I'm honest. I gave money to help another duck; gave him thousands; he was good to me when I was on my uppers and I mean to repay him. I was grateful. I signed a paper that gave him everything I had. I was in Paris. There's where my bonds went to. I was a struggling artist'" (xviii 332). The relationship between Geary and Vandover, then, becomes hardly conceivable outside these discursive ploys. Vandover's success in extorting money from Geary—"Lend me a dollar" (xviii 331)—relies on Geary's failure to understand Vandover: "I couldn't keep away from the cards. Of course, you can't understand that" (xviii 332). This strategy is all the more compelling because it comes back a few pages later, only this time it is reversed. The same game is, in fact, recreated to designate a different winner. Accompanying Vandover to his new work place at the workers' cottages across the street from the boot and shoe factory, Geary explains to his old chum—who is also his adversary—the secret behind his success in turning the property that Vandover used to own from a liability to an asset: "'That was *my* idea,' observed Geary, as they approached the row, willing to explain even though he thought Vandover would not comprehend" (xviii 340). In spite of his awareness of the incommunicability of his discourse, Geary is nonetheless keen on explaining to Vandover that the success of his investment is attributable to his sound decision and intuitive judgement. The purpose of the information he volunteers about the clarity of his vision is not to provide clarification but to perpetuate ambiguity and increase confusion, and thus to prolong the game he has been playing.

Such as it is, then, the narrative is infused with instances of what may be termed, after Guy Debord, "diversion" (208), a communication that cannot guarantee certitude, or better yet a discourse that lacks authority because its truth does not depend on any outside guarantee but is, instead, grounded in its own indefiniteness. Norris is disposed to provide his readers with clues about certain moments or episodes in the novel, but to deprive them of absolute certainty. In so doing, he calls on his readers to reinterpret and reevaluate the reality that the novel represents. Again, the fate of the bonds provides an eloquent example. Although Geary consents to help his old friend, he never acquires a definite knowledge of the fate of the bonds and seems to be satisfied at the end with Vandover's contention that "somehow, they all went" (xviii 332); Geary is, in fact, more intrigued by the whole mystery of Vandover's degeneration than he is preoccupied by the true fate of the bonds: "Geary leaned back in his chair listening to Vandover, struck with wonder, marvelling at that which his old chum had come to be" (xviii 333). Norris' own commentary on Vandover's recklessness stands out less as an assertion than a probability, and in that sense is less revelatory than ludic: "Of the many different stories that Vandover has told about the disappearance of his bonds, the one that was probably truest was the one that accounted for the things by his passion for gambling" (xviii 336–37). By withholding the truth the omniscient narrator is playing games with the reader. Not unlike Geary, the reader of the novel does not get a clear-cut answer on how Vandover has squandered his money but is, instead, faced with a plethora of possible scenarios. Even when later in the novel the narrator informs the reader of the real fate of the bonds after he has been playing with his or her expectations, the assertive thrust of his account is undermined by the circumstantiality of the incident which led to their loss:

> one day, about six months before his visit to Geary's office, Vandover saw
> that the proprietor of the Reno House had set up a great bagatelle board in a

corner of the reading room. A group of men, sailors, ranchmen, and fruit vendors were already playing. Vandover approached and watched the game, very interested in watching the uncertain course of the marble jog-jogging among the pins. The clear little note of the bell or the dry rattle as the marble settled quickly into one of the lucky pockets thrilled him from head to foot; his hands trembled, all at once his whole left side twitched sharply.

From that day the fate of the rest of Vandover's little money was decided. (xviii 337)

The passage is oxymoronic, to say the least, insofar as it juxtaposes two different, even antithetical, investments. The reliability of the bonds—"U.S. bonds are always good" (xv 262)—is undercut by the uncertainty associated with gambling and the risk from which the player cannot be shielded.

The playfulness of the interaction between Vandover and Geary points to a number of swerves or atypical moments that are not on a par with the proclaimed realism of the novel. Given Vandover's mendacity, the text calls on the reader to make speculations, formulate hypotheses, and enact choices. To get an insight into the real character of Vandover, one has to consider an expanded world of possibilities, evaluate a number of alternatives, and consider a set of variables. The peculiarity and unpredictability of Vandover, in fact, turns the reader into a player-reader. Reading is no longer a matter of simple unfolding; the story does not just report the events but compels the reader to construct them.[12] To read the novel is to confront the challenge of deciphering the "pliable character" (xii 207) of Vandover. The depiction of Vandover early in the novel poses one such challenge: "Little by little, the crude virility of the young man began to develop in him. It was a distressing, uncanny period. Had Vandover been a girl he would at this time have been subject to all sorts of abnormal vagaries, such as eating his slate pencil, nibbling bits of chalk, wishing he were dead, and drifting into states of unseasoned melancholy" (i 8–9). In exploring the possible transmogrifications of Vandover, Norris is playing a counterfactual game with his reader. Portraying Vandover as a girl anticipates the feminization of Vandover later in the story; at the same time, this counterfactual game undermines the "realism" of that story.

The playfulness that the foregoing analysis exemplifies can be partially attributed to the complexity of reality itself. Realist representation is invested in the very artifice of the text for the simple reason that if that text purports to represent reality, it has to reproduce reality in its full complexity. This is precisely what Norris finds most

intriguing in the nature of the real: "the story writer must go to real
life for his story. You can never think out, or invent or imagine a tale
that will be half so good as the things that have 'really happened.'
The complications of real life are infinitely better, stronger and more
original than anything you can make up" (*Literary* 51).[13] This vision
of the complexity of the real has long been the subject of
appreciation.   In a short essay occasioned by the posthumous
publication of *Vandover and the Brute*, John Macy captures this
distinctive trait in Norris' fiction: "He is never guilty of the young
writer's vice of seeming to 'do a description.' He uses his eyes and is
perhaps youthfully conscious that he sees life in an individual way
and is not victim of other people's trite observations" (36).   Norris
hardly allows his language to reduce the complexity of reality or
diminish its vitality. His fiction stands out less as a portrait of the real
than as an experience of reality.   From Norris' standpoint, an
adequate representation of reality has to capture the real in its
complexity, elusiveness, and even playfulness. This aspect of Norris'
naturalist vision is particularly emphasized in a curious short story
based on a trip to South Africa. The story contains the following
exchange between a timekeeper in a diamond mine and the imagined
author:

> "Here's something you can tell your paper. You'll never see a Zulu finish a
> meal without washing his teeth very carefully afterwards."
>   I answered that the details would be duly reported, but that I would not
> answer for its acceptance as truth. (Norris, *Collected Writings* 225)

The kind of objectivity the author advocates underscores a distinction
between the documentation of the real and the apprehension of the
real. The former is supposedly scientific and objective, the latter is
ambiguous and even subjective.   Norris' response to the Zulu
timekeeper not only denotes the complexity of reality but also points
to the arbitrariness of representation.
    In *Vandover and the Brute*, the playfulness of the text is
indistinguishable from the "pliable character" of Vandover himself
(xii 207). The unpredictability of the protagonist often produces a
textual predilection towards equivocality which places the reader in a
realm of uncertainty. One can see the collision, and even collusion, of
antithetical characteristics and incompatible traits that introduce a
pervasive element of surprise. The ensuing effect stems not so much
from the unreality of the new developments but from their
improbability. An incident towards the end of the novel illustrates this

contrariety. After having dinner with his two gambling companions, Ellis and the Dummy, on Thanksgiving eve, Vandover discloses to them his intention to go to a football game. Ellis' repeated attempts to dissuade Vandover from attending the game make him even more resolute:

> Ellis began to argue with Vandover against the folly of going anywhere in the rain.
> "*You* don't want to go to that game, Van. Just look how it's raining. I'll bet there won't be a thousand people there. They'll probably postpone the game anyway.... Better change your mind, Van." (xvi 291–92)

Norris devotes several pages to convey Vandover's excitement over this sports event, describing his meticulous preparations for the game down to the smallest detail—from cutting the string around a pasteboard box containing a new cheviot suit that Vandover is to wear to the most trivial detail about tying a couple of silk streamers bearing the college colors to his umbrella handle. The sense of anticipation mustered in this episode, however, is cut short by Vandover's whimsical attitude. In some incomprehensible way he gives up his original plan to see the football game to join in the game of cards he has been tangentially watching:

> Half an hour later he was still behind Ellis' chair. Ellis had become so fidgety that he was losing steadily. Once more he turned to Vandover, speaking over his shoulder, "Come on, come on, Van, go along to your football; you make me nervous standing there." Vandover pushed a ten-dollar gold-piece across the table to the Dummy, who was banking, and said:
> "Give me that in chips. I'm coming in."
> "I thought you were going to the game?" inquires Ellis.
> "Ah, the devil!" answered Vandover. "Too much rain." (xvi 294)

Vandover's state of mind is intriguing given his earlier stubborn resolution to attend the game in spite of the rain. This incident, along with other unaccountable moments in the novel, make Vandover almost a chameleon who slips from one character to another. He belongs to a well to do family, has a Harvard education, and has developed a taste for art and a disposition towards moral striving. As the novel unfolds, however, he not only loses his moral uprightness but also becomes *déclassé* and *désœuvré*. After the death of his father, Vandover becomes so peculiar as to resist typification. Little by little, he abandons his prayers, loses his wealth, and forsakes his art. He believed in God and yet "rejected a concrete religion" (xiv 218), owned property and yet lost it, possessed "the fundamental *afflatus* that underlies all branches of art" (i 12) and yet found himself unable to paint, eventually losing interest in his art altogether.

We should not conclude, however, that Vandover is not a "realist" character. The unintended events and unforseen developments that precipitate Vandover's degeneration are stunning, but not unrealistic. Because "society cared no longer what he did" (xiv 217), Vandover has indulged in a playfulness that is congenial to his pliable and adaptable character: "Drunkenness, sensuality, gambling, debauchery, he knew them all" (xiii 207). Bizarre as it may seem, the unfolding of events does not interfere with the consistency of Norris' protagonist. Vandover is not unprincipled but simply opportunistic: "His nature was not shallow. It had merely become deteriorated.... He had so often rearranged his pliable nature to suit his changing environment that at last he found that he could be content in almost any circumstances. He had no pleasures, no cares, no ambitions, no regrets, no hopes" (xi 159–xvi 278). Resulting from this kind of indifference, is a sense of unexpectedness that gives Vandover all the more credibility as a character; his realism lies precisely in his consistent inconsistency.

Such an ambivalence bears witness to a certain "roundness" at work in the novel that energizes, or at least relativizes, what is otherwise a flat realism.[14] The effect of roundness interferes with the predictability of the character and instills a certain episodic newness which interferes with the deterministic strain in the novel. At the same time, however, the realism of the novel is never undermined. The effect of roundness creates a tension in the narrative that does not go against the novel's realism in any radical way; at the same time it cannot be contained within the confines of a strict realism—it enhances the realism of the story while complicating it. Such an effect finds ample articulation in the numerous distortions that infuse the novel: the transmogrification of a middle class character into an impoverished brute, the deterioration of a promising artist into a debased hero, the transformation of an old friend into an adversary, the transmutation of property from one owner to another, and even the disfigurement of the landscape whereby houses are transformed into a factory. Complementing these distortions are a number of ambiguous moments that introduce a peculiar dimension into the novel: inaccessible information, shattered memories, faint recollections, tangential incidents, inconsistent characterizations, incomprehensible developments, obscure events, bizarre characters, uncontrollable diseases, and mysterious deaths.

The most astounding moment in the novel in which this playful dimension can be seen at work is probably the growing bestiality of Vandover, i.e., the degeneration of Vandover from a character who "had a capital ear for music" (i 2) to a barking dog. The starker the realism gets with the motifs of animalism and atavism the more gothic the novel becomes. Fancying that he is some kind of beast, Vandover ends up crawling on all fours, uncontrollably growling: "He was barking incessantly. It was evident that now he could not stop himself; it was like hysterical laughter, a thing beyond his control" (xvi 301). Acting under the influence of alcohol and suffering from lycanthropy, Vandover acts out of control, although not out of character. Such unaccountability makes Vandover a bizarre persona without necessarily undermining his realism. Thus, when Norris takes up the image of the howling Vandover again in Geary's office, he takes pains to convey a certain realism:

> "You ought to see me sometimes—*b-r-r-r-h!*—and I get to barking! I'm a wolf mostly, you know, or some kind of an animal, some kind of a brute.... See how long my finger nails are—regular claws; that's the wolf, the brute! Why can't I talk in my mouth instead of in my throat? That's the devil of it. When you paint on steel and iron your colors don't dry out true; all the yellows turn green. But it would 'a' been all straight if they hadn't fined me! .... Oh! I don't complain. Give me a dollar and I'll bark for you!" (xviii 333)

In this passage, Norris reiterates Vandover's grotesque animalism and exaggerated brutishness but at the same time endows his character with a realistic appeal. The passage starts with a depiction of Vandover as a wolf and ends with the same image. In between is a curious rhetorical move in which Vandover, who has long abandoned his art, makes use of an analogy that bears witness to an artistic sensibility: "'When you paint on steel and iron your colors don't dry out true; all the yellows turn green'" (xviii 333). As the character of Vandover starts to reach the limits of credibility, Norris instills the scene with a dose of reality. The metaphor of the paint echoes a comment about Vandover's artistic sensibility earlier in the novel: "His indulgent luxurious character continually hungered after subdued, harmonious colors" (xvi 280). By reminding the reader that Vandover is not only a brute but a brute who is a failed artist, Norris restores the realism of the scene. Charles Walcutt aptly captures the effect of this move in his reading of the novel: "At any time, Vandover might take a turn for the better" (121). At the point where Vandover's dog-like behavior seems to start undermining the realism of the novel, a counter-effect is introduced; by reminding the reader that the barking Vandover is the failed artist we have known all along, Norris keeps the story within the limits of possibility. This is an aspect in Norris' writings which even his contemporaries have found intriguing: "Norris' imagination was strong enough to endow his personages with individual temperaments, motives, habits of thought and modes of speech; they lead their own lives; they seem to be out of control. And that is the most difficult, the most wonderful illusion that a creator of fiction can produce" (Macy 36). Walcutt concurs: "The events which thrust him down are more coincidence than the acts of fate that destroy some of Hardy's characters. But nevertheless they are presented with such a wealth of convincing detail that the average reader accepts them as probable" (121). The story achieves a kind of ludic realism that wards off the suspicion of the reader as to the fictive nature of the real without compromising Vandover's complexity.

Seen from this perspective, the main question that naturalism poses is not how the text copies reality but how it convinces the reader that it does.[15] As Miles Orvell puts it, "*Vandover and the Brute* raises in dramatically unexpected form the question of how real realism could be. Or, perhaps, How *unreal* realism could be?" (116). There is something grotesquely incomprehensible about Vandover which Norris has taken pains to convey throughout the novel:

> The boys called him "skinny-seldom fed." His appetite was enormous. He ate heavy meat three times a day, but took little or no exercise.... At times the strangest and most morbid fancies took possession of him, chief of which was that every one was looking at him while he was walking in the street.
>
> Vandover was a good little boy. Every night he said his prayers, going down upon his huge knees at the side of his bed.... Till very late he kept his innocence, the crude raw innocence of the boy, like that of a young animal, at once charming and absurd. (i 8–9)

The passage is intriguing because it stresses Vandover's atypicality. He is skinny and yet has an enormous appetite; he is a little boy and yet has huge knees; he has grown up with the spiritual comfort of prayers and yet entertains the wildest fantasies; he is charming and yet absurd. The peculiarity of Vandover that the passage conveys forces the reader to consider the possible implication of reality as a lived experience rather than reality as a pre-given. With Vandover, we move from referential reality (i.e., mimetic realism) to performative reality (i.e., ludic realism).

The curious unfolding of events at the end of the novel further intensifies the sense of unexpectedness that distinguishes Vandover. Not only has Vandover's character become incomprehensible, but the denouement of the story itself turns out to be unexpected, engendering a number of swerves: "Vandover was evicted from the Lick House three days after he had stolen young Haight's money. Instead of paying his bills with the amount, he gambled it away in a back of a new café on Market Street with Toby" (xvii 314). Such swerves seem so insistent that as Vandover started "to lead a haphazard sort of life ... he was so irregular that he could never be depended upon" (xvii 314–15).16 Vandover himself has not failed to sense his own irregularity: "I was so irregular" (xviii 332), he admits to Geary towards the end of the novel. Accounting for the rest of the story becomes as uncertain a task as following the swerves of Vandover and projecting his possible developments. The unpredictability of the protagonist is thus reinforced by the inexplicability of the text. The irregularity of Vandover is such that a forceful depiction of his character would entail an open-ended story. To be true and faithful to its complex protagonist, Norris' naturalist novel comes close to being a *roman d'aventure*.17

CHAPTER THREE

The Strategy of Desire in *McTeague*

The Economico-Libidinal Nexus of Desire

Particularly insistent in Frank Norris' *McTeague* is a curious overlapping between political and libidinal economies. Trina's affection for her "Old bear" (viii 137) is hardly conceivable outside the economic perspective that encompasses the novel: "Trina's emotions had narrowed with the narrowing of her daily life. They reduced themselves at last to but two, her passion for her money and her perverted love for her husband when he was brutal" (xvi 310). One can, in fact, discern a structural affinity between what she finds attractive in the dentist and what she finds appealing in gold. Trina, Norris writes, "took an infinite enjoyment in playing with McTeague's great square-cut head" (viii 135). Later in the novel, she experiences a similar urge to palpate her gold: "She would plunge her small fingers into the pile with little murmurs of affection, her long narrow eyes half closed and shining, her breath coming in long sighs.... Next she laid herself upon the bed and gathered the gleaming heaps of gold pieces to her arms, burying her face in them with long sighs of unspeakable delight" (xix 354–59). This smothering effect reproduces the same thrill Trina has previously experienced with the dentist: "On occasions they sat like this for an hour or so, 'philandering,' Trina cuddling herself down upon McTeague's enormous body, rubbing her cheek against the grain of his unshaven chin, ... or putting her fingers into his ears and eyes. At times ... she would clasp his thick red neck in both her small arms" (xii 252). The image of a miser teetering between a desire to feel her gold and a desire to play with her husband, between a joy in "polishing the duller pieces till they shone ... [then] running her palms over them, fairly quivering with pleasure" (xix 356–57) and a joy in "kissing the bald spot on the top of his head" (xii 252), this interplay bespeaks a fetishism that is hard to ignore.

An episode half-way through the novel further crystallizes the ways in which Trina's infinite passion for the dentist and her immense passion for gold are brought into one extended experience. After one of the several fights over money, Trina feels remorse about offending McTeague because of her excessive miserliness. Trina at first refuses to share the expenses of the contract for the new house McTeague has misleadingly been led to sign, but then "it occurred to her how pretty it would be to come up behind him unexpectedly, and slip the money, thirty-five dollars, into his hand, and pull his huge head down to her and kiss his bald spot as she used to" (x 208). Trina's monetary delight in McTeague cannot be disengaged from her sexual delight in money, which is tantamount to saying that economy and desire are mutually reinforcing. The slippage between the two registers is intriguing: Trina is not giving up her money but only giving up one pleasure for another. She is willing to forsake part of her money only insofar as she finds a provisional compensation for her loss in the brutishness of McTeague—in playing with his huge head and experiencing his coarse features.

The linkage between the passion for McTeague and the passion for gold can be pushed even further. It is clear from the course of the novel that Trina has a strong influence over her husband. She manages to change his habits, refine his taste, ameliorate his life style, and raise his expectations. She manages to "improve" the brutish McTeague, transforming his "crude and primitive nature" (xix 365), in such a way and "with such slowness that the dentist was unconscious of any process" (x 190). This process, as Norris describes it, is one of substitution: "The little animal comforts which for him constituted the enjoyment of life were ministered to at every turn, or when they were interfered with ... some agreeable substitute was found.... She broke him of the habit of eating with his knife, she caused him to substitute bottled beer in the place of steam beer" (x 190). The language and dynamics of this gradual conversion alert the reader to strong economic overtones. The rift between the ideal McTeague and the real McTeague is akin to the discrepancy between conferred value and material reality which, according to Marx, gives money its distinctive quality: "The coin is only a symbol whose material being is irrelevant" (*Grundrisse* 226). The idolization of gold and the idealization of McTeague point to a system of value that is distinctively invested in a symbolic existence. Both McTeague, as the image of the denaturalized brute, and gold, as the abstract image of wealth, convey a common and even unified syntax that accounts for the permeability of Trina's desire. A fascinating line in a short story that Norris published in the San Francisco *Wave*, a few years prior to the publication of *McTeague*, translates this prevailing permeability into a quasi-aphorism: "as lovers of gold, we were lovers of each other" (*Collected Writings* 103). The dentist that Trina loves and cherishes is not so much the character we encounter at the opening of the novel but a molding of her own imagination: "Instead of sinking to McTeague's level as she had feared, Trina found that she could make McTeague rise to hers" (x 186–87). It is true that she loved the dentist with "a blind unreasoning love that admitted no doubt or hesitancy" (x 183), but she loved him "not because she fancied she saw in him any of those noble and generous qualities that inspire affection. The dentist might or might not possess them, it was all one with Trina. She loved him because she had given herself to him freely, unreservedly; had merged her individuality into his; she was his, she belonged to him forever and forever" (x 183). Her love for McTeague, as Norris points out, increased and intensified "not for what he was, but for what she had given up to him" (x 186). Trina's devotion is not to a real object of desire; she does not love McTeague for what he is but for what she has invested in him emotionally. The McTeagues' conjugal life, then, is wrapped in a misleading transparency that revolves around a real couple but an imaginary relationship. In the same way the value of money lies beyond its inert form, the value of McTeague, in Trina's eyes, lies outside his innate characteristics. Trina's relationship with her money, much like her relationship with her husband, points to a non-referential reality—a reality that is based on the elimination of empirical determination and the ignoring of physical properties. The condition of substitution ·rests on qualities that are neither intrinsic to the character of McTeague nor contingent on the materiality of gold but are, instead, located in the imaginative and dreamy mind of the miser and, beyond that, in the status system and culture of a socio-symbolic that thrives on mediated interactions and indirect exchange.

Such as it is, then, Trina's twin experience is sustained by a unified mode of symbolization the structuring principle of which deserves more than a cursory attention. For Jean-Joseph Goux, an analysis of the socio-symbolic is possible only within the logic of the general equivalent. The point of entry to an inquiry that seeks to extract the lowest common denominator of any designated socio-historical formation is the value form, simply because the mode of symbolization is most pronounced in the economic perspective. In other words, the relations of exchange provide a reliable index for a system of relations that encompasses all spheres of vital activities. Following Marx's analysis of the genesis of the money form, Goux crystallizes four forms of value: (1) the *elementary form* which presupposes an original and simple equation between one commodity and another, (2) the *extended form* which brings the commodity into a social relation not just with another commodity but with the world of commodities in general, (3) the *generalized form* whereby the value of commodities and their reciprocal relations are expressed in terms of a standardized and socially recognized form, and finally (4) the *money form* whereby a specific commodity (historically gold) is instituted as a norm which acquires the status of an idealized standard. In a society that thrives upon this latter form of organization, money "enters circulation as the only adequate equivalent of the commodity, as the absolute form of existence of exchange value, as the last word of the process of exchange, in short as money, and money in its distinct role as a *universal means of payment*" (Marx, *Contribution* 190). Money becomes a general or universal equivalent around which all other commodities express their value.

In Goux's formulation, however, gold is not the only object to acquire monopoly as a general equivalent. The symbology that sustains a particular value form is not confined to the economic sphere but cuts across the different registers of the social body. The theoretical configuration of a fixed standard makes possible the identification of a series of equivalences, in fact, a "whole interplay of substitutive formations" (Goux, *Symbolic* 10). Some points of syntactic correspondence can be noted, for instance, between the genesis of the money form and the genesis of the phallic form. The development of the money form in the economic register is homologous, in every point, with libidinal development in the sexual register. Thus, to the elementary, extended, generalized, and money forms correspond, respectively, the oral, anal, phallic, and standardized phallic phases which mark the development of infantile sexuality as Freud conceived it. Stated differently, the progressive stages of socio-economic formations correspond to the successive phases that the subject undergoes: "The succession of economic forms ... would be not only a progression through modes of production and exchange but also the constructive inscription of the contemporary subject's psychic apparatus" (Goux, *Symbolic* 74). Within the specificity of the capitalist mode of production, the systematic solidarity between gold, as the general equivalent of all objects of labor, and the phallus, as the general equivalent of all objects of desire, involves a coherent system of reproduction of relations obeying a unified mode of symbolization—that of the *mono* form.

The structural affinity between these two major signifiers, gold and the phallus, finds ample expression in Trina's desire. Although the innumerable references to gold are enough to dwarf any other motif, phallic images are not wanting. The over-valuation of the chamois sack is as much an attachment to the phallus as it is an attachment to gold:

> Long since the little brass match-box had overflowed. Trina has kept her surplus in a chamois-skin... Just now, yielding to an impulse which often seized her, she drew out the match-box and the chamois sack, and emptying the contents on the bed, counted them carefully ... and rubbed the gold pieces between the folds of her apron until they shone... She took a ten-dollar piece from the heap and put the rest away... The bag was shrunken and withered, long wrinkles appeared running downward from the draw string... She returned the money to the bag and locked it and the brass match box in her trunk, turning the key with a long breath of satisfaction. (x 209–10)

In this curious passage, phallic images and references to gold intersect in such a way that makes the distinction between the two almost imperceptible. The images of an "overflowed," "shrunken," and "withered" substance characterized by superfluity and excess, on the one hand, and lack and devaluation, on the other, converge in such a way that the economic and the libidinal registers co-construct each other. In its alternations of abounding and diminishing, expanding and contracting, gold is portrayed like a tumescent phallus in its tendency to alternate between an erect and flaccid state. In the same way gold constitutes "the material of abstract wealth" (Marx, *Contribution* 180), the phallus constitutes "the image of vital flow" (Lacan, *Écrits* 287). The former represents abundance and richness, the latter epitomizes excess and superfluity. That which makes gold the privileged signifier of value also makes the phallus the privileged signifier of desire. It should not escape the reader that the social monopoly that both objects acquire entails not only a process of

centralization but also one of subordination; in the same way gold can
be instituted as an equivalent only through its separation from relative
value, the phallus can acquire a primacy only through the acceptance
of the concept of castration.   In other words, the exclusion of a
specific commodity or a sexual object is what endows it with a certain
sovereignty.   Such is the ambivalence that defines these privileged
value forms: their ascendancy to power bestows on them not only the
status of a norm but also the status of an outside signifier—whence
their transcendental quality.   The phallus, as Goux explains, "is the
general equivalent, the standard, and the unit(y) for all objects of
drive—for all objects, as these acquire relative value only through the
phallus.   The phallus transcends its status as part object in the same
way the gold transcends its commodity status" (*Symbolic* 22).   In
their ascendence to the role of standard measure of erotic and
economic value, both the phallus and gold become transcendental
signifiers.

   This remarkable isomorphism between libidinal and political
economies induces us to relocate, with an informed precision, the
nodal point around which libidinal economy is articulated in the
novel. As the foregoing analysis suggests, the libidinal investment lies
not so much with the figure of McTeague but with the phallic
function as such. The persistence of phallic images in the absence of
McTeague makes this analytical move even more insistent. If towards
the end of the novel the image of infinitude that Trina has once
cherished in McTeague has failed her, gold never fails her: "She had
her money, that was the main thing" (xix 360).   If McTeague is a
transient source of pleasure, gold is a perpetual one.   Against the
limits of McTeague, Norris sets the unlimited possibilities of gold as
the "imperishable commodity" (Marx, *Grundrisse* 149). Gold is a
continuous fuel for the imagination and a burning source of desire,
for even commodities, as Marx puts it, "aspire to gold as their
hereafter" (*Contribution* 115).   The potency of money rests on a
certain infinitude that makes it "the lord and god of the world of
commodities" (Marx, *Grundrisse* 221). It becomes hardly surprising,
then, that as the novel unfolds, Trina no longer relates to her failing
dentist but to her unfailing go(l)d: "Trina had become more
niggardly than ever since the loss of McTeague's practice. It was not
mere economy with her now. It was a panic terror lest a fraction of a
cent of her little savings should be touched" (xiv 274). Gold has
become Trina's only passion: "little by little her sorrow over the loss
of her precious savings overcame the grief of McTeague's desertion.
Her avarice had grown to be her one dominant passion; her love of

money for the money's sake brooded in her heart, driving out by degrees every other natural affection" (xix 354). In front of money, the dentist becomes a dim memory. For Trina, the transition is complete and the substitution is satisfying: "Trina even told herself at least that she was happy once more. McTeague became a memory—a memory that faded a little every day—dim and indistinct in the golden splendor of five thousand dollars.... Her passion for it excluded every other sentiment" (xix 360). What is interesting about this gradual substitution is that the eclipse of McTeague from Trina's life has not eradicated the libidinal economy at work in the novel. Trina's economics of desire are charged with a libidinal investment that goes beyond a simple metaphorical correspondence between McTeague and gold. The point is not that, in the absence of Trina's husband, "Money has become her lover" (Freedman 57) or that "gold acts as a caressing lover" (Cain 211), but that money itself is inherently phallic. Marx's analysis of the miser's passion for money leaves little to be said: "The hoarder therefore sacrifices the lusts of the flesh into the fetish of gold" (*Capital* 231). The over-investment at work in Trina's desire unfurls two parallel developments: to talk about the sexualization of money is to posit a conceptual parallel between the hegemony of money (as the privileged signifier of value) and the hegemony of the phallus (as the privileged signifier of desire)—or, more pointedly, to trace a systematic solidarity between monetaricentrism and phallocentrism.

The bed-scene where the wallowing Trina experiences an erotic *frisson* provoked by a desire for gold bespeaks a "lust for gold" (Marx, *Capital* 229) that eloquently captures the double bind of the pleasure principle: "Not a day passed that Trina did not have [her little brass match-safe] out where she could see and touch it. One evening she had spread all her gold pieces between the sheets, and had then gone to bed, stripping herself, and had slept all night upon the money, taking a strange and ecstatic pleasure in the touch of the smooth flat pieces the length of her entire body" (xix 360–61). The phantasmic mutations in this scene depict the infinitude of desire at the heart of the symbology of gold. Money, in general, and gold, in particular, have an exceptional power to unleash imagination: "The consumption of pearls is desired *as a function of their concept* (as the general form of wealth) and not as a function of their material being, for their form of universality and not their quantitatively limited exchange value or their qualitatively bounded use-value" (Goux, *Symbolic* 207). What Trina finds most appealing in gold is the absence of a "definite limit," in fact the absence of all "inherent

limits" (Marx, *Contribution* 176).[1]   The hoarding drive, as Marx
explains, is "boundless in its nature. Money is independent of all
limits, that is it is the universal representative of material wealth
because it is directly convertible into any other commodity" (*Capital*
230–31). The passion for gold does not point to a specific object but
to a transcendental state—a beyond. Behind Trina's hoarding instinct
lies an endless desire that constantly turns her money into a
"glittering, splendid dream" (xvi 308). In the hoarder's insatiability
one can discern the very strategy of the commodity in its tendency to
harness desires, stimulate needs, and proliferate wants—to produce
"imaginary appetites capable of making (economic) demand
potentially infinite" (Goux, *Symbolic* 208). Trina's passion for gold
is only the confirmation of this logic: "I'm going to get more" (xvi
308). The miser's keenness to continuously save gold is governed by
the same principles that lead the capitalist to engage in perpetual
production in order to increase and enlarge his initial capital. If the
miser is a capitalist *ad gloriam*, miserliness is capitalism *ad infinitum*:
"the hoarding of money for the sake of money is the barbaric form
of production for production's sake" (Marx, *Contribution* 179). The
passion to save—"to be awful saving" (xv 285)—is a passion for
"future money" (Marx, *Contribution* 187). Thus, what Trina has
always pales in front of what she might have: "It was passion with her
to save money.... [Her fortune] was a nest egg, a monster, roc-like
nest egg, not so large, however, but rather it *could be larger*" (x 188;
my emphasis). Insofar as the hoarder is driven by the compulsion to
repeat, by the urge to generate more surplus value, the passion for
gold becomes an endless pursuit.

This is the theoretical juncture where political and libidinal
economies converge in the novel—*jouissance*. Money, writes Marx,
"is not only *an* object of passion for riches; it is *the* object of that
passion" (*Contribution* 176). If the possessor of gold is "master of
all he desires" (Marx, *Capital* 229), it is because gold contains all
possible *jouissances* in *nuci*. The object of *jouissance* sought in gold
or pearls, writes Goux, is "the qualitative capacity to buy *all
jouissances*... They are consumed as the abstract potential of *all
jouissances*" (*Symbolic* 207). Gold is associated with prodigality and
boundlessness; it exhibits what may be termed, after Lacan, "the
exigency of infinitude" (*Encore* 15). In its libidinal manifestation,
this regime of *jouissance* is governed by the same infinitude that
characterizes gold. At the heart of both lies an appetite that is
stimulated by an absence and sustained by a dissatisfaction.
Jouissance has to be understood as taking place within a lack, i.e., in

relation to a lost object. *Jouissance*, writes Lacan, is "that which serves nothing.... Phallic *jouissance* is the obstacle which prevents man from enjoying (*jouir*) the body of the woman" (*Encore* 10–13). The realm of *jouissance* is the realm of the impossible, and it is only through repetition that the subject can hope to reclaim the lost object. To that extent desire and entropy go hand in hand.[2]   In this compulsion to repeat lies also the key to Trina's "passionate eagerness to continue to save" (xiv 274). Trina's greed exceeds her passion for gold; it symbolizes excess itself. Trina, insists Norris, clung to her gold "with a tenacity that was surprising" (ix 154). Her avarice has become a "mental disease" (xix 357). In her excessive passion for gold, the hoarding Trina has become a hysterical Trina.

But what does the hysterical Trina want? What does any hysteric want? The answer to this question has to be conceived within the triangle of desire: the desire of the hysteric is simply a desire for the phallus, which is tantamount to saying that it is an insatiable desire. In other words, the desire of the hysteric is an Ur desire for the father.[3] But since the access to the father is inconceivable, this desire is articulated around a substitutive formation, through "a complex dynamics which enables the hysteric to surreptitiously slide, there where it pertains, ... the imaginary phallus" (Lacan, *Transfer* 288). In this way, phantasm functions as a support for this unsatisfied desire. In fact, pleasure itself becomes the limit of *jouissance*: "desire is a defence, a prohibition against going beyond a certain limit" (Lacan, *Écrits* 322). This fundamental proposition is crucial insofar as it provides a summation for the economic principle around which much of the novel revolves. Trina, Norris insists, did not only have a strong passion for saving gold, adding a little every day, but also "counted it and recounted it" (xi 209). In her insatiable desire, the hoarder, much like the hysteric, is committed to an endless repetition. If desire is inseparable from repetition, it is because repetition opens up the possibility to redouble and intensify desire—to prolong it indefinitely and incessantly. Such is the frenetic motion of a desire equally at work in political and libidinal economies: an over-investment that makes surplus-enjoyment a corollary to surplus-value.

Passions for Drinks, Appetites for Food, and Orgies of Gold

One of the distinctive features of Norris' naturalism is the revelation of the body. In his fiction, the body is almost always thematized; it is associated with appetite, excretion, liquids, digestion, rape, death, and regeneration. Even more intriguing is Norris' fascination with the voracious body, a theme that is intimately connected with what Donald Pizer calls "atavistic ferocity" (*Novels* 71). The images of degeneration, primitivism, and atavism are often undistinguishable from images of craving, eating, and devouring. In *Vandover and the Brute*, for instance, Vandover undergoes a phenomenal degeneration, succumbing to the brute within him, and is ultimately eaten away by the disease he contracts. Such animalism carries over to *The Pit* where bulls and bears are engaged in fierce competitions and ferocious games. Likewise, *The Octopus* has a predatory theme at its core. This is evident not only in the scene where Behrman, the railroad agent and speculator, is buried alive beneath the wheat, but also in the metaphor of the wheat itself. In the words of John Macy, Norris' unfinished epic of the wheat depicts "the history of an empire of vast migrations, conquests, and disasters, controlled, as all national movements and private destines have been controlled, by the mute motive of hunger" (37).

This motif may be more developed in Norris' fiction, but is not limited to it. It is part of a predatory theme that can be pointed out throughout naturalism. The starkest rendering of this theme is probably the deadly fight between two sea creatures at the opening of Dreiser's *The Financier*. Watching a lobster slowly but surely tear apart a squid in a fish-tank, Frank Cowperwood learns a lesson which stayed with him all his life. He has come to realize early in his childhood that life is essentially a battle between the strong and the weak: "The incident made a great impression on him. It answered in a rough way that riddle which had been annoying him so much in the past: 'How is life organized?' Things lived on each other—that was it. Lobsters lived on squids and other things. What lived on lobsters? Men, of course! Sure, that was it! And what lived on men? he asked himself... Sure, men lived on men" (i 8–9). The Darwinian overtones of this monologue are unmistakable. By emphasizing the predatory theme, Dreiser is suggesting that one has little or no control over the evolutionary process that entangles nature, including human nature. The episode is a vivid exemplification of the principle of natural selection where the strong survive and the weak die. In naturalism, individuals are often portrayed as powerless creatures who are either crushed by a hostile environment, subjected to hereditary forces, or victimized by appetites over which they have little or no control.[4]

But there is more. Naturalism cannot be reduced to a literary application of social Darwinism. When naturalists were drawn to the scientific writings of their time, as Irving Howe perceptively points out, "they were really looking for cues with which to understand the experience of human beings.... They hoped that the 'advanced' philosophical theories would help explain or justify why their own sense of life had darkened so visibly since the Victorians" (221). Richard Hofstadter concurs. In his view, social Darwinism, in general, and Herbert Spencer's doctrine of natural selection, in particular, provided a theoretical justification for the harsh reality imposed by capitalism, and even a scientific rational to *laissez-faire* capitalism: "The most popular catchwords of Darwinism, 'struggle for existence' and 'survival of the fittest,' when applied to the life of man in society, suggested that nature would provide that the best competitors win, and that this process would lead to continuing improvement" (*Social* 6). But this is only one level of analysis—the ideological level. In *McTeague*, the various images of eating, voracity, and hunger lend themselves to a more complex and more systematic analysis. Examining the correspondence between culinary and pecuniary desire or, more specifically, the coalescence between the rabid desire for food and the morbid desire for gold can lay bare the structure of the socio-economic system around which much of the novel revolves.

Confronted with "Trina's persistent stinginess" (xvi 309), McTeague takes up drinking: "'Miser... You're worse than old Zerkow, always nagging about money, money, and you got five thousand dollars. You got more ... and you won't drink any decent beer. I ain't going to stand it much longer.' ... His anger against Trina, heated by the whiskey he had drank, flamed up afresh. What a humiliating position for Trina to place him in, not to leave him the price of a drink with a friend, she who had five thousand dollars!" (xv 291–93). If Trina resists spending money, McTeague resents deprivation from drinking. As the novel unfolds, Norris sets the drinking McTeague in counter-distinction to the hoarding Trina: "His old-time affection for his 'little woman,' unable to stand the test of deprivation, had lapsed by degrees, and what little of it was left was changed, distorted, and made monstrous by the alcohol" (xvi 309).

Disparate as they may be, however, the two practices are not antithetical. A close consideration will suggest that McTeague finds in drinking what Trina finds in saving. Trina "would wake at night from a dream of McTeague revelling down her money" (xix 355) and McTeague himself cannot help "feasting continually" with Trina's money (xvi 307). It is in this fashion that the dentist has squandered the money that Trina took pains to save over the years: "He had spent her money here and there about the city in royal fashion ... feasting and drinking for the most part with companions he picked up heaven knows where" (xix 364). Towards the end of the novel, hoarding and drinking—which have been the subject of many a quarrel—collapse into a single experience. Norris leaves little to comment upon in his artful imbrication of the two registers: Trina's passion for money is "a temptation such as drunkards only know" (xix 357). This metaphor resonates throughout Norris' writings. In *The Pit*, for instance, it is used even more pointedly to dramatize the speculator's passion for more money: "I tell you the fascination of this Pit gambling is something no one who hasn't experienced it can have the faintest conception of. I believe it's worse than liquor, worse than morphine" (iv 131). In *McTeague*, however, the linkage between gold, on the one hand, and food and drink, on the other, exceeds a metaphorical value; the two registers are, in fact, related within a structural affinity that warrants a closer attention to minor images and small details pertaining to gluttony and parsimony.

In one of the incessant arguments about money between the dentist and his wife, the following exchange takes place:

> "But fifty dollars is fifty dollars, Mac. Just think how long it takes you to earn fifty dollars. Fifty dollars! That's two months of our interest."
> "Well," said McTeague, *easily*, his mouth full of mashed potato, "you got a lot *saved up*." (xii 250; my emphasis)

At first reading, the scene is a reflection on the superficiality of the characters' lives and preoccupations. A more careful consideration, however, will uncover a curious and even cunning effect behind this spontaneity. The images of Trina's miserliness are interjected not only with images of a masticating mouth but also with the utterances of a speaking mouth. Theoretically, these two activities delineate two spheres of orality that center around the same organ, the mouth, but are not fully compatible. The uttering of words is even antithetical to the ingestion of food: speaking consists in expelling breath and giving it an articulate form while eating involves an inward movement and a process of decomposition. What is interesting in the case of McTeague is that the conflation between the two activities is unproblematic. The chewing of the potato never hampers McTeague's articulateness or muffles his words: although his mouth is "full" with potato, Norris insists, he speaks "easily" (xii 250). The ensuing effect is one of continuous (re)production that brings together the chewing McTeague and the saving Trina. More particularly, the invocation of money ("saved up") is literally traversed by the reference to food ("potato") in such a way that the image of the stuffed mouth ("his mouth full of mashed potato") actualizes the hypothetical profit ("two months of interest"). It is as if the unfettered process of mastication facilitates the reproduction of value.

Read in light of this latent economic theme, the billiard ball episode, where Marcus Schouler mouths a ball and then challenges McTeague to out-mouth him, acquires an additional significance. The scene stands out as a perversion that is distinctly oral in nature:

> Ten minutes after his renunciation of Trina Sieppe, Marcus astounded McTeague with a tremendous feat.
>
> "Looka here, Mac. I know somethun you can't do. I'll bet you bits I'll stump you." They each put a quarter on the table. "Now watch me," cried Marcus. He caught up a billiard ball from the rack, poised it a moment in front of his face, then with a sudden, horrifying distension of his jaws crammed it into his mouth, and shut his lips over it. (iv 57)

The scene is intriguing not because of its unexpectedness but because of its ambiguity. The pecuniary desire associated with this oral perversion is probably the least recondite. No sooner has McTeague succeeded in cramming the ball in his mouth than he "reached for the money and put it in his vest pocket" (iv 58). Getting the money in the pocket is contingent on getting the ball in the mouth. What emerges is an ingenious quasi-simultaneity between openings. There is, in fact, a confluence between the distension of the jaws and the multiplication of value, between stuffing the mouth and filling the pocket.

This confluence is reproduced with even more insistence later in the novel. In his flight through the mountains McTeague is fascinated with the diggers' extraction of gold from the entrails of the earth:

> On near approach one heard the prolonged thunder of the stamp-mill, the crusher, the invisible monster, gnashing the rocks to powder with its long iron teeth, vomiting them out again in a thin stream of wet gray mud. Its enormous maw, fed night and day with the car-boy's loads, gorged itself with gravel, and spat out the gold, grinding the rocks between its jaws, glutted, as it were, with the very entrails of the earth, and growling over its endless meal, like some savage animal, some legendary dragon, some fabulous beast, symbol of inordinate and monstrous gluttony. (xx 380)

The over-coded images of food indulgence stand out as a travesty of

McTeague's own oral perversion. The restless and energetic search
for gold is indistinguishable from the image of a feasting stamp-mill
with its gaping maw and its enormous desire to devour. The outcome
of this monstrous gluttony is an anthropomorphic body out of
proportion—a grotesque body. The juxtaposition of an irresistible
appetite for food and an orgy of gold instills the scene with the image
of excess in such a way that the desire for gold becomes the desire of
the replete body. At the same time, the ingenuity of the scene feeds
on a tension between interiorization and exteriorization, between
pleasure and repugnance, between an oral desire (eating) and a fecal
desire (excretion). This double bind is already implicit in the billiard
ball episode. The second ambivalence that marks McTeague's oral
perversion emerges precisely out of this intriguing confluence
between the mouth and the feces: in order to win the quarter from his
opponent, McTeague has to extricate the ball from his mouth. The
investment of money takes the form of an over-investment of the
body. McTeague's pecuniary desire is, thus, played off in the
intersection between an oral and a fecal desire in such a way that the
body finds itself entangled in a compulsion to repeat: that which is
inserted in the mouth is subsequently spewed out. What emerges is an
auto-productive process whereby the mouth consumes without
consuming—the ball is engorged only to be disgorged.[5] The pursuit
of profit becomes a pursuit of pleasure whereby the playful body
oscillates between the control of the sphincters and the release of
pressure, between repletion and excretion, between discharge and
congestion.

McTeague's spasmodic experience is intriguing not only because
it recalls the parlor scene where McTeague fills the tooth of the
etherized Trina with gold and then leans over to kiss her "grossly, full
on the mouth" (ii 31), but also because it describes an oral frustration
that produces and sustains pleasure. Unraveling the lineaments of the
ensuing (dis)pleasure requires a Lacanian detour. In his seminar on
Plato's *Banquet*, Lacan inquires as to the nature of an "oral
exigency," only to enjoin that "It is an exigency to be fed" (*Transfer*
238). This provisional answer, however, is not void of theoretical
difficulties because the mouth designates two different, though often
indistinct, spheres of orality. The mouth is not only the locus of need
but also the point where a drive is firmly inscribed. In other words,
the desire for food is charged with another desire; hunger not only
expresses an instinctual need for self-preservation, it also represents a
sexual drive. Freud's analysis of infantile sexuality makes the link
more conspicuous: "The child's lips, in our view, behave like an

erotogenic zone, and no doubt stimulation by the warm flow of milk is the cause of the pleasurable sensation. The satisfaction of the erotogenic zone is associated, in the first instance, with the satisfaction of the need for nourishment. To begin with, sexual activity attaches itself to functions serving the purpose of self-preservation and does not become independent of them until later" (7:181–82). Freud's analysis of infantile sexuality points to an imposing conclusion: it is not only nourishment that is sought from the Other—theoretically the mother—but the very body of the nourisher. However, the dynamics of desire are such that satisfaction is constantly denied. The oral exigency is always answered in reverse so that what ensues is not an appeasement but a conflict. In Lacan's words, satisfaction "must be refused, so that it can be reached on the inverted ladder (*l'échelle renversée*) of the Law of desire" (*Écrits* 324). An oral exigency, then, does not lead to satisfaction but, instead, results in the confrontation of two exigencies:

> What would apparently be a better answer to the exigency to be fed than letting oneself be fed? We know, however, that it is in the very mode of confrontation between the two exigencies that this abysmal gap, this fissure, appears.... As soon as a conflict erupts in the relation of nourishment, in the encounter of the exigency to be fed and the exigency to let oneself be fed, it so happens that this exigency, wrapped in desire as it may be, cannot reach a state of satisfaction without necessarily eradicating that desire first; that it is precisely because this desire that wraps need does not vanish that the subject, hungry as he may be, ... refuses to let himself be fed and, in some ways, refuses to disappear as desire upon being satisfied as need; that the extinction or elimination of this exigency in satisfaction cannot be achieved without putting an end to desire. (Lacan, *Transfert* 238–39)

The inversion that Lacan points out explains the ways in which letting oneself be fed does not result in satiation but in mere titillation—such is the secret of desire: the subject does not seek satisfaction but dissatisfaction. Seen from this perspective, McTeague's oral perversion reveals the very strategy of desire in its tendency to withhold pleasure, to prolong itself incessantly and indefinitely. What ensues is not satisfaction but repetition, reproduction, and excess. Even the *denouement* of the billiard ball episode does not bring about an appeasement of desire but the stimulation of another oral exigency. The outcome of the excessive orality that McTeague experiences is an indulgence in drinking: "All at once the ball slipped out of McTeague's jaws... On the strength of the occasion, Marcus Schouler invited the entire group to drink with him" (iv 58).

In light of the preponderant nature of desire, the often conceded preeminence of need becomes open to scrutiny. The dynamics at work in the billiard ball episode even lead us to reverse the assumed priority of need over desire. Contrary to what we tend to believe, it is need that is, paradoxically enough, parasitical upon desire and not the other way around. This reversal is verifiable not only in the context of libidinal economy, but also that of political economy. Under capitalism, biological needs retreat in front of induced wants. Capitalism, as Slavoj Zizek has aptly pointed out, is caught in a loop: "producing more than any other socio-economic formation to satisfy human needs, capitalism nonetheless also produces even more needs to be satisfied; the greater the welt, the greater the need to produce" (*Tarrying* 209). It is true that the strategy of desire consists in unleashing needs, but it does so by appropriating them in the most controlled and calculated way. What emerge are not needs *per se* but needless need; needs as such become synonymous with the need to reproduce, multiply, reiterate, and keep in motion. In this sense, vital needs become mere functions and effects of the system—if there are needs, writes Baudrillard, it is "only because the system needs them" (*For a Critique* 82).[6]

The oral exigency that characterizes this early episode finds its way to the novel on more than one occasion. For Norris, the passion for food and drink is key to understanding the phenomenal McTeague: the dentist's "only relaxations were to eat, to drink steam beer, and to play upon his concertina" (ii 28). His unremitting appetite corroborates his brutishness: "He would retire to a bit of level turf around an angle of the shore and cook his fish, eating them without salt or knife or fork. He thrust a pointed stick down the mouth of the perch, and turned it slowly over the blaze. When the grease stopped dripping, he knew that it was done, and would devour it slowly and with tremendous relish picking bones clean, eating even the head" (xviii 333–34). The references to food and drink not only capture the grotesque character of McTeague in the most blatant way, but also discretely enhance the economic theme. Such a complementarily gives a special significance to what otherwise would be two unprivileged moments in the novel.

The first instance takes place in McTeague's office upon Trina's unexpected win in the lottery: "The company begun to be very gay. Chairs and tables were brought in from the adjoining rooms, and Maria was sent out for more beer and tamales, and also commissioned to buy a bottle of wine and some cake for Miss Baker, who abhorred beer" (vii 114). In this scene, the rejoicing in money is also a gastronomical delight. Even more fascinating are the ways in which the Dental Parlors are transformed into a banquet scene: "The 'Dental Parlors' were in great confusion. Empty beer bottles stood on the movable rack where the instruments were kept; plates and napkins were upon the seat of the operating chair and upon the stand of shelves in the corner, side by side with the concertina and the volumes of 'Allen's Practical Dentist.' ... They drank and feasted in impromptu fashion" (vii 114–15). The abundance of money (five thousand dollars) is translated into an abundance of food (orgiastic excess). The becoming-rich (winning the lottery) is almost indistinguishable from the becoming-gorged (feasting).

The second instance of the juxtaposition of pecuniary and culinary desires articulates the exact same logic, albeit in its inverted form: the scarcity of money is enhanced by a shortage of food. The impoverished McTeague is often portrayed as a starving McTeague. His climactic encounter with Trina, after he has stolen her money and squandered it, is a case in point. The first appeal he makes to her is to provide him with food:

> standing just on the edge of the shadow thrown by one of the cherry trees was McTeague. A bunch of half-ripe cherries was in his hand. He was eating them and throwing the pits at the window...
>
> "Say, Trina," he exclaimed ... "let me in, will you, huh? Say, will you? I'm regularly starving..."
>
> "No," she whispered back at him. "No, I will not let you in."
>
> "But listen here, Trina, I tell you I am starving, regularly—"
>
> "Hoh!" interrupted Trina scornfully. "A man can't starve with four hundred dollars, I guess."
>
> "Well—well—I—well—" faltered the dentist. "Never mind now. Give me something to eat... I ain't had anything to eat since—"
>
> "Where's the four hundred dollars you robbed me of when you deserted me?" returned Trina, coldly.
>
> "Well, I've spent it," growled the dentist. "But you can't see me starve. Trina, no matter what happened. Give me a little money, then."
>
> "I'll see you starve before you get any more of *my* money... I won't give you any money—never again—not a cent."
>
> "But do you know that I'm hungry?" (xix 361–62)

This is only part of a protracted exchange between Trina and her husband. The actual conversation fills the space of three pages with cross references to food and money, hunger and hoarding, eating and saving. The scene is as much a remark on McTeague's need to consume food as it is a commentary on Trina's persistent desire both to consume and to be consumed by gold: "she even put the smaller gold pieces in her mouth" (xvi 308). Trina's desire to consume gold not only explains why she starts to begrudge the money McTeague spends on food towards the end of the novel, but also suggests that her refusal to satisfy McTeague's hunger is indicative of the insatiability of her own desire for gold.[7]

The interplay between these two oral exigencies—consuming food and gold—becomes even more poignant later in the novel: "the gigantic golden molar of French gilt, enormous and ungainly, sprawled its branching prongs in one corner of the room, by the footboard of the bed. The McTeagues had come to use it as a sort of substitute for a table" (xviii 337). In its double function as tooth and table, the golden tooth reproduces and reinforces the McTeagues' intense desire. In fact, the imposing image of the golden molar with its branching prongs conveys, in the most grotesque way, the growing encroachment of desire (sign) over need (food). The insatiable desire for gold is recapitulated in the image of endless voracity in such a way that the consumption of food becomes indistinguishable from the consumption of gold.

The confluence between the two registers is far from being accidental. A close examination of a banquet scene at the Sieppes', half-way through the novel, makes the link between the desire for food and the desire for gold even more conspicuous:

> What a wonderful supper that was! There was oyster soup; there were sea bass and barracuda; there was a gigantic roast goose stuffed with chestnuts; there were egg-plants and sweet potatoes... There was calf's head in oil, over which Mr Sieppe went into ecstasies; there was lobster salad; there were rice pudding, and strawberry ice cream, and wine jelly, and stewed prunes, and cocoanuts, and mixed nuts, and raisins, and fruit, and tea, and coffee, and mineral waters, and lemonade.
>
> For two hours the guests ate; their faces red, their elbows wide, the perspiration beading their foreheads. All around the table one saw the same incessant movement of jaws and heard the same uninterrupted sound of chewing. (ix 168–69)

Against the abundance of food, Norris sets a gargantuan appetite. Eating does not satisfy hunger but increases the desire for food. McTeague, in particular, is possessed by a relentless culinary desire:

"McTeague *ate for the sake of eating*, without choice; everything within reach of his hands found its way into his enormous mouth" (ix 169; my emphasis). What is intriguing about this indulgence is that McTeague's approach to food is homologous to Trina's passion for gold: "Trina looked longingly at the ten broad pieces in her hand. Then suddenly all her intuitive desire of saving, her instinct of hoarding, her love of money for the money's sake, rose strong within her" (x 209). Norris portrays Trina's relation to gold in exactly the same terms—the same equation—he uses to describe McTeague's approach to food: Trina has been "*saving for the sake of saving*, hoarding without knowing why" (viii 134; my emphasis). Both characters are impelled by an appetite that falls "beyond the limits of ordinary wants" (Marx, *Contribution* 179). If Trina saves for the sake of saving, McTeague eats for the sake of eating. What stands out is not need but greed. McTeague's attitude towards food is, in fact, characterized by the same orgiastic excess that designates Trina's attitude towards money. They both epitomize the law of surplus value in action—for capitalism, as Lefebvre has put it aphoristically, "produces for the sake of reproducing" (*Pour connaître* 244), engendering a perpetual cycle whereby money begets money. Both the gluttonous McTeague and the hoarding Trina, are caught up in infinite desire. Hoarding and feasting converge in such a way that the thirst for gold manifests itself as an appetite for food and *vice versa*.

The overlapping between oral pleasure and pecuniary delight, between McTeague's relish for food and Trina's passion for gold, figures even more persistently in the subplot. In the numerous encounters between Maria and Zerkow, the juxtaposition of fantasies about gold and bouts of drinking is more than accidental. References to whisky and gold constantly intersect:

> Zerkow had made Maria sit down to the table opposite him—the whiskey bottle and the red glass tumbler with its broken base between them—and had said:
>   "Now, then, Maria, tell us that story of the gold dishes again." ...
>   "What gold plate?" said Maria, frowning at him as she drank her whiskey. "What gold plate? *I* don't know what you're talking about."
>   "... Why you told me about it a hundred times."
>   "You are crazy, Zerkow," said Maria. "Push the bottle here, will you?"
>   "Come, now," insisted Zerkow...
>   "I don't remember nothing of the kind," protested Maria, reaching for the bottle. Zerkow snatched it from her. (xii 241–42)

Here the frivolous invocation of gold is intermittently infused with casual references to drink. Maria is literally regaling her host with a story about gold. The passage is strewn with two distinct objects of desire, but is motivated by a single appetite. Thus, when Zerkow cannot extort the words from Maria he snatches the bottle form her. Although initially Zerkow is positioned to Maria in a relation of exchange—as a junk collector—the relationship of exchange *stricto sensu* is gradually extended to other forms of reciprocity. The two are not only exchanging commodities but also bandying drinks, words, and fantasies. Whether he is a junk collector, a hallucinating "searcher after gold" (xii 243), or a confabulating host, Zerkow is driven by the same indulgence in exchange: "'No junk, hey? But you're welcome for all that. You'll have a drink, won't you?'... After the two had drunk together Maria produced the gold 'tape'" (vii 125)—a tape of non-cohesive gold she has previously stolen from McTeague. The passion for drinks and the passion for gold are interlaced in such a way that the indulgence in the one is also an indulgence in the other. Thus, drink functions as an aperitif that spurs a metaphoric hunger for gold which, in turn, stimulates an appetite for food. Infatuated with the "golden piece[s]" (xii 240), Zerkow listens to the story of "that wonderful service of gold dishes" (xi 214) that Maria's family "used to eat off of" (xii 241), his "lips trembling" and "his fingers hooking themselves into claws" (vii 126). For Zerkow, as for Maria, the desire for gold is never sundered from the image of a banquet—it is gold in the form of a service with its bowels, plates, knives, and forks:

> Then he plied her with questions—questions that covered every detail of that service of plate. It was soft, wasn't it?... The handles of the knives, now, were they good too? All the knife was made from one piece of gold, was it?... Did Maria ever polish the plates herself? When the company ate off this service, it must have made a fine noise—these gold knives and forks clinging together upon these gold plates. (vii 127)

Zerkow's desire for gold bespeaks an orgiastic pleasure that is embodied in the cherished gold plate: "You could bite into a plate and leave a dent," Zerkow tells Maria (vii 127). Zerkow's metaphoric hunger points to the contrived character of desire while his phantasmic biting of gold highlights the insulation of that desire from real needs. Zerkow's craving for gold does not entail satisfaction but dissatisfaction in the guise of a boundless orgy. Both the recovery of the gold plate and the satisfaction of an oral desire are unthinkable because they entail a *post festum*. The possibility of satiation raises a question that Baudrillard has well formulated: "what happens after the orgy?" (*Transparence* 11).

The Economy of Language and the Language of Economy

It is interesting that Norris invests the economic theme that defines *McTeague* in the morbid desire of Zerkow long before the five thousand dollars from the winning lottery ticket transform Trina from a "pure girl" (vi 88) to a "nasty little old miser" (xv 291). The numerous references to gold that imbue the subplot revolve around an infamous figure—"the red-headed Polish Jew" (vii 124) who is "crazy ... after money and gold and those sort of things" (xi 214). Zerkow's obsession is significant not only because it anticipates and extends the mania for gold, but also because it does so on grounds that are distinctly cultural and religious. The identity of Zerkow becomes even more resonant when set against that of Maria Macapa, the Mexican woman he is involved with: "'But what *do* those two see in each other?' cried Trina. 'Zerkow is a horror, he's an old man, and his hair is red and his voice is gone, and then he's a Jew isn't he?'" (xi 214). Equally insistent is a contrariety between the Jewish Zerkow and the Christian McTeague. The dentist's cultural identity is particularly notable in a climatic confrontation between Trina and McTeague after this latter has stolen her precious gold and squandered it to the last coin. Impoverished, desolate, and hungry, McTeague makes an appeal to Trina the tone of which is overtly Christian: "I'm regularly starving, and I haven't slept in a Christian bed for two weeks.... I ain't had a thing to eat since yesterday morning; that's God's truth" (xix 361–63). The Christian values that transpire in McTeague's supplication for food, be it suffering, sacrifice, or sharing, stand in marked distinction to the miserliness of Trina, and by extension the parsimony, usury, and shrewdness associated with the infamous Zerkow. The Polish Jew, as Walter Benn Michaels reminds us, is "described by Norris as 'a man who accumulates, but never distributes,' he buys junk without ever selling it" (*Gold Standard* 153).

Such a reading is even more tempting in light of a curious passage in *Vandover and the Brute*—often considered as a companion piece to *McTeague*—in which the Christian and anti-semitic invocations acquire an allegorical or, at least, a quasi-allegorical dimension. Succumbing to a "certain little weakness" (v 65) in his character, Vandover embarks on a life of self-indulgence which culminates in the seduction of Ida Wade, a "fast girl" who later commits suicide for fear of being pregnant. Deeply troubled by the outcome of his debauchery, Vandover seeks an escape from the thoughts that have been hounding him: "He made up his mind to read a little before going to bed.... His interest in the book was gone in a moment, and he took up another of his favorite novels, the story of a boy at the time of Christ, a Jewish boy unjustly condemned to the galleys, liberated afterward, and devoting his life to the overthrow of his enemy, whom at last he overcame and humbled, fouling him in a chariot race, all but killing him" (xv 239). What is interesting about this story is the stereotypical depiction of the victim. The animosity between the Christian and the Jew that the story highlights suggests that the key to the victimization and the retribution of the boy rests within his Jewishness. Cultural identity becomes both the cause and justification for his action. The victim is unjustly condemned because he is a Jew, which in turn accounts for his hunger for revenge.

The same observation can be extended to *McTeague*. According to S. N. Verma, the depiction of Zerkow as a Jew who is mad with a lust for gold echoes a cultural attitude towards Jews: "Racists of the time were particularly afraid of the Polish Jew" (136). For Donald Pizer, the key to the connection between the tangential story of the gold plate in the subplot and the central theme of the main plot lies precisely in the racial identity of Norris' characters: "Zerkow is a Jew, Maria of Latin blood, and Norris characterizes them along racial lines. (Norris' Chinese are crafty, his Latins hot-blooded, his Jews miserly, his Anglo-Saxons adventurous, and so on). Zerkow's avarice is as much a rational 'reversion to type' as is Trina's. The subplot therefore reinforces the main plot not only by foreshadowing the tragic effects of avarice, but also by reintroducing the theme of the racial source of that flaw" (*Novels* 73). Pizer's argument implies that the kind of biological determinism that informs the novel is further sustained by cultural determinism; the characters are subdued not only by their environment but also by their ethnic heritage. John Conder concurs; in his view, gold and the Jew are mutually inclusive: "Since Norris uses stereotypes to convey his cultural determinism, he doubtless means Zerkow's greed to have its origin in his Jewish heritage.... He is a Polish Jew who wandered westward from Poland to California. As a Polish, he is already a social outcast" (73).

This line of analysis, however, is fraught with a number of theoretical difficulties. The coalescence of the economic theme and the Jewish figure, in fact, raises more problems than it settles, the most

insistent being an essentialist assertion of cultural identity. Walter
Benn Michaels has aptly outlined the skewed premise of such an
essentialist position: "instead of who we are being constructed by
what we do, what we do is justified by who we are" ("Race" 783).
Given that identity categories, as Judith Butler reminds us, "are never
merely descriptive, but always normative" (15–16), the claim that
Zerkow acts the way he does simply because he is a Jew strikes the
reader as impotently prescriptive. To say that Zerkow idolizes gold
because he is a Jew and he is a Jew because he idolizes gold is to take
for granted what should be the object of inquiry. The complexity of
the strategy of desire, as the preceding sections suggest, induces us to
problematize, and even resist, a reading constructed around cultural or
religious stereotypes. Far from being a systematic analysis, the
identification of the imagery of gold with the figure of the Jew
amounts to little more than a justification that risks entrapping the
analysis into a semanticization of the economic theme in a way that
leaves untouched its constitutive structure. The question that needs to
be addressed is not what the economics of desire in the novel signify,
but how they signify. To that extent, Zerkow's desire for gold will be
read not as an expressive desire but as a productive one which
reproduces Trina's own morbid desire for gold.

An exchange between Maria and Zerkow, shortly after Trina has
won the lottery, crystallizes a slippage between Trina's passion for
gold and Zerkow's infatuation with the gold dinner set:

> "Five thousand dollars" [Zerkow] whispered... "Think of it, Maria, five
> thousand dollars all bright, heavy pieces—"
>
> "Bright as a sunset," interrupted Maria, her chin propped on her hands.
> "Such a glory, and heavy. Yes, every piece was heavy, and it was all you
> could do to lift the punch-bowl. Why, that punch bowl was worth a fortune
> alone—"
>
> "And it rang when you hit it with your knuckles, didn't it?" prompted
> Zerkow. (vii 126)

The confluence between the gold pieces that Trina has won in the
lottery and the gold service that Maria is supposed to have had seems
to be contrived but nonetheless ingenious. Zerkow reacts with the
same intensity to both objects of desire. At some point, the reader is
even left unclear as to whether the pieces Zerkow invokes refer to
Trina's gold pieces or Maria's gold service. The overlapping between
the two objects of desire makes them not only indistinguishable but
also exchangeable. What starts as a conversation, the occasion of

which is a visit that Maria paid to the junk collector for the purpose of selling him gold foil, leads to an invocation of Trina's newly won gold pieces, and ends up as a celebration of Maria's gold service.

Zerkow's bewilderment in front of the gold Maria steals from McTeague notwithstanding, the "half-mythical" (v 64) story of the gold plate almost dwarfs other references to (real) gold. In his fantasy, Zerkow is seized by a "perverted mind" (xii 240) experiencing the gold plate not as an object but as mere words. In the absence of the real object, desire takes the form of a logorrhea which points to an increasing erosion of the real. The reproduction of words is invested in a repetitive movement which, as Norris insists, is characterized by a mechanical regularity: "He's gettun regularly sick with it, [Maria told Trina] ... Sometimes he has regular fits" (xvi 311). The pleasure that Zerkow draws from Maria's recital of her story is immense. It leads him into a state of ecstacy. "[S]weating with desire" (xii 241), Zerkow is entangled in an incessant cycle of repetition so intensive that he can neither stop nor control himself: "'Go on, go on, go on,' cried Zerkow... shutting his eyes in ecstasy.... He tormented Maria into a second repetition of the story— into a third" (vii 127–128). Maria tells the story of the hundred pieces over and over again, and Zerkow lives it over and over again: "Zerkow has asked Maria to tell him the story of the famous service of gold plate for the hundredth time.... 'Come, now,' insisted Zerkow ... 'There were more'n a hundred pieces, and every one of 'em gold'" (xii 240–42). Maria's recital, Norris concludes, has "come to be Zerkow's mania" (xii 241). Thus, even when Maria is unable to remember the story, it is Zerkow himself who keeps repeating the same excited words: "the idea of the gold plate had passed out of [Maria's] mind and it was now Zerkow who labored under its hallucination" (xii 243). Gold becomes a hysterical reverie: "'The way he goes on,' Maria told Trina, 'is somethun dreadful. He ... got a fever every night—don't sleep, and when he does, talks to himself. Says "more'n a hundred pieces, an' every one of 'em gold." ... He's just gone plum crazy'" (xvi 311).

The gold plate, then, is present only in the form of a conversation that constantly obscures what it passionately invokes. In their ritualistic invocation, Maria and Zerkow ultimately mystify that which they adore. The story of the gold plate amounts to little more than the rehearsed recital of mere words that deny what they designate as soon as a referent is designated—an articulation that disarticulates. The morbid desire for gold designates a complete dislocation perpetuated through a ceaseless stream of words.[8] The "fever of excitement" (vii 127) over gold becomes a provocation with no definite invocation, a titillation with neither etiology nor teleology—it does not know what it invokes, but cannot stop invoking that which it does not know: "'It ain't anywhere. What gold plate? What are you talking about? I don't remember nothing about no gold plate at all.... I don't know, I don't know,' cried Maria... 'I would tell you, Zerkow, if I knew; but I don't know nothing about it. How can I tell you if I don't know?'" (xii 242–44). The story of the gold plate exists not because it is verifiable, but because it is incessantly repeated. Derrida's deconstructive analysis of negative theologies can shed some additional light on this point. For Derrida, "not to say" involves, to a certain extent, denial, deferral, and even titillation: "Those people, adepts of negative theology or of deconstruction ... must indeed have a secret. They hide something since they say nothing, speak in a negative manner, respond 'no, it's not that, it's not so simple' to all questions, and say that what they are speaking is neither this not that, nor a third term.... But since this secret obviously cannot be determined and is nothing, as these people themselves recognize, they have no secret. They pretend to have one in order to organize themselves around a social power founded on the magic of speech that is suited to speaking in order to say nothing" ("How to Avoid Speaking" 19). Translating the paralogism that Derrida points out into the context of Norris' novel, one may say that the perpetual reiteration of the story of the gold plate does not necessarily indicate that there is a secret but rather points to the imposition of the form of the secret over its content. What prevails is simply the logos.

The logocentric nature of Zerkow's and Maria's desire makes the reference to Lacan almost inevitable. For Lacan the subject's desire is unknown; desire is the expression of a longing for the return to an origin which, if recovered, would entail the dissolution of the subject. Simply put, desire is that which can never be satisfied. Such is the case, then, desire has to be understood as a principle of linguistic displacement. In Lacan's formulations, the linguistic field—which is also the field of the Symbolic Order—is the dimension by which the subject's desire is articulated: "the unconscious is structured around language" (*Four* 20). Language always signifies a rupture between the signifier and the signified, which means that linguistic signification takes the form of a series of substitutions that can never reclaim an original meaning. Because language has the property to slide around its own incapacity to signify an object, that object exists only as a pure lack. The representation of desire is therefore marked by a drifting which entails a set of substitutions and repetitions but promises no satisfaction. Zerkow's desire for an object that never existed is a perfect elucidation of the dynamics of a desire that is insatiable. The lacking object (i.e., the gold plate) is realized and realizable only within repetition (i.e., the infinite invocation of the story of the gold plate).

It should not go unnoticed that the ensuing repetition has an economic resonance. The repetition that entangles Zerkow and Maria not only revolves around an object of value (gold) but is itself structured around the law of value. In other words, the reiteration of the story is structurally akin to the reproduction of value. This affinity between the libidinal and linguistic registers, on the one hand, and the economic register, on the other hand, is far from being imposed. Lacan himself has pointed out a correlation between surplus-enjoyment and surplus-value. Both are forms of reproduction and both entail a ceaseless repetition.[9] The correlation that Lacan posits, however, is somewhat problematic because it fails to capture the specificity of this compulsion to repeat. Lacan's project extends Freud's seminal proposition that the Oedipus complex is a founding concept; it rests on the assumption that the subject is constituted in language and that desire is structured as a chain of metonymic associations.[10] To the extent that he endows repetition with a near-universal quality, Lacan falls short of reinscribing the compulsion to repeat within a logic which, as Goux explains, subordinates the different types of value to the dominant socio-symbolic. For Goux, it is possible to establish a congruence between libidinal and political economy "only by grasping the global mode of symbolizing, the *form of exchange* which cuts across economic libidinal, intersubjective, signifying, and political registers" (*Symbolic* 128–29). From this standpoint, it is not enough to trace homologies between different levels of signification. In order to be theoretically viable, these disparate forms of value have to be united within a symbolic logic. In Norris' novel, this symbolic logic is structured around the logic of capitalism: "Capitalism can be defined as the reproduction of the 'general equivalent' from all levels of sociality, including the libidinal level, the signifying level, and the economic level" (Goux, *Symbolic* 129).[11]

The implications of this proposition can further be extended by a closer examination of the compulsion to repeat in the novel. The linguistic exuberance that characterizes the speaking Maria depicts almost the same superfluity that characterizes the feasting McTeague and the hoarding Trina. Norris' miser, we are told, has a strong passion for money, "saving for the sake of saving" (vii 134). Few chapters later, McTeague's passion for food is presented in the same terms: "McTeague ate for the sake of eating" (ix 169). What ensues is a single effect—tautology. Tautology, writes Roland Barthes, is a "verbal processus that consists in defining the same by the same" (*Mythologies* 240). McTeague eats for the sake of eating and Trina saves for the sake of saving—beyond this tautology, Norris offers no explanation but, instead, appends a series of redundant enunciations: Maria not only explains the same by the same, but also sets into a perpetual movement an empty same against an empty same. Maria's linguistic desire corresponds to no referent and refers to no specific need. The novel is imbued with a number of repetitive movement, but these movements are sustained by an Ur-repetition. The ensuing tautology is the very tautology of capitalism in its drive towards endless production, in its commitment to "the necessity to produce anything, to obey a compulsion to reinvest at any price" (Baudrillard, *Échange* 40). In the case of Maria, enunciation persists only as a pointed negativity invested in a flat tautology insofar as tautology is "a double murder: the murder of the rational because it resists, and the murder of language because it betrays" (Barthes, *Mythologies* 241). Within language, the object of desire does not yield its secret but instead undergoes further mystification, thus provoking more words. Tautology puts the object of desire within language but not within reach; at the same time, the withholding of the object of desire is what ensures circulation. Such is the "law of reversal" that Blanchot finds most intriguing in language: "as soon as we assert that language contains the secret ... we have to add that the secret is beyond language; if this secret is what language continuously invokes without ever invoking, or, better yet, what allows it to articulate itself, it is on the condition that it remains outside the discourse" (*Amitié* 178). Thus, Zerkow's desire for gold is stimulated by language but language itself is sustained through an insatiable desire. The story of the gold plate not only startles his imagination but also tantalizes him: "The more his mind dwelt upon it, the sharper grew his desire" (vii 128).

Seen from this perspective, the minute details with which the story of the gold plate is recited acquire a new valence. The story is repeated with an algebraic exactitude—the same images and the same words are transmitted over and over again: "She can describe it just as though she saw it, and she can make you see it, too, almost... [Zerkow]'s made Maria tell him the story of that plate over and over again, and Maria does it and is glad to, because he's the only one that believes it. Now he's going to marry her just so's he can hear that story every day, every hour. He's pretty near as crazy on the subject as Maria" (xi 214–15). The sameness of words, however, disguises a certain deficiency of meaning, for both characters are "crazy over a lot of dishes that never existed" (x 214–15). The exactitude with which the story is recited conceals the approximation of a truth that never reaches certitude. The irrecuperable gilded object of desire and the unattainable truth about the gold service become one and the same: "Zerkow's avarice goaded him to believe that [the gold service] was still in existence, hid somewhere, perhaps in that very house, towed away there by Maria.... It was somewhere somebody had it, locked away in that leather trunk with its quilted lining and round brass locks" (xii 234–40).

It is not hard to see that the ambivalence that characterizes the subplot extends the strategy of desire at work in the main plot. The uncertainty that warps Maria's story is homologous to the (im)possibility of *jouissance* that marks Trina's relation with her gold pieces. The unavailability of truth and the inaccessibility of *jouissance* in *McTeague* are two sides of the same coin. They both epitomize the cycle of desire as Leclaire unravels its lineaments:

> *jouir*? It is the effect of apprehending truth with the other. More specifically, it is to listen and to perceive, with the senses and with judgement that open up on escapes and their paradoxical articulation, a relation of incompatibility that does not cease to play itself, through the other, between the system (of signifiers) of the body and the system of the discoursing discourse. *Jouir* is the cumulative effect of an apprehension of nothingness, of trifles which, much like the immobile axis of a wheel, animate the dynamics of the relations. (*Rompre* 193)

While recalling Trina's experience with money, Maria's story both recapitulates and reinforces its condition. Trina makes *jouissance* her ultimate object of desire, and Zerkow seeks truth as his grail. Like *jouissance*, truth is a residue of the effect of language, or as Lacan put it, "truth ... is the sister of this forbidden *jouissance*" (*Envers* 76).[12] As affines both truth and *jouissance* are sustained by the law that forbids. If the former implies renunciation, the latter engenders annulment: "'It's gone—gone—gone,' chanted Maria in a monotone. Zerkow dug his nails into his scalp, tearing at his red hair. 'Yes, yes, it's gone, it's gone—lost forever! Lost forever!'" (vii 128). In spite of this inhibition, Zerkow's search does not end. The compulsion to repeat that marks Zerkow's fervor bespeaks a fear of the threat of cessation. Hence he yearns to reclaim and re-experience his object of desire: "Look out for yourself, my girl. I'll hunt for it, and hunt for it, and hunt for it, and some day I'll find it—*I* will, you see—I'll find it, I will find it; and if I don't" (xii 243). But as Zerkow himself is not tardy to realize, the only way he can experience his object of desire is through the entropic dimension of language: "And if I don't [find it], I'll find a way that'll make you tell me where it is. I will make you speak" (xii 243). The only possibility of access to his object of desire lies in the prolongation of enunciation.[13] Zerkow's hallucination, Norris insists, has "developed still further" (xii 240). The recital of the story of the gold plate does not result in a disclosure of truth but in a "continued ill success" (xii 244).

In light of these observations, the mystery that envelops the character of Maria early in the novel starts to unfold. When asked about her name, the Mexican woman consistently answers: "Name is Maria—Miranda—Macapa" (ii 21). The way Maria utters her name is intriguing. It is invested in a repetition that is hard to ignore. The sequence of names "delivered in a rapid undertone" (ii 21) coupled with a resounding alliteration alerts the reader to a compulsion to repeat that is very much akin to the compulsion to repeat generated by the lost gold plate. The congruity between the two instances becomes even more acute when considering the curious litany which Maria always attaches to her name: "'Name is Maria—Miranda—Macapa.' Then, after a pause, she added, as though she had but that moment thought of it, 'Had a flying squirrel an' let him go'" (ii 21). What is striking about this passage is the affinity between the flying squirrel and the lost gold plate. Both objects stand for a sham reality; both of them have been once in Maria's possession but are now irrecuperable. Norris describes the squirrel that Maria invokes as a "mythical squirrel" (ii 21); a few chapters later, he uses the same adjective to describe the "mythical gold plate" (v 64) her wealthy parents used to own. The affinity between these two mythical objects is far from being accidental. Maria's nostalgia for the squirrel translates her nostalgia for the gold plate. Associating the release of the squirrel with her name becomes an occasion for experiencing her lost object of desire: "Invariably Maria Macapa made this answer. It was not always she would talk about the famous service of gold plate, but a question as to her name never failed to elicit the same strange answer…. 'Name Maria—Miranda—Macapa.' Then, as if struck with an after thought, 'Had a flying squirrel an' let him go'" (ii 21).

The Semiotic Violence of Desire

In an early study on Norris, Warren French has identified an interesting tension in *McTeague* between the real and the symbolic or, more pointedly, between the thing-handler and the symbol-handler. In his view, the novel voices an unsettling suspicion towards, and even a reaction to the tyranny of signs during a time when the country was witnessing a momentous change from a society of production to a society of consumption. French's achievement lies not so much in his suggestion that the novel is an attack on the increasing tyranny of signs and symbols, but rather in the formal linkage he draws between this suspicion towards symbols and the increasing abstraction that late nineteenth century capitalism nurtures: "An attack upon 'symbol-handling' has extraordinary value as a period document, for McTeague, Trina, and Norris were far from alone in their difficulties in manipulation of symbols. Indeed much of the history of this country and most of the rest of the world during the past century has been one of decreasing demand for 'thing-handlers.' The steady diminishing demand for unskilled workers and the shortage of mathematicians are only the most obvious signs of a widespread situation" (74). Cursory as it may be, French's observation alters the reader to the hegemonic impact of a mode of symbolization that is marked by an increasing tendency towards abstraction.

The proportion and ramification of this linkage between the profusion of signs and the abstraction of the economy deserve a close attention. A convenient starting point is Trina's attitude towards money. Cogitating with herself, Trina experiences a strong suspicion towards the value of the check that represents her deposited five thousand dollars. She is afraid that in its representative form, the scrip that Uncle Oelbermann has given her holds no guarantee for her deposited metallic coins. What Trina fears most is a destitution of value:

> Trina told herself that she must have her money in hand. She longed to see again the heap of it upon her work-table, where she could plunge her hands into it, her face into it, feeling the cool smooth metal upon her cheeks. At such moments she would see in her imagination her wonderful five thousand dollars piled in columns, shining and gleaming somewhere at the bottom of Uncle Oelbermann's vault. She would look at the paper that Uncle Oelbermann had given her, and tell herself that it represented five thousand dollars. But in the end this ceased to satisfy her, she must have the money itself. She must have her four hundred dollars back again, there in her trunk,

in her bag and her match-box, where she could touch it and see it whenever she desired. (xix 355–56)

It is clear that Trina favors the present and real measure of value for the transcendental and symbolic one. She is against the reduction of her gold to an abstract monetary sign—"just a piece of paper" (xiii 265). She resents the possibility and condition of the disappearance of gold from circulation. The substitution of fiat money for gold means the despotism of signs that have no intrinsic value in and of themselves, signs that are charged only by virtue of their symbolic valence. Such as it is, then, Trina's obsessive attachment to her gold is a reaction against the manipulation of signs and the indifference of representation.

But this is so only in appearance because in reality Trina's experience with gold depicts a relationship which, although contingent on the materiality of money, is nonetheless symbolic in essence. What is not clear to Trina is that, even in possession of her gold, she is already circulating in a world of signs that are detached from that which they signify. The apparent potency of metal coins should not obscure the symbolic character of gold. It is enough here to recall Marx's observation that, even in its metallic form, money serves as a symbol of itself: "money as gold ... can be replaced by any other *symbol* which expresses a given quality of its unit, and ... in this way symbolic money can replace the real because material money as mere medium of exchange is itself symbolic" (*Grundrisse* 212). In other words, money is always already abstract, and the power of that abstractness is embodied in the sensuality of Trina's gold. The implication of this nuance can readily be discerned in a monologue that Trina ventures half-way through the novel. Undecided whether to give McTeague a golden or a silver coin, Trina wonders "what difference does it make in the appearance and weight of the little chamois bag!" (x 209). The nominal value of the pieces of gold, as Trina has not been tardy to suspect, is independent of their real content or natural substance; if gold has acquired a high value it is only as the impersonation of commodities and the embodiment of labor-time. Marx's analysis of the representative quality of metallic money confirms Trina's unspoken suspicion of the symbolic character of her gold pieces: "Their function as coins is therefore in practice entirely independent of their weight, i.e. it is independent of all value. In its form of existence as coin, gold becomes completely divorced from the substance of its value" (*Capital* 223). To say that, in circulation, coins lose some of their weight without losing their value is tantamount to saying that they can be replaced by any "token of value" (Marx, *Contribution* 202). To that extent, the transmogrification of money from a "symbol of commodity" (gold pieces) into a "symbol of itself" (a piece of paper), is only a transmutation from a "sign of exchange value" into a "conscious sign of exchange value" (Marx, *Grundrisse* 144).

Seen from this perspective, Trina's fortune and McTeague's misfortune depict a twin experience. The dynamics of Trina's pecuniary practices can, in fact, be discerned in McTeague's professional undertaking.[14] The unexpected letter that McTeague receives from City Hall is a turning point in the novel: Marcus "got the law on him so's he couldn't practice anymore" (xxi 392). Even McTeague's twelve-year practice cannot efface the fact that he has never received a diploma from a dental college: "McTeague would be obliged to stop work, no matter how good a dentist he was" (xiii 263). But, as Trina wonders, what "difference does a diploma make, if you are a first class dentist?" (xiii 262). It is not enough to be a good dentist or to know "how to operate" (xiii 262) in order to practice dentistry. It is not skill that is the gauge of a dentist's proficiency but a diploma—"a kind of paper" (xiii 261). Lacking a diploma, McTeague is powerless in front of the violence of the sign.

McTeague's response to Trina's decision to invest her five thousand dollars makes the linkage even more conspicuous: "when Trina had begun to talk of investments and interests and per cents, he was troubled and not a little disappointed. The lump sum of five thousand dollars was one thing, a miserable little twenty or twenty-five a month was quite another; *and then someone else had the money*" (vii 132; my emphasis). What has escaped McTeague, however, is that even in possession of the hoarder, money is "an external thing" (Marx, *Grundrisse* 147) simply because its value depends on the law of an intervening third. Strictly speaking, Goux explains, "the value of signs lies exclusively in what the law bestows on them" (*Monnayeurs* 181). The law that forces the unlicensed McTeague to abandon practicing dentistry is also the law of the signifier. It is not real value that authenticates the dentist but the law:

> "But it's the law"
> "What's the law?"
> "That you can't practice or call yourself a doctor, unless you've got a diploma." (xiii 261)

Thus, when in the midst of this confusion one of McTeague's patients calls on the office of the dentist to have a bicuspid pulled, Trina confronts McTeague again with the imposition of the law: "But you can't... you've got to quit" (xiii 262). What the diploma means is that the relationship between the dentist and his patient is not a bi-partite relationship but one that necessarily engenders a third party. Outside this external mediation, even the gilded sign cannot signify: "Ain't I a doctor? Look at my sign, and the gold tooth you gave me" (xiii 261). There is a disjunction between how the sign functions and what it means, a disjunction that makes the sign valueless outside its signifying function.

Both Trina's relationship with her money and McTeague's relationship with his clients, then, depict the same problematic of representation. They both testify to the imposition of the law in its "role of regularization" (Goux, *Monnayeurs* 185); they both point to the irrevocable need to resort to the mediating function of a third party that facilitates exchange by effacing differences. The law that impels the hoarder to enter exchange through a medium of circulation—what Marx calls "a mere sign" (*Contribution* 145)—is also the law that compels McTeague to enter the medical profession through a diploma—what may be termed a "form of appearance" (Marx, *Capital* 188). The convertibility of Trina's check and the exchangeability of McTeague's diploma function as two sides of the same coin. This generalization is well articulated in the *Economic and Philosophic Manuscripts* of the young Marx: "that which mediates my life for me, also mediates the existence of other people for me" (166). Under capitalism, social relations are no longer intersubjective but transsubjective, which is tantamount to saying that relations between people are mediated by relations between things—such is the fetishistic character of the dentist's experience in a society that has "thoroughly stripped signs of their cryptophoric coating" (Goux, *Symbolic* 122).

Among the several signs that the novel expounds, the golden molar is probably the most representative of the fetishistic character of McTeague's world. For McTeague, the gilded sign represents a special object of desire: "Even Trina and the five thousand dollars could not make him forget this one unsatisfied longing" (viii 131). Coated with French gilt, the thing, Norris tells us, is "overpowering," "gigantic," "dazzling," and "with some mysterious light of its own" (xiii 147–50). In front of the golden sign, McTeague is literally dwarfed: "big boned and enormous as he was, [he] shrunk and dwindled in the presence of the monster" (viii 147). This enthralling sign points to a value that exceeds its materiality: "The dentist circled about that golden wonder grasping with delight and stupefaction, touching it gingerly with his hands as if it were something sacred" (viii 148). Norris' description of McTeague's gilded object of desire not only reproduces Trina's reverence for gold "as something almost sacred and inviolable" (ix 154) but also reenacts Marx's own depiction of the commodity as a "sensuous" and "supra-sensible" thing (*Capital* 165). Surrounded with "magic and necromancy," the commodity, Marx writes, is "a very strange thing, abounding in metaphysical subtleties" (*Capital* 169, 163). Likewise, the golden tooth is both what it is and more than what it is—an "unsatisfied desire" (v 83).

The disposition of the fetish to replace something by invoking it as a substitute infuses the novel with a logic that extends beyond the disaffected sign. To say that the fetish is a substitute is also to say that it designates a whole relationship. The dynamics of this relationship can be discerned in the initial response the other dentist receives when trying to talk McTeague out of his sign: "What would the other dentist, that poser, that rider of bicycles, that courser of greyhounds, say when he should see this marvelous molar run out from McTeague's bay window like a flag of defiance? No doubt he would suffer veritable convulsions of envy; would be positively sick with *jealousy*" (viii 148; my emphasis). McTeague measures the value of the golden molar against the impact it has on the other dentist. The jealousy that the sign is likely to arouse in his rival depicts elements that correspond to Baudrillard's theorization about the concept of castration: "If one does not lend his car, his pen, his wife, it is because these objects are, within jealousy, the narcissistic equivalent of the ego: if this object is lost, if it deteriorates, castration is inevitable. Bottom line, one does not lend his phallus" (*Système* 139). McTeague's possession of the golden sign engenders the possible deprivation of the other dentist. Read from the perspective of Baudrillard, the acquisition of the golden sign is structurally akin the to acquisition of the phallus, the loss of which engenders castration. This becomes evident when the other dentist offers to buy the sign from McTeague; the latter not only stubbornly refuses to sell his big gilded sign, but becomes outraged at the proposition to the point of violence. Covetous of this object of "jealousy" (viii 148), the unnamed dentist has not just disparaged and denigrated the jobless McTeague, but also threatened to castrate him. McTeague's sizzling response leaves little to be said: "You can't make small of me" (xiv 278). What is implicit in the argument between the two dentists becomes explicit in the exchange that follows between Trina and her neighbor. Empathizing with McTeague's loss of his job, Miss Baker offers her consolation to Trina: "It's just like cutting off your husband's hands, my dear" (xiv 279).

This observation is all the more imposing in light of a key moment that takes place later in the novel. In the same way McTeague's sign is a symbolic castration of the other dentist, Trina's money presents a threat of castration for McTeague himself: "His hatred for Trina increased from day to day... She couldn't make small of him" (xix 367). To be made small or denigrated is not just an attitude that embitters McTeague, but a derision he cannot tolerate. McTeague feels castrated precisely when finding out that Trina has sold his concertina. The deprivation of this object of desire is homologous to the loss of the phallus. McTeague himself cannot conceive of the possibility of such a loss: "Trina had sold his concertina—had stolen it and had sold it—his concertina, his beloved concertina, that he had had all the time. Why barring the canary, there was not one of all his belongings that McTeague had cherished more dearly. His steel engraving of 'Lorenzo de' Medici and his Court' might be lost, his stone pug dog might go, but his concertina!" (xix 369–70).

Seen from this perspective, the proliferation of signs becomes both a precaution against the threat of castration and a promise for the fulfillment of desire. In both political and libidinal economies, the outcome is a compulsion to renew one's experience. The fetishist always has an additional object to seek. In the words of Lacan, the object of desire "is encountered and is structured along the path of a repetition—to find the object again, to repeat the object. Except, it never is the same object which the subject encounters. In other words, he never ceases generating substitutive objects" (*Ego* 100). In the case of Norris' protagonist, this compulsion to repeat manifests itself as a fascination with signs—the world of McTeague is, in fact, saturated with a travesty of signs, gilded and plain alike: the pipe, the concertina, the bird in the gilded cage, and the golden tooth.[15] Even in times of dire need, McTeague stubbornly refuses to part with his canary and sell his concertina: he opposes Trina's "entreaties and persuasions with a passive inert obstinacy that nothing could move. In the end Trina was obliged to submit. McTeague kept his concertina and his canary, even going so far as to put them away in the bed room, attaching to them tags on which he had scrawled in immense round letters, 'Not for Sale'" (xiv 276–77). And it is the loss of the concertina that triggers McTeague's anger and initiates the sequence of events leading to the murder of Trina.

Syntactic Involutions and Negative Precipitations

The compulsion to repeat that entangles the saving Trina and the hallucinating Zerkow sets the tone for the whole novel. The sense of regularity and rhythmic repetitiveness that marks Trina's hoarding instinct can even be noted in her everyday life: "the new life jostled itself into its groves. A routine began" (x 192). Her relationship with McTeague does not so much depict a happy union as it delineates an unbroken cycle of monotony: "Year after year, month after month, hour after hour, she was to see this same face, with its salient jaw, was to feel the touch of those enormous red hands, was to hear the heavy, elephantine tread of those huge feet—in thick gray socks. Year after year, day after day, there would be no change, and it would last all her life" (x 185). The sense of persistence and regularity that emanates out of this pleonasm hardly escapes the reader. Norris dramatizes the story of Trina and McTeague through distinct verbal reiterations. The reigning lethargy is not just described but enacted as a linguistic repetition; the monotony of Trina's life is recouped in the consecutiveness of the words: "A week passed, then a fortnight passed, then a month" (xvi 303). Trina's life drags and so does the prose—more of the same life, and more of the same words. Again, this repetitiveness is tightly connected with the economic production of value with which the novel throbs. The repetitive language constantly reminds the reader of Trina's persistent passion for money: "I'm going to get more, more, more; a little every day" (xvi 308). The cumulative effect that transpires from both the concatenation of words and the accumulation of money gives the impression that this repetition is unfailing and even uncontrollable. McTeague's nonchalance only adds to the force of this cadence: "He never questioned himself, never looked for motives, never went to the bottom of things.... As time went on, McTeague's idleness became habitual" (x 188–xix 309).

To content oneself with the observation that the novel revolves around repetition, however, is not only to reduce the complexity of the story to a pure determinism, but also to impoverish the category of repetition itself.[16] Repetition, as E. K. Brown has aptly pointed out, is double edged: "Repetition is the strongest assurance another can give of order; the extraordinary complexity of the variations is the reminder that the order is so involute that it must remain a mystery" (115). A close attention to *McTeague* will uncover that the continuities that drive much of the action are not without curious discontinuities. Repetition is not simply entropic; at certain points, it inclines towards a negative entropy or a "negentropy," to borrow Michel Serres' neologism ("Estime" 116). In the tautological model that orders Norris' novel, and for which Trina's pecuniary desire is the pointed manifestation, disruption and discontinuity chase reproduction and accumulation. What this proposition means, in part, is that the dynamics of the novel revolve around an experience that cannot be fully conceived within an unfailingly repetitive model. If the concept of repetition is to be retained as a viable theoretical paradigm capable of unfurling the entangled dynamics of the novel—and by extension the dynamics of capitalism—it has to be qualified. One can hardly ignore Serres' caveat that "repetition is death. It is the fall into the similar. The always already is only a cemetery where entropy rots matter away. Fortunately, the rare exists, exceptions come about, novelty appears" (*Parasite* 122). A repetition that is invariably tautological is an unproductive, even counter-productive repetition. Only when it is innovative, only when it challenges its own logic, can repetition sustain that which it reproduces. In this sense, difference is essential to the efficacy of any repetitive movement.

McTeague is a case in point where language is structured around a principle that imitates the logic of reproduction only to challenge it. In other words, language seems to—and it does to a certain extent—create and recreate the economic thrust of the novel, but it does so in a contentious way. A crisis towards the end of the novel provides an eloquent instance of this internal linguistic subversion:

> One day as she sat in her room, the empty brass match-box and the limp chamois bag in her hands, she suddenly exclaimed:
> "I could have forgiven him if he had only gone away and left me my money. I could have—yes, I could have forgiven him even *this*"—she looked at the stumps of her fingers. "But now," her teeth closed tight and her eyes flashed, "now—I'll—never—forgive—him—as—long—as—I —live." (xix 354)

The repetition in this monologue is fractal, to say the least. The continuity of language is punctuated with gaps or moments of silence that undermine the firmness which the tone of the speaker seeks to maintain. Trina's resolution is supposed to be an assertion, even a vow never to forgive McTeague; and yet, the commitment it proposes is gradually dissipated in the intermittence of language. In fact, the stammering in the last sentence undercuts Trina's resolution to remember that McTeague has stolen her hoard. There is an unspoken tension between the performative character of language and the assertive intention of the speaker. What is even more interesting is the fact that this passage relies on the logic of accumulation only to subvert it. Trina, we are told, has an obsessive desire to save a little every day, filling her brass match-safe which "answered the purpose of a saving bank" (x 188). Even when deprived of her hoard, Trina remains caught up in this compulsion to repeat; she would mourn her losses with the same regularity that commits the miser to repeated savings: "Day after day she took them from her trunk and wept over them as other women weep over a dead baby's shoe" (xix 354). What is intriguing is that repetition is retained within a vacuity. The illusionary impact of language thrives on a certain negativity. Language nullifies its referent not by discarding it, but by draining its vigor in repetition in a way that leads to an empty production—it is as if language is confronted with its limit. The sentence that follows makes this reversal even more conspicuous: "Her four hundred dollars were gone, were gone, were gone" (xix 354). The repetition of the word "gone" points to the unavailability or disappearance of money, but it does so by using the very logic and language of accumulation. The repetitive construction replicates Trina's hoarding experience, only this time it dramatizes the loss rather than the multiplication of money. Repetition starts to produce the reverse of its intended effect. Although the motion of the sentence is modeled on the drive of the hoarder, the outcome is not a multiplication of money but an intensification of emptiness and desolation.

A consideration of Trina's extreme moments of passion will only add more force to these propositions. Out of the monotonous routine of Trina's daily life appears a notable paroxysm that announces a disconcerting experience. Anxious about her future, Trina lapses into a "momentary revolt" (x 186) that interrupts the predictive sameness of her life. Her sudden eruptions even stimulate a disconcerting confusion: "At times, a brusque access of passion would seize upon her" (xii 252). The violence of Trina's desire for McTeague points to the violence of her desire for gold: "Trina looked longingly at the ten broad pieces in her hand. Then suddenly all her intuitive desire of saving ... rose strong within her" (x 209). Trina's "brusque outbursts of affection" (x 187), in fact, reenact the intensification of her miserliness: playing with her gold pieces, later in the novel, she experiences a "brusque access of cupidity" (xix 358). What is more interesting is that these moments of perversion are often reinforced by textual agitations. The mechanically repetitive character of Trina's life is suddenly suspended by moments of disruption invested in a curious faltering. Flirting with McTeague, she is suddenly seized by a violent squall of passion:

> "Oh Mac, dear, love me, love me *big*! I'm so unhappy."
>
> "What—what—what—" the dentist exclaimed, starting up bewildered, a little frightened."
>
> "Nothing, nothing, only *love* me, love me always and always."
>
> But this first crisis ... passed, and Trina's affection for her "old bear" grew in spite of herself. She began to love him more and more. (x 186)

The gesticulations that suffuse the exchange between Trina and McTeague introduce a mini-crisis that interferes with the syntactic continuity of the text and bends the linearity of the action. The whirls of frantic passion that accompany Trina's "mania" (xix 357) are verbally reproduced as a volatile stammering that involuntarily entangles language in a perplexing disequilibrium; in other words, her quasi-derangement takes the form of a syntactic disarray.[17]

The effect that ensues from these verbal quirks induces us to examine more closely the implication of some other syntactic anomalies in the novel. Particularly distinctive in *McTeague* is the dispersed recurrence of a negative structure construed *via* a syntactic inversion: "Never had Marcus made her feel like that" (vi 88). Taken at face value, this inversion is hardly unusual; but when used to the point of calling attention to itself, the reader starts to suspect that there is more in Norris' language than meets the eye. The effect that this particular syntactic involution introduces can be initially gauged when set against a comparable structure that occurs later in the novel. Norris' depiction of Trina's pecuniary desire provides an eloquent instance: "Never, never, never," insists the miser, "should a penny of that miraculous fortune be spent" (x 188). The redundant "never" reinforces Trina's resolute stinginess. The passion of the miser to continue to save is reproduced in the continuous flow of words. There is a coincidence between the accumulation of money and the proliferation of words; both instances are marked by a certain predictability and regularity. Unlike this structure, the syntactic involution identified earlier introduces an irregularity, even a disorientation. What Trina experiences with McTeague defies the steady affection that characterizes her relationship with Marcus. Correlatively, what McTeague finds in Trina exceeds anything he has experienced so far: "Never until then had McTeague become so well acquainted with a girl of Trina's age.... With her the feminine element suddenly entered his little world" (ii 26–27).   The transposition of the elements of the sentence engenders a diversion in the expectation of the character and the anticipation of the reader.

A similar inversion occurs later in the novel. Here, the intensity that characterizes the life of McTeague and Trina develops into a kind of precipitation at the syntactic level: "Never had she looked so pretty" (xiii 258).   The morpho-syntactic arrangement of the sentence dislodges what it introduces.   The emphatic modifier confirms the thetic statement it precedes only to exceed it.   The abrupt "never" that opens the sentence not only generates a condensed experience, but also announces a swerve in the unfolding of events.   It interrupts the flow of events not by denying the insistence of the character's experience but by taking it to an unpredictable resolution. The statement asserts that Trina has reached the apogee of her beauty as much as it implies a new turn.   The unexpected drawing of the lottery that has put five thousand dollars in Trina's possession only enhances this sense of aberration: "never have I seen fortune so happily bestowed as in this case" (vii 118–19), exclaimed the agent who announced the winning ticket.   There is an inexplicable tendency, even an agitation that is constructed around a manipulative temporality.   The sentence does not so much negate as it presents that which it negates.   This fore-presentation of the negative produces an atypical effect whereby something is taken away before it is given: "Never in his life had sleep seemed so sweet to him" (xxi 421), writes Norris describing the last peaceful moment McTeague will ever have in the desert before the novel reaches its climax.   The inversion fulfills its purpose by simultaneously negating that which it so emphatically asserts.   Read in light of the subsequent development of the story line, the sentence implies not only that McTeague has enjoyed such a sound slumber, but also that he will never be at rest again.

The outcome is the instillation of counter-moments or, what I call, moments of intensity.   *McTeague* is not wanting in these tendencies towards intensification complemented by sudden agitations that constantly usher in new limits.   In essence, the intensive designates "any linguistic means that makes it possible to take a certain notion to its limit or to transcend it" (Sephiha 113).   An intensity delineates a swerve that points to an over-development; it bespeaks an asymmetry between a rhythmic experience and an exceeding experience. Intensity, as Blanchot defines it, "is an excess, an absolute disruption" (*Writing* 46).   It is the point where repetition spawns a discordance that establishes a contact with a limit: "Never had McTeague been so excited" (iv 54).   An agonistic element is clearly at work: "never had he made so long a speech" (iv 54). The syntactic inversion establishes an internal dialectic between affirmation and negation that is on a par with the dialectic of desire in which the possibility of fulfillment is always accompanied by the mark of its prohibition. The internal dynamics of the prose intimately reproduce the contradictory movement which enables desire to impose itself *via* a simultaneous recognition of its negation. The outcome of these syntactic inversions is a negative assertion—an assertion that effaces that which it negates as soon as it asserts it because the only way to affirm it is by transgressing it.

Norris uses the same syntactic structure to describe a climax in the life of the McTeagues: "Never afterward were the two so happy as at that moment" (vi 91). The disintegration of the characters' experience is invested in a syntactic displacement. The ordered and normative unity of lexemes breaks away, not only engendering a disruption in the linear sequence of words but also interfering with the predictability of events. A syntactic intensity is superimposed on an emotional intensity in such a way that the emotion of the character becomes the very motion of language—it is as if, "the logos," as Deleuze puts it, "starts to derail" (*Proust* 208).[18] Thus when Trina looks retrospectively and nostalgically at her relationship with McTeague, the same statement is reproduced without inversion: "She had never been happier before in all her life" (xviii 345). The reversion to a consecutive arrangement of lexemes points to the lack of maximization. In other words, the absence of the emotional intensity eliminates the linguistic intensity. Conversely, the inverted structure announces an unpredictable development that disrupts the linearity of the narrative; it introduces a generative tension—an excitement—even in the most trivial daily events: "All the flat knew the feud between the dogs, but never before had the pair been brought face to face" (xi 216). The confrontation between the two dogs engenders an unexpected *denouement*: "they did not come together, and the distance of five feet between them was maintained with an almost mathematical precision.... Gradually and with all the dignity of monarchs they moved away from each other" (xi 217). What is even more interesting is the way in which the suspended confrontation between the two dogs results in a suspended "never" that is upheld by a false sense of anticipation: "'Well, I *never!*' exclaimed Trina in great disgust. 'The way those two dogs have been carrying on you'd 'a' thought they would 'a' just torn each other to pieces when they had the chance'" (xi 217). The impact of this incident, however, is not limited to the encounter between the two pets; it is carried with more weight a few pages later to dramatize the breach between McTeague and Marcus: "Never had the quarrel between the two men been completely patched up" (xi 220). The ruffling syntax is charged with an indignation that announces an imminent crisis and a precipitous development. Something has gone awry; Marcus has, in fact, betrayed his friend. The letter McTeague has received from City Hall heralds the end to his career: "It was like a clap of thunder. McTeague was stunned, stupefied. He said nothing. Never in his life had he been so taciturn" (xiii 263–64).

Seen from one perspective, these various moments of intensity reflect Norris' long-recognized sensibility to language. One of the characteristics that distinguish his writings, as John Macy has observed upon the publication of *Vandover and the Brute*, is the ability to create a "sensory reality" in the scenes he describes: "he knew how to present persons as if they had an air on all sides of them, streets as if they could be walked upon, even an entire city, San Francisco, as an organization with a life and visage particularly its own" (36). But there is more. The depiction of McTeague's flight in the desert, for instance, conveys more than an authorial control over language; it points to an irreducible element of madness—in the Deleuzian sense of flux or intensity—that protrudes even the most highly crafted passages. Thus, at the end of the novel, the fore-mentioned inversion recurs with a new force to designate not only sudden and incomprehensible developments, but also a frantic experience. The madness of language and the paranoia of McTeague become two effects of the same experience: "Never had the mysterious instinct in him been more insistent than now; never had the impulse toward precipitate flight been stronger; never had the spur bit deeper. Every nerve of his body cried aloud for rest; yet every instinct seemed aroused and alive, goading him to hurry on, to hurry on" (xxii 422). What ensues is an image of a character who, in his flight, is caught up in the very density of language. McTeague is not only under the spell of "something behind him" (xxii 426) but under the very spell of language. The pursuit of the fugitive dentist is recreated in the internal dynamics of the prose, in the very creepiness of the words: "A score of black, crawling objects were following him, crawling from bush to bush, converging upon him. *'They'* were after him, converging upon him, were within touch of his hand, were at his feet—*were at his throat*" (xxii 427). The tension in this passage not only crystallizes a rhythmic dimension in Norris' prose, but also points to a connection between the ensuing rhythm and the negative moments that infuse the novel. Repetition achieves an order which is so involute that it resists closure.

Tarrying with the (Il)logic of Capitalism

With the death of Trina, a new setting is introduced. Burdened with the murder of his wife and loaded with her gold, McTeague flees San Francisco for the wide open spaces of Placer county. The vast spaces that attract the dentist at the end of the novel stand out in a marked distinction to the claustrophobic spaces he has to endure while living with the stingy Trina. The image of the degenerated, lacerated, and shrinking "little old miser" (xv 291) confining herself to rat-holes is superseded by scenes of an enchanting vastness. Towards the end of the novel, the setting is no longer that of houses, parlors, rooms, and operating chairs, but one of open, natural, and unoccupied spaces. The fugitive McTeague circulates freely *extra muros*:

> As far as one could look, uncounted multitudes of trees and manzanita bushes were quietly and motionlessly growing, growing, growing. A tremendous, immeasurable life pushed steadily heavenward without a sound, without a motion. At turns of the road, on the higher points, cañons disclosed themselves far away, gigantic grooves in the landscape, deep blue in the distance, opening one into another, ocean deep, silent, huge, and suggestive of colossal primeval forces held in reserve... Here and there the mountains lifted themselves out of the narrow river beds in groups like giant lions rearing their heads after drinking. The entire region was untamed. (xx 379)

On these images of untamed and immeasurable spaces is grafted the interminable search for gold: "there were men in these mountains ... now with hydraulic 'monitors,' now with drill and dynamite, boring into the vitals of them, or tearing away great yellow gravelly scars in the flanks of them, sucking their blood, extracting gold" (xx 380). The juxtaposition of the exhilarating experience of space and the enthralling experience of the precious metal is reenacted, with even more forcefulness, in the concluding episode of the Western desert.

The association between gold and the desert on the point of extension may at first seem paradoxical. What characterizes gold is not the extension of space but rather the opposite. In essence, gold is a reduced space: "As mediums of circulation, gold and silver have this advantage over other commodities, that their high specific gravity which condenses much weight in little space, corresponds to their economic specific gravity which condenses relatively much labor-time, i.e. great quantity of exchange value in a small volume" (Marx, *Contribution* 210). But if gold is a precious metal, it is precisely because its ability to condense much weight in little space ensures its mobility. The physical compressibility of gold, coupled with its abstractness, facilitates its circulation, thus endowing it with the "ability to appear as rapidly as to disappear" (Marx, *Contribution* 210). In circulation the real substance of gold is obfuscated. Money is a substance that has neither an individual characteristic nor an intrinsic value: "If commodities could speak, they would say this: our use-value ... does not belong to us as objects" (Marx, *Capital* 176–77). Such is the double-bind of money: the presence of an absence.

This ambivalence at the heart of the symbology of money is formally reproduced in McTeague's experience of the desert. There is a certain vacuity that makes circulation in space almost interchangeable with monetary circulation. In the metaphor of space lies all the ambiguities of the commodity: "The emptiness of primeval desolation stretched from [McTeague] leagues and leagues upon either hand. The gigantic silence of the night lay close over everything, like a muffling Titanic palm. Of what was he suspicious? In that treeless waste an object could be seen at half day's journey distant. In that vast silence the click of a pebble was as audible as a pistol-shot. And yet there was nothing, nothing" (xxi 411). The desert is a space where traces are evanescent and where events are incorporeal: "The heat grew steadily fiercer; all distant objects were visibly shimmering and palpitating under it. At noon a mirage appeared on the hills to the northwest.... On he went, straight on, chasing the receding horizon; ... the horizon, that always fled before him" (xxi 419–28). This sense of haunted presence is no less insistent in the fantastic character of money: "The body of the coin," writes Marx, is "but a shadow" (*Contribution* 142). In the uncanny character of the desert and the mystery of the commodity one can discern not a definite object but the insidious presence of a quasi-object, an a-thing, that simultaneously embodies and dissimulates.[19] Both, the topology of the desert and the morphology of gold bespeak a spectral disincarnation that is hard to ignore.

There is yet another way in which the spatial element and the economic metaphor co-construct each other. Money is characterized not only by its enigmatic quality, but also by its infinitude: "Money appears then no less an object than a source of passion for riches" (Marx, *Contribution* 176). For the most part, this infinitude in Norris'

novel is invested in the figure of the miser. With the death of the
hoarding Trina, this boundlessness is reinstated in the spatial
configuration of the novel. Here the desert becomes the main locus
of the story while McTeague is its main focus. The spendthrift dentist
we encounter early in the novel is a figure associated with enclosed
and confined spaces, more specifically the mine: "The miner's idea
of money quickly gained and lavishly squandered, persisted in his
mind" (xvi 307). In this context, money has limits: squandering his
wife's painstakingly saved money, McTeague "suddenly found
himself at the end of his money" (xix 365)—the same money that
exemplifies Trina's boundless desire. The change of scenery in the
concluding chapters, however, is not without significance; it
adumbrates a new configuration of McTeague's relation to gold. It is
interesting that the fugitive dentist first seeks refuge in the mine but
soon abandons it and heads towards the desert. In this latter setting,
Trina's money regains its infinite quality. In the openness of space,
money is again the symbol of boundlessness. The pardoner's
exclamation as he catches a glimpse of McTeague's loaded canvas
sack economically captures this sense of unfailing abundance: "An'
me asking you if you had fifty dollars! ... You carry your mine right
around with you, don't you" (xxi 398). The image a coal mine,
which has so far been a defining experience for the dentist, is
ingeniously superseded by a gold mine. The unlimited possibilities
that the discovery of gold opens for McTeague recreate Trina's
insatiable desire for gold: "now he had suddenly become rich; he had
lighted on a treasure—a treasure far more valuable than the Big
Dipper mine itself. How was he to leave that?" (xxi 411).
McTeague's fascination with the newly found quartz reproduces,
almost verbatim, his infatuation with the enthralling scenic spaces that
suddenly unfold in front of his eyes: on the edge of Death Valley,
"Cribbens and the dentist sat motionless in their saddles, looking out
over that abominable desolation, silent, troubled" (xxi 401). The
sight of the precious metal, a few pages later, generates a comparable
effect: "The two watched it with the intensest eagerness" (xxi 406).

The spatial organization of the novel, then, makes the affinity
between Trina and McTeague more conspicuous than it may initially
seem. The dentist's absorbing spatial experience is homologous to
the miser's engrossing experience with gold. Both the omnipotence
of money and the prodigality of space are incarnations of excess and
immensity—what I call the spatio-extensive. For the fugitive
McTeague, the desert is not just a space but an *espace vital*; in the
same way, gold for the hoarder is "the glittering incarnation of [the]

innermost principle of life" (Marx, *Capital* 230). There is no need to push the parallel further. It is enough to juxtapose Norris' description of the amplitude of the alkaline desert—

> League upon league the infinite reaches of dazzling white alkali laid themselves out like an immeasurable scroll unrolled from horizon to horizon (xxi 424–25)

and Marx's characterization of the hoarder in his progressive conquest of space—

> He is in the same situation as a world conqueror, who discovers a new boundary with each country he annexes. (*Capital* 231)

The topology of the desert reenacts the passion of the hoarder, for the "hoarding drive," as Marx puts it, "is boundless in its nature" (Marx, *Capital* 230). Like the "illimitable leagues of quivering sand and alkali" (xxi 420) that McTeague pauses more than once to behold, hoarding is "an endless process" (Marx, *Contribution* 176). If money is "independent of all limits" (Marx, *Capital* 230), the desert is a "gigantic landscape" (xxi 419) with no geometry, no center, and no circumference.[20] In its endless extension, the desert unfolds the ceaseless possibilities of (re)production.[21] In the abundance of space one is constantly reminded of the boundlessness of money: "McTeague's eyes wandered over the illimitable stretch of alkali that stretched out forever and forever to the east, to the north, and to the south" (xxi 401).[22]

In contemplating Norris' desert, however, the reader experiences not only a sense of endlessness fostered by the absence of geographical markers, but also an exaggeration of space. It is interesting to note, along with Donald Pizer, that Norris "broadens Death Valley to over three times its width" (*Novels* 82). The exaggerated representation of the desert is all the more intriguing given the author's commitment to realist representation, for Norris, much like other naturalists, fully researched his novels. Such deviation alerts the reader to a salient element in the organization of space. Norris himself emphasizes the idiosyncracy of the desert experience of his protagonist: "A new life began for McTeague" (xxi 402). McTeague's new setting involves an unsettling experience. The *tableau semi-vivant* with which the novel closes, where McTeague is chained to the dead body of Marcus in the immensity of the desert, depicts more than an infinitude of space. Out of this spatial element emerges an additional but less propitious dimension whereby the desert is transfigured from a space of pure extension to a saturated space that propels a negative precipitation of events

But what exactly does it mean to talk about a negative precipitation of events? For Deleuze, negation is that which overrides all laws; negation needs "no foundation and is beyond all foundation, a primal delirium, an original and timeless chaos solely composed of wild and lacerating molecules" (*Masochism* 25). But this is only one level of negation, the impersonal level. It is a pure negation in the sense that it is absolute. The other and less totalizing level of negation is what Deleuze calls partial negation. Here, Deleuze insists, negation pervades but only as the underside of affirmation, and in this sense tends toward a state that is never fully achieved because its is constantly surpassed: "Destruction is merely the reverse of creation and change, disorder is another form of order and the decomposition of death is equally the composition of life. The negative is all-pervasive but the process of death and destruction that it represents is only a partial process" (*Masochism* 24). Rather than a radical destruction, this latter concept of negativity designates a structure the envisaged unity of which is not static but mobile. At the same time, this motility is not a matter of simple inversion but an intrinsic, restless movement. The negative precipitation that erupts is constitutive of the system in the sense that it traverses the movement of completion towards which the system usually tends.

In *McTeague*, this negative dimension instills the novel with counter-developments. "Gigantic" and "colossal" (xxi 419) as it may be, the Western desert where McTeague freely circulates turns suddenly into a space of negativity. Against the images of extension and boundlessness is mustered a "counterrhythm of space" (Graham 53). It is as if all the openness of the desert becomes entrapping: "McTeague might get away, but where to, in heaven's name? A rat could not hide on the surface of that glistening alkali" (xxii 437). McTeague is a prisoner not only of his deed, but also of space. No sooner does McTeague find his freedom in the desert than the desert closes on him: "Marcus was dead now; McTeague was locked to the body. All about him, vast, interminable, stretched the measureless leagues of Death Valley" (xxii 442). If with McTeague's first murder, the reader is taken from constricted spaces to open spaces, with his second murder, the space of abundance develops into a space of negativity—literally Death Valley. The implication of this negativity can be more pointedly conveyed when related to the economic perspective that informs the novel. The relationship between the economic logic and the spatial element becomes observable when treating the latter as "a mode of symbolic narration," to borrow Don Graham's phrase (11). In other words, the language of reproduction and repetition at the heart of political economy is formally recreated in the spatial metaphor of propagation and expansion. It follows that the counterrhythm of space is an implicit commentary on the negative developments that intrude the system (i.e., capitalism).

The specific forms that this disconnection takes require a more detailed analysis of McTeague's flight. Complementing the oscillation between flux and counter-flux, between evasion and death in the novel, is a notable tension between regularity and irregularity. McTeague's spatial experience, in fact, propels a circuit of intensities whereby the spatio-intensive interferes with the spatio-extensive. The end of the novel is full of paths of escape and images of flight, but it is also infused with impasses, blocked passages, and thwarted escapes—in fact, a whole topography of obstacles. The ensuing intensities, however, are not pure or absolute negations; they emanate out of an ordered flight. The fugitive McTeague does not travel at random but follows an itinerary. In its earlier phase, his escape through the mountains is barely an adventure, for his moves are coordinated with such a regularity and his trajectory is mapped out with such a precision that little is left to randomness. McTeague does not have to pry open new paths but only discern old traces. Even after years of absence, McTeague finds his trail with relative ease, in fact with an instinctual guidance: "Twice again the dentist left the road and took to the trail that cut through deserted hydraulic pits. He knew exactly where to look for these trails" (xx 382). His flight is both systematic and intuitive: "not once," insists Norris, "did his instinct deceive him. He recognized familiar points at once" (xx 382). Even in the desert, McTeague is not travelling at random, but following trails, keeping "along the edge of the hill where these trails are" (xxi 417). In the cartography of the desert McTeague can still discern ordered paths and consistent trajectories: "The trails were numerous, but old and faint; and they have been made by cattle, not by men. They led in all directions but one—north, south and west; but not one, however faint, struck towards the valley" (xxi 417). The destination of these traces can even be surmised: "The cattle trails seemed to be drawing together toward a common point" (xxi 421).

The consistency of these codes, however, starts to break down with Norris's fugitive. Flight is still systematic—i.e., McTeague is still bound to Mexico—but is no longer predictable or accountable.

Confronted with the dentist's aberrant trajectory, the sheriff and his men "could hardly believe their eyes" (xxii 433). Insofar as it does not follow the trodden paths inscribed on the surface of the desert, McTeague's flight ceases to be linear: "it swerved abruptly," observed the sheriff's horsemen (xxii 433). Suddenly, McTeague's wilder path introduces a deviation. McTeague started unintelligibly to incline in alien territory, to circulate outside possibilities inscribed in the existing trajectories: "Then once more he sat forward. But there was a change in the direction of McTeague's flight. Hitherto he had held to the south ... but now he turned sharply at right angles" (xxi 423). In his unpredictable swerves, McTeague acts just like his mule under the influence of loco-weed. In the desert, madness—in the Deleuzian sense of escape—is a general state affecting both the mule and its rider. McTeague moves out of range, and his mule acts out of the norm: it "ran a few steps, halted, and squealed again. Then, suddenly wheeling at right angles, set off on a jog trot to the north, squealing and kicking from time to time" (xxi 417). Norris himself has not excluded the possibility of a negative development whereby an experience is intensified by the eruption of irregularities: if the mules "'get to eating that, they'll sure go plum crazy'" (xx 401–02). Both the frantic behavior of the mule and the abrupt swerves of McTeague suffuse the end of the novel with an unpredictable precipitation of events. An unaccountable and chaotic dimension, in fact a certain madness, gradually imposes itself: "It seemed as though he were bitted and ridden; as if some unseen hand were turning him toward the east; some unseen heel spurring him to precipitate and instant flight" (xxi 412).

In light of this precarious movement, Norris' question towards the end of the novel—"Flight from what?" (xxi 412)—acquires an added valence. In order to answer this question, let us recapitulate some of the key points that the foregoing analysis has crystallized. It is obvious that the imposing presence of gold makes much of the thrust of the novel revolve around economic value. As such, this preoccupation with the motif of gold is hardly surprising given that the author is himself the son of a San Francisco jeweler. What is important about this motif, however, is that it provides the central metaphor for a symbology that exceeds the field of political economy *tout court*. Retracing the economic perspective in a number of practices, motives, and themes has made it possible to unravel the encroachment of the language of production in apparently autonomous registers. If economic value is the epicenter of the novel, it is because the lived totality of Norris' characters has undergone an economico-politicization. In this sense, economic value is pervasive precisely because it is formally reproduced within and outside the economic sphere. In *The Production of Space*, Henri Lefebvre provides a useful theoretical mediation between reproduction *stricto sensu* and formal reproduction: "When reproduction is treated as a concept ... it brings concepts in its wake: repetition, reproducibility, and so on" (102). Seen from this perspective, the proliferation of redundancies becomes itself a production of surplus value. The compulsion to repeat at the heart of the system becomes a general experience in the novel. Such a generalization assumes that all excesses are alike; that desire is not only pecuniary, but also culinary, linguistic, and semiotic. At the same time, the analysis of syntactic involutions and spatial intensities in the novel has enabled us to sharpen or qualify this proposition. It is obvious that the strategy of desire is not only repetitive but also intensive. The various moments of disruption, flux, and discontinuity at work in the novel suggest that the system's movement towards completion is always interfered with by the possibility of dissolution.

This interplay between regularity and irregularity is not limited to the desert episode. McTeague's volatile experience of space bespeaks the proliferation of intensities spawning paths of non-linear propensities that can be seen at work even in Trina's pecuniary desire, and more specifically in the intensification of her hoarding instinct. Greed, writes James Caron, has turned Trina into "an automaton" (294)—a machine, so to speak, the engine of which is money. Norris himself refers to Trina's money as "a-god-from-the machine" (ix 154). Such a characterization is hardly inappropriate, for accumulation among hoards, as Marx points out, is a "Sisyphean task" that knows no limits (*Capital* 231). McTeague makes it a point to note the regularity of Trina's avarice: "Trina, you're getting to be regular stingy.... Trina, you're a regular little miser" (xii 250–51). Even Trina concedes that she has "become a regular little miser" (x 210). Yet, Trina's hoarding, as Norris takes pains to convey, is not only instinctive but also excessive: "She loved her money with an intensity she could hardly express" (xvi 308). In her perverse desire, Trina had become "a strange woman" (xvi 310), or better yet an unpredictable woman. Her desire has reached a catastrophic level. With Trina's repeated withdrawal of her "capital" (xix 357) from Uncle Oelbermann at the end of the novel, comes the possibility of disrupting the "machine-like regularity" (xix 353) that has marked her hoarding experience: "'But this is very irregular, you know, Mrs McTeague,' said the great man. 'Not business like at all'" (xix 356).

The indeterminacy of the system, the possible irregularity that threatens the machine-like regularity in the field of political economy, intersects with Trina's whirls of passion. The hysterical fervor that occasionally seizes the hoarding Trina is a symbolic form of disorder that formally reenacts the transgressive character of capitalism. The irregularity that instills the miser's passion for repeated savings reenacts the principle of excess and irrationality that is inherent in the system. In her utter perversion, Trina, in the words of William Cain, becomes "a classic study of capitalism gone mad" (211). Her passion for money has developed into a "veritable frenzy" (xix 355); her pecuniary desire has become a perverse desire:

> Trina began to draw steadily upon her capital, a little at a time. It was a passion with her, a mania, a veritable mental disease...
>
> It would come upon her all of a sudden. While she was about her work, scrubbing the floor of the house; or in her room, in the morning ..., a brusque access of cupidity would cease upon her... At times, she would leave her work just as it was, put on her old bonnet ΄of black straw, throw her shawl about her, and go straight to Uncle Oelbermann's store and draw against her money. (xix 357–58)

Inscribed in Trina's passion is a certain indeterminacy that engenders the same threat of irrationality and unaccountability that marks the experience of the hallucinating Zerkow, the hysterical Maria, and the bewildered mule. What these clustered instances have in common is the tendency to act in an unpredictable way. In their proclivity to exceed and transgress, they recapitulate the image of Norris's fugitive in his flight. But the flight of McTeague itself reenacts the flux, in fact the intensity of capitalism—it is not just McTeague who is running away, it is a runaway system. Seen from this perspective, the real question is not "Flight from what?" (xxi 412), but instead, whether a system that is free from flight is ever conceivable. At least theoretically, the concept of a closed system—i.e., a system that permits nothing to escape its hold—is reductive simply because, as Baudrillard reminds us, a "system that approaches the threshold of perfection is a system that lies on the brink of its collapse" (*Échange* 11).

CHAPTER FOUR

A Rhythmanalytical Approach to the
Problematic of Everydayness in *Sister Carrie*

To read *Sister Carrie* is to come across a rhythm that is hard to ignore. The novel, as Ellen Moers pointed out long ago, abounds with images of motion and movement: "Rhythmic effects of every variety (the train, the carriage horse, the shuffling feet of the bums, the rocking chair) are scattered through the novel so profusely that its lyrical quality becomes at times almost too rich" (519). This rhythmic effect is particularly important because it lays bare some fundamental elements about the economic structure around which much of the novel revolves. Despite what appearances may suggest, the economic theme is not limited to Carrie's ambition "to gain in material things" (i 2) or the natural inclination of her imagination to "trod a very narrow round, always winding up at points which concerned money, looks, clothes, or enjoyment" (vi 48). It is associated with all that which is repetitive and pleonastic—in fact, it is associated with rhythms as such. Highlighting this aspect in the novel enables us to explore the ways in which capitalism functions at the formal level. The study of rhythms is, indeed, a study of capitalism in its most insidious effects.[1]

This rhythm can be observed in the various aspects of everyday life that the novel depicts. Carrie's experience with the Hansons, for instance, reveals a distinctively monotonous and iterative pace: "She felt the drab of a lean and narrow life.... She was glad to be out of the flat, because already she felt that it was a narrow, humdrum place, and that interest and joy lay elsewhere" (ii 12–iv 31). Later at the shoe factory Carrie experiences the same monotony. Dreiser even uses the same term—humdrum—to describe both experiences: "At this task she laboured incessantly for some time, finding relief from her own nervous fears and imaginings in the humdrum, mechanical movement of the machine.... At the shoe factory she put a long day, scarcely so wearisome as the preceding, but considerably less novel" (iv 43–vi 49). As if the mechanical movement that entangles the factory workers is not enough, Dreiser draws our attention to the overwhelming motion that animates the street: "All during the long afternoon she thought of the city outside and its imposing show, crowds, and fine buildings" (iv 38). There is a curious continuity between the running machine and "the hurrying throng which filled the sidewalks" (iii 16), between the accelerated pace in the work place and the pace of life in the city. It is as if the movement of the "clattering machines" (xliv 417) in the factory is commingled with "the clatter and clang of life" (i 8) in the city. What prevails is a measured rhythmic motion that brings together the ceaseless energy inside the factory and the endless movement outside it. Even when the machines are brought to a halt at the end of the day, the motion that Carrie so intensely experiences at work is hardly interrupted. The mechanical movement dies way only to cede to the intense movement of the people "pouring out of the building" (iii 26) and "hurrying with the same buzz and energy-yielding enthusiasm" (iv 39). Almost every aspect of the city and every detail about its dwellers enhance this rhythmic movement that pervades the novel: "She gazed into the lighter street ... and wondered at the sounds, the movements, the murmur of the vast city" (ii 10). The more Carrie becomes familiar with metropolitan life, the more this sense of motion imposes itself: "labourers tamping by in either direction, the horse-cars passing crowded to the rails with the small clerks and floor help in the great whole sale houses, and men and women generally coming of doors and passing about the neighborhood.... Trucks were rumbling in increasing numbers: men and women, girls and boys were moving in all directions" (iv 32). The pace of the city is insistent to such an extent that to "join in the great, hurrying throng ... becomes a desire which the mind can scarcely resist" (Dreiser, *Theodore Dreiser* 95).

I focus on the various aspects of everyday life that the novel exposes because, in many ways, everyday life is the meeting place of all repetition. It is true that everyday life has always existed as the basis of every society but it did so in ways that are drastically different from the modern era. In a society that thrives on rationality, planning, and measurability everyday life has acquired a new significance. For Henri Lefebvre, such a historical development calls for a subtle but important distinction between daily life (*la vie quotidienne*), on the one hand, and the everyday (*le quotidien*) and its corollary everydayness (*la quotidienneté*), on the other hand: "Let us simply say about daily life that it has always existed, but permeated with values, with myths. The word *everyday* designates the entry of this daily life into modernity: the everyday as an object of programming, whose unfolding is imposed by the market, by the system of equivalences, by marketing and advertising. As to the concept of 'everydayness,' it stresses the homogenous, the repetitive, the fragmentary in everyday life" ("Toward" 87, n. 1). The everyday does not simply refer to perfunctory functions, but instead designates the common denominator of these functions; it means by its sequence rather than its substance.[2] Stated differently, the everyday is invested in a certain realism but cannot be confounded with that realism, nor can it be reduced to an enumeration of the mundane tasks and daily preoccupations that entangle the individual: "The deployment of time is such that the day is fragmented and chopped into small segments. The pursuit of realism consists in a detailed description of these segments; focusing on such activities as eating, dressing, cleaning, moving about; and listing commonly used objects or products. Although it may seem scientific, such description cannot seize the essence of the everyday simply because the everyday does not consist in a series of time lapses but, instead, their concatenation, i.e. their rhythm" (Lefebvre, "Projet" 194). An analysis that focuses on the petty and humdrum realities around which everyday life revolves can neither seize their full significance nor uncover their specificity. The everyday does not lie in the mundane activities individuals perform but in the concatenation of these activities. The everyday, writes Lefebvre, "refers to repetition in daily life, to that which repeats itself consistently" ("Toward" 78). What matters for the study of everydayness is not the prism of the activities one undertakes but their sequence, not their sum but their rhythm—what Dreiser intuitively called "the flow of common everyday things about" (xx 180).

This rhythm, however, is more complex than it appears; it conjures up two temporal modalities that are deceptively similar—one that is cyclical, the other linear. I use the term *linear* here in a specific way; the distinction is not between a time that flows in a line as in a river and a time that flows in a circle as around the surface of the globe. Both the linear and the cyclical refer to a repetitive movement, but in each case repetition is motivated by different dynamics. While in the

former time is locked in a specific sequence, the prototype of which is
production for the sake of production, in the latter time unfolds within
a sequence that refers to the order of existence (i.e., the movement of
life and death). Cyclical time has furnished the axis around which
everyday life has always been organized. Cyclical time is neither
cumulative nor circular (in the sense that no two seasons are ever the
same), but instead regular and recurrent; it is associated with
regeneration and renewal. It should not go unnoticed, however, that
the distinction between the natural and the post-natural rests on an
assumption that needs to be qualified. Setting linear time against
cyclical time assumes that the latter is unproblematically natural (and
thus normative) while in reality this naturalness is a matter of degree.
Even the natural—or what is considered the raw material of everyday
life—is coded; it is historically bound. Natural time, as Cornelius
Castoriadis reminds us, is not timeless: "Time is never instituted as a
purely neutral medium or receptacle for external coordination of
activities. Time is always endowed with meaning" (50). What we
often perceive as natural time, does not have an absolute but a relative
value, because society always provides the framework according to
which time is arranged.

   With this caveat in mind, we can now return to the rhythm that
defines modern everyday life. With the hegemony of capitalism, the
generalization of monetary economy, and the consolidation of the
socio-symbolic that sustains it, cyclical time has gradually lost its
depth (i.e., its ritualistic component), giving way to a more linear time,
or what may be termed a time of indefinite progress. What this means
is that everyday life still revolves around repetition, but the ensuing
rhythm is specific to an age of mechanical reproduction—it is
impelled by the compulsion to repeat that is at the core of capitalism.
With the exigency of a socio-symbolic structured around the
production of surplus-value, the non-cumulative process upon which
cyclical time has always thrived is folded into a cumulative process in
which accumulation becomes the Ur-repetition. In a fluid society
where the motion of capitalism has permeated cyclical alternations, the
movement of birth and death (the law of nature) is increasingly
undermined by the process of production and destruction (the law of
value). Broadly speaking, the time that defines the modern era is a
time that tends to efface the repetitive movement induced by cycles
and to instill a new type of repetition; it is a time that is subjected to
the measurable temporality of the clock and the routine of the
working day. Behind the hours, days, weeks, months, seasons, and
years stands an experience that is increasingly undermined by the

type of temporality dictated by the division of labor and the automation of production. In an age of rationality, planning, and specialization, cyclical time is reconfigured into such functional categories as pledged time (the time spent in the factory), free time (time devoted for leisure), and compulsive time (other demands that city life calls for such as moving about and the like). In this reconfiguration, life is calculated and programmed in order to fit a controlled timetable in ways that have not been previously experienced.[3]

However, it would be wrong to assume that cyclical time has completely disappeared under the spell of linear time. The institutionalization of this new temporality does not mean the total evacuation of natural cycles but the imposition of an intensely programmed everyday life. Sociality is still entangled in natural cycles, but these have been profoundly altered in accordance with the dominant mode of production. Therein lies the intricate character of everyday life in the modern world. It is the meeting place of all repetitions, but these repetitions are played off in the intersection between a cyclical and a linear temporality. To put it somewhat differently, repetition is not void of natural dimensions (such as hunger, need, and satisfaction), but these are increasingly brought under the exigency of rational categories (such as repetitive gestures, monotonous acts, and programmed consumption). As Lefebvre explains, the distinction between the two temporal modalities is not clear cut: "This rhythm takes the form of a regulated time governed by rational categories but revolves around the least rational in the human being: the lived, the sensual, and the corporeal. On the various natural rhythms of the body (breathing, hunger, thirst) are superimposed—not without momentous effects—rhythms that are rational, numeric, quantitative, and qualitative" (*Éléments* 18).[4]

The conflictual unity between these two temporal modalities can be readily discerned in the different approaches to eating and sleeping in the opening chapters of *Sister Carrie*. In the factory, lunch time is decided not by the time when the worker is hungry but by the time when the machine stops; in other words, it is dictated by labor time. During her first day at work in the shoe factory, Carrie experiences a disjunction between natural needs and external constraints imposed by the organization of work: "Carrie got up and sought her lunch box. She was stiff, a little dizzy, and very thirsty" (iv 36). Carrie's new experience at work entails a perturbation of the natural inclination of the body: "It is no easy thing to get up early in the morning when one is used to sleeping until seven and eight, as Carrie had been at home" (iv 31). Carrie's initial difficulty to adjust to the new conditions imposed by her work experience, in particular, and city life, in general, puts into perspective the tension between that which is social and programmed and that which is innate and natural. There is, in fact, an instinctual resistance from the body to bend to a new pace of life. Unaccustomed to this new rhythm, Carrie's body fails to respond in the manner Hanson's body unreservedly does: "She gained some inkling of the character of Hanson's life when, half asleep, she looked out into the dinning-room at six o'clock and saw him silently finishing his breakfast" (iv 31). Over time, however, Carrie's natural habits started to cede to the exigency of a more conditioned life style. Her adaptation to the new pace imposed by city life well articulates the dynamics of this compromise between a primary nature and a second nature: "During the remainder of the week it was very much the same. One or two nights she found herself too tired to walk home, and expended car fare. She was not very strong, and sitting all day affected her back. She went to bed one night before Hanson" (vi 50).[5]

The significance of such a compromise becomes even more evident when setting these ordered practices against a rare moment of spontaneity early in the novel. When encountering Sister Carrie in downtown Chicago, Drouet does not hesitate to invite her to have lunch with him: "Let's go and have something to eat" (vi 54). While admittedly Drouet is driven by a genuine appetite and an insistent hunger, the demands of the body are soon undermined by an ordered movement that tacitly extends linear time. The movement in the street that attracts Drouet while eating impinges on the spontaneity that initially characterizes this restaurant episode: "Drouet selected a table close by the window, where the busy rout of the street could be seen. He loved the changing panorama of the street—to see and be seen" (vi 54). The reference to food inside the restaurant is strewn with references to the movement of the crowd outside it in such a way that the exigency of the body (the hungry Drouet) almost retreats in front of the pace of city life (the thronging crowd).

The study of everyday life in the novel is important not only because it makes it possible to identify a certain rhythm that is structurally akin to the motion of capitalism, but also because it sheds some additional insights on the historical specificity of realist aesthetics. The fragments of reality that lay bare the structure of everyday life in the novel constitute the same themes, elements, and motifs around which naturalism revolves—the banal, the mundane, the insignificant, and the common. It is partly through novelistic realism and naturalism that everyday life has eminently entered into our reflection. One may even argue that naturalism contributed to reversing the bias that everyday life is unworthy of exploration because of its triviality. Seen from one perspective, there is nothing more obvious than everyday life, but this proffered obviousness is misleading; the everyday is, in fact, the locus of a deceptive simplicity. In the words of Lefebvre, there is "power concealed in everyday life's apparent banality, a depth beneath its triviality, *something extraordinary in its very ordinariness*" (*Everyday Life* 37). From this vantage point, an analysis of the structure of everyday life not only requires a careful consideration of insignificant details and mundane activities that are often taken for granted, but also calls for a systematic method capable of unfurling the hegemony of everydayness.

The type of analysis I would like to suggest is not without precedent. A prototype for the study of the deceptive triviality of everyday life can be readily discerned in Marx's analysis of the mystery of the commodity. Marx's chief concern is repetition—as a mechanism of production in the widest sense—because that which recurs often dissimulates the trace of its repetitiveness: "the constant repetition of exchange makes it a normal social process" (Marx, *Capital* 182). One may even argue that the thrust of Marx's critique of political economy is a critique of the misleading transparency of everyday life. In the same way reification points to a relationship which we take for granted, the everyday designates a process that presents itself as natural: "It is only through the habit of everyday life that we come to think it perfectly plain and commonplace, that a social relation of production should take on the form of a thing" (Marx, quoted in Lévi-Strauss 95). Habits are essential in conceiving of the hegemony of the everyday because they foster the ability to accept unquestioningly one's existing conditions. A remarkable passage early in *Sister Carrie* lays bare the role habits play in the structure of everyday life:

> Habits are peculiar things. They will drive the really non-religious mind out of bed to say prayers that are only a custom and not a devotion. The victim of habits, when he had neglected the thing which it was his custom to do, feels a little scratching in the brain, a little irritating something which comes out of being out of the rut, and imagines it to be the prick of conscience, the still, small voice that is urging him ever to righteousness. If the digression is unusual enough, the drag of habit will be heavy enough to cause the unreasoning victim to return and perform the perfunctory thing.

'Now, bless me,' says such a mind, 'I have done my duty,' when, as a matter
of fact, it has merely done its old unbearable trick once again. (viii 75)

Behind the different types of activities required by everyday life there
is a habitual commitment to a certain conformity, monotony, and
sameness.   To talk about the everyday is to talk about a habitual
system of constraints, or, better yet, a compulsion to repeat.[6]

An examination of Carrie's impression of New York can extend
the implication of these observations: "For a long while she
concerned herself over the arrangement of New York flats, and
wondered at ten families living in one building and all remaining
strange and indifferent to each other" (xxi 277).   Domestic urban
spaces are divided in discreet locations whereby city dwellers live in
proximity to each other but do not know each other.   The flats are
designed in such a way as to bring the inhabitants together while
keeping them apart.   In spite of such detachment and differentiation,
however, these individualized spaces are the locus of an enormous
tautology.   People are isolated in apartments and enclosed in private
spaces and yet behind this social isolation there is a strong and
unescapable conformity which commits them to monotonous gestures
and repetitive movements.   Individuals are caught up in what may be
termed, after Sartre, a serial relationship.[7]   In seriality one's act is
characterized primarily by its relation to the acts of other people
doing the same thing.   The other is present in one's action but this
presence is discrete and even illusory.   Fredric Jameson's analysis of
seriality well articulates this paradox:

> In seriality, what I happen to be doing, reading a newspaper, waiting for a
> bus, opening a can, pausing for a red light, is characterized primarily by its
> identity with the acts of other people in those situations... Somehow I feel
> that I am no longer central, that I am merely doing just what everybody else
> is doing, that the center of my act is elsewhere, outside me, in other people.
> But, and this is the crucial point, *everybody else* feels exactly the same way
> about it. In seriality, in Sartre's language, "each is the same as the Others
> to the degree that he is Other from himself." ("Seriality" 76–77)

Society enables its members to pursue their business as usual while, at
the same time, it compels them to do so—or, as Jameson puts it,
submits them to a "collective impotence and helplessness" (*Marxism*
248).

An incident half way through the novel can further elucidate the
ways in which individuals come into connection with each other only

in determined ways:

> Some time in the second year of their residence in Seventy-eight Street the
> flat across the hall from Carrie became vacant, and into it moved a very
> handsome young woman and her husband, with both of whom Carrie
> afterwards became acquainted. This was brought about solely by the
> arrangement of the flats, which were united in one place, as it were, by the
> dumb-waiter. This useful elevator, by which fuel, groceries, and the like
> were sent up from the basement, and garbage and waste sent down, was used
> by both residents of one floor; that is, a small door opened into it from each
> flat.
>
> 　If the occupants of both flats answered to the whistle of the janitor at
> the same time, they would stand face to face when they opened the dumb-
> waiter doors. One morning, when Carrie went to remove her paper, the
> newcomer, a handsome brunette of perhaps twenty three years of age, was
> there for the same purpose. (xxxi 280–81)

Dreiser's depiction of this urban setting reveals an interesting
paradox. The organization of space disguises the relationship
between people. Behind the apparent disconnection so characteristic
of city life lies a misrecognized, but nonetheless essential
connectedness. The setting makes the coincidence between Carrie's
habitual activity of collecting the paper and that of her neighbor a
pseudo-coincidence. The episode, in fact, crystallizes a curious
paradox that lies at the heart of the everyday; everybody is doing the
same thing at about the same time, but everybody is seemingly alone
in doing it—what is at stake is not difference but indifference.[8]
　Dreiser's description of the alluring world of the commodity that
imposes itself on the defenseless and covetous Carrie rearticulates, in a
forceful way, this indifference: she "passed along the busy aisles,
much affected by the remarkable displays of trinkets, dress goods,
stationary, and jewelry. Each separate counter was a show place of
dazzling interest and attraction. She could not help feeling the claim
of each trinket and valuable upon her personally.... Carrie began
wandering around the store amid the fine displays... Her woman's
heart was warm with desire for them. How would she look in this, how
charming that would make her!" (iii 20–vii 64).　Carrie's
exclamations in front of the opulence she witnesses in New York both
echo and extend her initial fascination with the department store:

> It was not often that she came to the play stirred to her heart's core by
> actualities. To-day a low song of longing had been set singing in her heart

by the finery, the merriment, the beauty she had seen. Oh, these women who had passed her by, hundreds and hundreds strong, who were they? Whence came the rich, elegant dresses, the astonishingly coloured buttons, the knick-cknacks of silver and gold? Where were these lovely creatures housed? Amid what elegancies of carved furniture, decorated walls, elaborate tapestries did they move? Where were their rich apartments, loaded with all that money could provide? In what stables champed these sleek, nervous horses and rested the gorgeous carriages? Where lounged the richly groomed footmen? Oh, the mansions, the lights, the perfume, the loaded boudoirs and tables! New York must be filled with such bowers, or the beautiful, insolent, supercilious creatures could not be. (xxxii 287)

The overwhelming sense of theatrical excess Carrie experiences in this part of New York points to a certain surreality.[9] Chicago is "a wonder," (i 8) Drouet tells Carrie. Later in the novel Carrie—who has herself been "the victim of the city's hypnotic influence" (vii 75)—conveys the same impression to Ames: New York is "quite a thing to see" (xxxii 291).

In Carrie's infatuation with the city one can see the lure of the commodity. To deal with the world of commodification is to deal with the problem of appearance and disappearance. The commodity, insists Marx, is an a-thing; it is something obvious and yet complex, tangible and yet intangible. In *Sister Carrie*, the city not only turns the real consumer (driven by genuine needs) into a consumer of illusions (motivated by created desires) but is itself the pointed manifestation of this illusion. Such is the case, then, the analysis of the logic and strategy of the commodity collapses into the analysis of a more imposing phenomenon—what may be termed, after Guy Debord, the spectacle. Here the oscillation between the thing and its representation, between reality and make-belief, is even more intriguing. For Debord, "the principle of commodity fetishism, the domination of society by 'intangible as well as tangible things,' ... reaches its absolute fulfillment in the spectacle, where the tangible world is replaced by a selection of images which exist above it, and which simultaneously impose themselves as tangible *par excellence*" (36). What this proposition means, in part, is that production in capitalism can no longer be contained within a base and superstructure model; there is no primary and secondary process of production—production takes place everywhere (although it is a production of illusion). The logic of the commodity seizes all aspects of sociality, thus extending the hegemony of capitalism beyond mechanisms of large diffusion. To deal with the spectacle is to deal with an extended and even atopical space of production: "the spectacle feels at home nowhere, because the spectacle is everywhere" (Debord 30). The spectacle cannot be isolated or demarcated, because it is embedded in the minutiae of everyday life: "The spectacle is the moment when the commodity has attained the total occupation of social life. Not only is the relation to the commodity visible but it is all one sees: the world one sees is its world" (Debord 42). Because capitalism functions in extended structures, because it infiltrates every aspect of sociality, everyday life becomes part of a programmed and controlled consumption.

This line of analysis crystallizes the increasing hegemony of signs—a phenomenon which Dreiser himself has not failed to notice: "Signs were everywhere numerous" (ii 7). The city becomes the space where not just goods and commodities but also signs and symbols proliferate:

> The walk down Broadway, then as now, was one of the remarkable features of the city. There gathered, before the matinée and afterwards, not only all the pretty women who love a show parade, but the men who love to gaze upon and admire them. It was a very imposing procession of pretty faces and fine clothes. Women appeared in their very best hats, shoes, and gloves, and walked arm in arm on their way to the fine shops or theaters strung along from Fourteenth to Thirty-fourth streets. Equally the men paraded with the very latest they could afford. A tailor might have secured hints on suit measurements, a shoemaker on proper lasts and colours, a hatter on hats. It was literally true that if a lover of fine clothes secured a new suit, it was sure to have its first airing on broadway.... Men in flawless top-coats, high hats, and silver-headed walking sticks elbowed near and looked too often into conscious eyes. Ladies rustled by in dresses of stiff cloths, shedding affected smiles of goodness and the heavy percentage of vice. The rouged and powdered cheeks and lips, the scented hair, the large, misty, and languorous eye, were common enough. With a start she awoke to find that she was in fashion's crowd, on parade in a show place—and such a show place! Jewelers' windows flamed along the path with remarkable frequency. Florist shops, furriers, haberdashers, confectiones—all followed in rapid succession. The street was full of coaches. Pompous doormen in immense coats, shiny brass belts and buttons, waited in front of expensive salesrooms. Coachmen in tan boots, white tights, and blue jackets waited obsequiously for the mistresses of carriages who were shopping inside. The whole street bore the flavour of riches and show. (xxxi 284–86)

In this remarkable passage the system is exposed to its barest detail.

Almost every aspect of the city is commodified, displayed, and advertised. The distinction between the spectacle and the spectators becomes hardly sustainable: "Carrie found herself stared at and ogled" (xxxi 285). People come together to watch and to be watched: "To stare seemed the proper and natural thing" (xxxi 285). At the same time, the pronounced visual character of the city is deceptive. As Debord warns us, the proliferation of images and signs hides the most important truth about the spectacle—its illusory reality: "The spectacle is not a collection of images, but a social relation among people, mediated by images" (5). The implication of this observation goes even further. Seeing and being seen, which traditionally have been associated with intelligibility, have become a trap whereby representations are often mistaken for the things themselves.[10] One consequence of this spectacularization is that the thing and its representation are commingled in such a way that real consumption is almost indistinguishable from the consumption of the signs associated with these things. To the extent that buying is increasingly based on images, consumption has become both factitious (the consumption of things not stimulated by need) and fictitious (the consumption of things that are not real). Not only are commodities increasingly glorified by signs, but consumption itself is more and more related to signs and less and less associated with the goods themselves. In this process of spectacular consumption, as Sherry Weber explains, real experience is increasingly replaced by pseudo-experience: "Advertising makes the image a conscious fantasy, and we are consciously living out in our daily lives. We enter the environment as consumers, and the environment of which we are part becomes the ultimate commodity. Since pseudo-experience is not gratifying as experience, we find our pleasure in its pseudo-ness—in the process of image-making" (36–37).

An examination of the seductive offer Carrie receives from a representative of the Wellington Hotel to board with them can help elucidate the increasingly abstract nature of consumption—the ways consumption has become almost synonymous with the consumption of signs. For Carrie, the hotel suite is appealing because it has an irresistible fantastic element: "It was such a place as she had often dreamed of occupying" (xliv 413). In addition to its functional use, the suite is presented as a status symbol: "In the third room, or parlour, was a piano, a heavy piano lamp, with shade of gorgeous pattern, a library table, several huge easy rockers, some dado book shelves, and a gilt curio case, filled with oddities. Pictures were upon the walls, soft Turkish pillows upon the divan, foot-stools of brown plush upon the floor" (xliv 413). Such lavishness not only makes the hotel an object of wonder and fantasy but also turns Carrie herself into a commodity. Carrie's consumption becomes all the more important because it has the potential of stimulating consumption among her fans: "your name is worth something for us.... Every hotel depends upon the repute of its patrons. A well known actress like yourself ... draws attention to the hotel, and—although you might not believe it—patrons" (xliv 411). Sister Carrie is not only consuming commodities but has become herself a cherished commodity. In a society of the spectacle, consumption is turned into an identificatory process; the distinction between having and being is blurred in such a way that even the consumer is consumed.[11] Thus Carrie becomes a sign to be advertised and consumed—a sign of happiness, satisfaction, success, and affluence.

This line of analysis points to a number of consuming practices that are propelled by an increasing tendency towards abstraction. When we first meet Carrie, she is fascinated with the world of commodities; at the end of the novel, Carrie herself becomes a sign that is advertised and consumed. The novel can even be said to revolve around a vicious circle whereby every act of consumption effaces the one that precedes it, but in the process creates new commodities that extend the circuit. The emphasis gradually shifts from the display of commodities, to the consumption of commodities, to the display of consumption itself, to the consumption of signs of consumption. Such a progressive structuring makes consumption more a matter of form than a matter of content. One may even say that consumption does not satisfy the desire to consume, but endlessly renews it. The implication of such a titillation, as Dreiser points out, is that "the whole energy of our lives [is] turned into a miserable struggle for the unattainable, namely, the uninterrupted and complete gratification of our desires" (*Theodore Dreiser* 157).

This unattainability characterizes not only Carrie's desire but also the very structure of a system that is fundamentally pleonastic. I use the term pleonastic partly because it emphasizes a redundant movement that is at the heart of capitalism, and partly because it conveys a certain futility. The principle of production for the sake of production upon which capitalism thrives involves not only over-production (the priority of exchange-value over use-value) but also over-consumption (the pre-eminence of desire over need), which is tantamount to saying that the driving impetus of the system is not production *per se* but the process of production, not consumption but the process of consumption. In his *Contribution to the Critique of*

Political Economy, Marx eloquently captures the theoretical significance of this distinction: "a nation is at its industrial height as long as its main objective is not gain, but the process of gaining" (271–72). What matters is not the act itself, be it production or consumption, but the ensuing rhythm.

Seen from this perspective, the repeated invocation of the mirror acquires a new relevance: "The mirror convinced [Sister Carrie] of a few things which she had long believed. She was pretty, yes, indeed! How nice her hat set, and weren't her eyes pretty.... She looked into her glass and saw a prettier Carrie than she had seen before; she looked into her mind, a mirror prepared of her own and the world's opinions, and saw a worse. Between these two images she wavered, hesitating which to believe" (viii 73–x 87). In this narcissistic episode, the boundaries between living and dreaming, between reality and make-belief, are blurred in such a way that the object of desire becomes hardly conceivable independently of its double. Carrie's attraction to her image even bespeaks the increasing volatilization of the subject's representational link to reality in a society that has stripped signs of their charged valence. By contemplating her image in the mirror, Carrie is able to break away from the confines of her real situation. The mirror functions as a virtual, even utopian space that enables Carrie to be where she is not—a space that is indefinitely desired. Carrie, as Dreiser points out, "has the blood of youth and some imagination.... She could think of things she would like to do, of clothes she would like to wear, and of places she would like to visit. These were things upon which her mind ran" (vi 47). It must be noted, however, that this utopic strain in the novel is not parasitical upon the structure of desire, but consonant with it. There is, in fact, a structural affinity between the unreality that sustains utopia and the unattainability that motivates desire. Both the insistence of a desire that goes beyond the limits of ordinary wants and the promise of a satisfaction that is never achieved alert the reader to the integral part that imagination plays in the process of production. In a society of commodification, as Susan Buck-Morss observes, the "technological capacity to produce must be mediated by the utopian capacity to dream" (120). What desire and dreaming have in common is the absence of a definite limit and the perpetuation of dissatisfaction. Carrie, as Dreiser depicts her, is the epitome of such a titillation: "She longed and longed and longed" (xii 109).

A close consideration of Carrie's incessantly expanding wants can further elucidate the central role this imaginative element plays in the structure of desire:

> Her sister Minnie ... was too busy scrubbing the kitchen wood work and calculating the purchasing power of eighty cents for Sunday's dinner. When Carrie had returned home, flushed with her first success and ready, for all her weariness to discuss the now interesting events which led up to her achievement, the former had merely smiled approvingly and inquired whether she would have to spend any of it for car fare. This consideration had not entered in before, and it did not now for long affect the glow of Carrie's enthusiasm. Disposed as she then was to calculate upon that vague basis which allows the substraction of one sum from another without any perceptible diminution, she was happy. (iv 27)

The passage sets in motion two tensions. The first tension is between the restricted purchasing power of the money in Minnie's possession and the unlimited possibilities of the money that Carrie dreams of having but has not earned yet. The juxtaposition of the tight budget that preoccupies Carrie's sister and the unactualized profit that tantalizes Sister Carrie makes it possible to pass off as real that which is imaginary at best. Carrie's desire entangles the reader in a world of fantasy, but this fantasy does not undermine the realist thrust of the novel; in fact, the image of Minnie's parsimony draws much of its effect from the image of Carrie's extravagance and *vice versa*. The contrast between the two sisters is further dramatized a few paragraphs later: "If Carrie was going to think of running around in the beginning there would be a hitch somewhere. Unless Carrie submitted to a solemn round of industry and saw the need of hard work without longing for play, how was her coming to the city to profit them" (iv 29). From here emanates the second tension; the eighty cents Minnie possesses not only actualize the sum of money that Carrie dreams of having but also inflate it. Spending does not dispossess Carrie but, interestingly enough, increases the purchasing power of her money. The dynamics of this scene imply that Carrie is caught in an endless movement which makes her desire larger than what it is but smaller than what it can be; stated differently, what Carrie has always pales in front of what she can have.

The discrepancy between the real and imaginary is further conveyed in Carrie's excitement over the "two soft, green ten-dollar bills" (vii 59) she receives from Drouet. In this episode, Dreiser reiterates the same curious algorithm that enables his heroine to subtract one sum from another without any perceptual diminution: "She would get stockings, too, and a skirt, and, and—till already, as in the matter of prospective salary, she had gone beyond, in her desires,

twice the purchasing power of her bills" (vii 59). The intensity of
Carrie's desire not only recapitulates the relation between fantasy and
reality, but also points to an essential connectedness between unreality
and insatiability. On the one hand, it reveals a shift whereby the
retreat of the real in front of the imaginary reproduces the increasing
imposition of desire over need. The dynamics of this phenomenal
reversal is well articulated by Debord: "To the extent that necessity is
socially dreamed, the dream becomes necessary" (21). On the other
hand, the episode establishes an intimate connection between the
intensification of desire and the multiplication of value. The
insatiable character of Sister Carrie both reflects and extends the
unlimited power of money: "When Drouet was gone, she sat down in
her rocking chair by the window... As usual, imagination exaggerated
the possibilities for her. It was as if he had put fifty cents in her hand,
and she had exercised the thoughts of a thousand dollars" (xvi 147).

This line of analysis points to an important but hitherto
unaddressed question: what is it that ensures the hegemony of
everydayness? Identifying a repetitive structure or an insistent rhythm
at the heart of everyday life is only the elementary level of analysis.
To say that the novel stages a number of redundancies that replicate
the principle of production for the sake of production lays bare the
tautological structure of capitalism but does not put into perspective
the reproductive nature of this tautology. If one argues that everyday
life is repetitive in accordance with the logic and structure of
capitalism, one is still left with the necessary task of examining the
ways in which the system ensures its continuity in the absence of a
cyclical mechanism for change and renewal. A close attention to a
number of tangential scenes in the novel—tangential in the sense that
they are not quite on a par with the repetitiveness thus far identified in
the novel—will suggest an interesting correlation between
everydayness and non-everydayness. The latter does not provide a
real escape from the sameness of everyday life but rather reproduces
that sameness while disguising its real character.

Confronted with a rational time that orders and defines
everydayness, the characters find themselves constantly in search of
forms of non-everydayness that enable them to overcome sameness
and escape monotony. Dreiser's account of Hurstwood's family life
prior to the climactic money scam is a case in point. Throughout the
novel, Mrs. Hurstwood—a woman of bourgeois upbringing and high
social aspirations—is passionately looking for change and actively
seeking distinction. Her only preoccupation in the novel is the pursuit
of entertainment—taking vacations, making travel plans, going out,

and attending horse races.[12] All these activities seem to be driven by an effort to evade the mediocrity of everyday life:

> "Jessica must have a new dress this month," said Mrs. Hurstwood one morning.
>
> Hurstwood was arraying himself in one of his perfection vests before the glass at the time.
>
> "I thought she just bought one," he said.
>
> "That was just something for evening wear," returned his wife complacently.
>
> "It seems to me," returned Hurstwood, "that she's spending a good deal for dresses of late."
>
> "Well she's going out more," concluded his wife. (ix 84)

Acquiring a new apparel is not motivated by real needs but instead by the desire to experience something new.

Behind the characters' inclination towards producing change, however, is an unsuspected sameness. While in appearance acquiring a new dress provides Jessica with the opportunity for change, in reality it leads her to conform to a certain style and identify with a particular class. Far from breaking with the monotony of the everyday, Jessica is only trading one form of sameness for another. Her attempt to dissimulate and transform the everyday amounts to little more than an imaginary transgression. Likewise, Mrs. Hurstwood's interest in horse races—supposedly a non-everyday activity—is not so much an escape from sameness as it is a perpetuation of that sameness:

> Mrs. Hurstwood had never asked for a whole season ticket before, but this year certain considerations decided her to get a box. For one thing, one of her neighbours, a certain Mr. and Mrs. Ramsey, who were possessors of money, made out of the coal business, had done so. In the next place, her favorite physician, Dr. Beale, a gentleman inclined to horses and betting, had talked with her concerning his intention to enter a two-year-old in the Derby.... Her own desire to be about in such things and parade among her acquaintances and the common throng was as much an incentive as anything. (xv 130–31)

Eager to distinguish herself and to join high society, Mrs. Hurstwood pursues the same kind of signs Carrie enjoys in the city—signs of wealth, consumption, prestige, and success. The sense of change that is gained, however, is more apparent than real; the more change is sought, the more sameness imposes itself:

> Jessica had called her [mother's] attention to the fact that the races were not
> what they were supposed to be. The social opportunities were not what they
> thought they would be this year. The beautiful girl found going everyday a
> dull thing. There was an earlier exodus this year of people who were
> anybody to the watering places and Europe. In her own circle of
> acquaintances several young men in whom she was interested had gone to
> Waukesha. She begun to feel that she would like to go too, and her mother
> agreed with her. (xx 179)

While seeking change, the characters reproduce the condition of that
which they wish to evade. Differentiation does not seem to provide an
escape from everyday life, but an intensification of its monotony.

Seen from a larger perspective, the leisure activities that constantly
attract Mrs. Hurstwood and her daughter are the manifestation of a
more general passivity, the key to which is commodity fetishism.
Fetishism is a process of substitution in which value is transformed
from a charged sign to a disaffected sign. Ensuing from this transfer
of value is an objectification of social bonds. In other words, the
social character of men's labor appears to them as an objective
character stamped upon the product of that labor: "The mysterious
character of the commodity-form consists therefore simply in the fact
that the commodity reflects the social characteristics of men's own
labor as objective characteristics of the products of labor themselves,
as the socio-natural properties of these things" (Marx, *Capital*
164–65). The value of objects does not lie in their intrinsic quality
(use value) but instead emanates from their function as signs capable
of representing something else (exchange value). Ensuing from this
dissonance between form and content is an organized passivity that
can be seen at work in the different spheres of vital activities: "in
leisure activities, [organized passivity means] the passivity of the
spectator faced with images and landscapes; in the work place, it
means passivity when faced with decisions in which the worker takes
no part; in private life, it means the imposition of consumption, since
the available choices are directed and the needs of the consumer
created by advertising market studies" (Lefebvre, "Everyday" 10).[13]
With this observation we are once again confronted with a *modus
vivendi* that is impelled by the incessant need to invest and
(re)produce at any price. Thus, for instance, Mrs. Hurstwood's
emulation of her daughter depicts the same commitment to repetition,
the same principle of production for the sake of production at the
heart of capitalism: "Jessica wanted fine clothes, and Mrs. Hurstwood,

not to be outdone by her daughter, also frequently enlivened her apparel" (ix 84). A similar unrestrained desire can be seen at work in Mrs. Hurstwood's relation with her husband. When Hurstwood went on a trip to Philadelphia without taking her, as he usually did, she naturally "drove out more, dressed better, and attended theaters freely to make up for that" (ix 85). In this instance, as in the example of the horse races, the nature and meaning of leisure activities are profoundly altered. Leisure hardly provides a break from the everyday; it has lost the festive quality and expressive dimension that have always made it the logical consequence and natural reward for work. Leisure has become a productive socio-economic mechanism that enhances the compulsion to repeat at the heart of the system.

The implication of such a compulsion to repeat becomes even more evident in Carrie's attraction to fashion:

> In this dressing, Carrie showed the influence of her association with the dashing Mrs. Vance. She had constantly had her attention called by the latter to novelties in everything which pertains to a woman's apparel.
>
> "Are you going to get such and such a hat?" or, "Have you seen the new gloves with the oval pearl buttons?" were but sample phrases out of a large selection.
>
> "The next time you get a pair of shoes, dearie," said Mrs. Vance, "get button, with thick soles and patent-leather tips. They're all the rage this fall." (xxxii 289–90)

Underlying the desire to be fashionable is an attempt to dissimulate the everyday by infusing it with the unusual and the exceptional. Because it promises uniqueness and difference, fashion becomes a way of evading the monotony, sameness, and drudgery of everyday life. To be fashionable is to be able to recognize and avoid that which is common and conventional. Such a sensibility makes Mrs. Vance's role in the novel all the more significant. She not only gives the impression that she is invulnerable to the drudgery of everyday life; she also symbolizes the pressure of being fashionable. Thus, she instructs Carrie in great detail on what to wear, how to look, and where to go—in short how to cope with the weight of the everyday. The attention to details and minutiae promises uniqueness and difference: "Oh, Dear, have you seen the new shirtwaists at Altman's? They have some of the loveliest patterns. I saw one there that I know would look stunning on you. I said so when I saw it" (xxxii 290). The pursuit of fashion becomes a search for that which is missing from everyday life.

However, the claim that fashion provides an escape from the

hegemony of everydayness is only partially true. Carrie's attraction to fashion is, in more than one way, a form of pseudo-emancipation; it promises change, but this change is more apparent than real. Thus, while striving to break away from sameness, the characters find themselves caught in a frenzy for change: "Every fine lady must be in the crowd on Broadway in the afternoon, in the theater at the matinée, in the coaches and dining halls at night" (xxxii 295–96). The search for the new is no longer a means to an end but the end itself, which is tantamount to saying that the passion for fashion has itself become a way of life. Lefebvre has well captured the cynical movement which makes fashion a concept that is perpetually provisional: "Fashion? How many women are really fashionable? A handful of models, cover-girls and demi-goddesses who quake in their shoes lest they should cease to be fashionable because fashion, which they make, eludes them no sooner launched, and they must keep up with it or rather ahead of it in a perpetual giddy-making overtaking" (*Everyday Life* 103).

Seen from this perspective, fashion—or the transitoriness of fashion—becomes an essential mechanism for maintaining the system. What defines fashion is not so much its expressive quality but its productive value. The pressure for being fashionable can even be said to be structurally akin to the pressure for accumulating money; the former is motivated by change for the sake of change, the latter is driven by production for the sake of production. In both cases, what matters is not the end result but the process of repetition. The distinction between the old and the new, between the common and the exceptional, between the fashionable and the unfashionable becomes a strategy for ensuring continuous reproduction.[14] Rather than an index for change, fashion becomes a commentary on the lack of innovation. The search for the new, as Adorno suggests, does not challenge the repetitiveness so central to capitalism but further confirms it: "The cult of the new, and thus the idea of modernity, is a rebellion against the fact that there is no longer anything new. The never-changing quality of machine-produced goods, the lattice of socialization that enmeshes and assimilates equally objects and the view of them, converts everything encountered into what always was, a fortuitous specimen of a species, the *doppel-gänger* of a model" (*Minima Moralia* 235).[15] As a vehicle of desire, then, fashion carries within itself its own justification; it satisfies the very desire it creates, and in doing so enhances everydayness while giving the illusion of creating non-everydayness. What appears to be new is in reality old and, in many ways, predetermined. Fashion, writes Baudrillard, "embodies a compromise between the need to innovate and the other need to change nothing in the fundamental order" (*For a Critique* 51, n. 30). Innovation becomes a means for sustaining the exigency of production for the sake of production. In a society of commodification, fashion becomes a curious cultural paranoia that produces sameness in the name of difference; it gives the illusion of change while extending the tautology at the heart of the system. In a slightly different register, Lefebvre has adequately captured this apparent paradox: "Underneath its pretended and pretentious newness, *modernity* conceals the tedium of the repetitive, its self-satisfied cud-chewing and regurgitation, the redundancy which would have us believe in the intelligibility of this world. The redundant brilliance and the appearance of newness in everyday cultural repetition conceal total reproduction. Conversely, the reproduction of the old in the modern conceals the current society which is renewing and reproducing itself" (*Survival* 34). The illusory nature of this change makes fashion the apogee of unproductive expenditure. The ephemerality of fashion means not only that the new reiterates the old but also that commodities are produced to be destroyed.

It is precisely this futility that Thorstein Veblen—a contemporary of Dreiser—seized upon in his analysis of conspicuous waste:

> Even in its freest flights, fashion rarely if ever gets away from a simulation of some ostensible use. The ostensible usefulness of the fashionable details of dress, however, is always so transparent a make believe, and their substantial futility presently forces itself so badly upon our attention as to become unbearable, and then we take refuge in a new style. But the new style must conform to the requirement of reputable wastefulness and futility. Its futility presently becomes as odious as that of its predecessors; and the only remedy which the law of waste allows us is to seek relief in some new construction, equally futile and equally untenable. Hence the essential ugliness and unceasing change of fashionable attire. (177)

In an age of mechanical reproduction, destruction is no longer harbinger of a natural process of death and rebirth but the engine for a programmed process of repetition that reinforces the dominant mode of production. Capitalism thrives on a process whereby not only money begets money, commodities generate commodities, fashion creates fashion, but dissatisfaction itself becomes a commodity—Carrie, writes Dreiser, was "competing with herself" (xi 95).

Such a characterization induces us to take even more seriously the structural affinity between Carrie's restless desire and the numerous images of motion that pervade the novel.[16] It is obvious that as the novel unfolds, the attempt to escape the everyday entangles Dreiser's desiring character in a continuous and often uncontrollable motion. Carrie, it should be remembered, came to Chicago because she was "dissatisfied at home" (ii 13). Later in New York, "Carrie's dissatisfaction with her state" (xxxi 284) has not diminished; on the contrary, it has augmented. The reader is constantly reminded that "she had never achieved what she had expected.... She became restless and dissatisfied, not exactly, as she thought, with Hurstwood, but with life" (xxxii 287–xxxiii 304). These images of motion and restlessness culminate in the motif of the rocking chair—the image *par excellence* of a nomadic strain in the novel. The rocking chair, as many critics have pointed out, is associated with discontent, dreaming, drifting, and insatiability.[17] More specifically, rocking emblematizes the very strategy of desire in a society that encourages consumption but promises no satisfaction. The rocking chair is all the more significant because it extends the rhythmic movement that defines the novel; a chair that is continuously rocking but goes nowhere enacts the very tautology of capitalism. This link is even more explicit with Dreiser's depiction of the longing Carrie at the end of the novel:

> Chicago, New York; Drouet, Hurstwood; the world of fashion and the world of stage—these were but incidents. Not them, but that which they represent, she longed for. Time proves the representation false.... Thus passed all that was of interest concerning these twain in their relation to her. Their influence upon her life is explicable alone by the nature of her longings. Time was when both represented for her all that was most potent in earthly success. They were personal representatives of a state most blessed to attain—the titled ambassadors of comfort and peace, a glow which they represented no longer allured her, its ambassadors should be discredited. Even had Hurstwood returned in his original beauty and glory, he could not now have allured her. She has learned that in this world, as in her own present state, was not happiness. (xlvii 459–60)

The passage not only puts into perspective the problem of representation so central to the novel, but also reiterates the rhythmanalytical dimension that characterizes Carrie's desire. Carrie's insatiability, in fact, extends the repetitiveness of everyday life: "In your rocking-chair, by your window dreaming, shall you long, alone. In your rocking-chair, by your window, shall you dream such happiness as you may never feel" (xlvii 460).

The image of a rocking chair that moves but goes nowhere is associated not only with Carrie but also with Hurstwood:

> The rocking-chair in the dining room was comfortable. He sank into it gladly, with several papers he had bought, and began to read.... He buried himself in his papers and read. Oh, the rest of it—the relief from walking and thinking! What Lethean waters were these floods of telegraphed intelligence! He forgot his troubles, in part. Here was a young handsome woman, if you might believe the newspaper drawing, suing a rich, fat, candy-making husband in Brooklyn for divorce. Here was another item detailing the wrecking of a vessel in ice and snow of Prince's Bay on Staten Island. A long, bright column told of the doings in the theatrical world—the plays produced, the actors appearing, the managers making announcements. Fannie Davenport was just opening at the Fifth Avenue. Daly was producing "King Lear." He read of the early departure for the season of a party composed of the Vanderbilts and their friends for Florida. An interesting shooting affray was on the mountains of Kentucky. So he read, read, read, rocking in the warm room near the radiator and waiting for dinner to be served.... The next morning he looked over the papers and waded through a long list of advertisements, making a few notes. (xxxiv 316–17)

What is interesting about this passage is the motion it sets in place between the everyday and the non-everyday. It opens and closes with the same monotonous movement that reenacts the drudgery of Hurstwood's daily life but in between are flashes of unusual events. Reading the newspaper, Hurstwood comes across news which stand out from the humdrum reality of everyday life. A close consideration, however, will suggest that the common and the exceptional are more related than they seem to be. Behind the image of a passive reader seeking mindless entertainment from the gossip column one may detect a calculated effect. The vicarious experience of events in the newspaper seems to compensate for the lack of genuine difference imposed by the abominable sameness of the quotidian; it provides a surrogate for a non-everydayness that is missing from everyday life. The everyday, writes Blanchot, "is that which refuses to be different.... The everyday is without events; in the newspaper, this absence of eventfulness is compensated by dramatic stories" (*Entretien* 362–63). Like fads and fashions, the type of (pseudo-) drama the reader comes across in the newspaper creates a space where the everyday is challenged only to be reconfirmed.

The sameness that marks everyday life and the drama that fills the space of the newspaper, then, are propelled by the same logic. The vacuity of the quotidian is, in fact, on a par with the emptiness of the sensational: "They'll get notice in the papers again—they always do" (xv 131–32). If in everyday life nothing much happens, in the newspapers what happens amounts to little or nothing. This conclusion becomes even more imposing when noting the occasional references to the *fait divers* in which Hurstwood finds much amusement:18 "In the meantime Hurstwood encountered a humorous item concerning a stranger who had arrived in the city and became entangled with a bunco-steerer. It amused him immensely, and at last he stirred and chuckled to himself. He wished that he might enlist his wife's attention and read it to her" (xxii 197). The unusual incidents and dramatic stories that find their way to the newspaper carry all the more weight when considered against the background of entrapment and drudgery which Hurstwood's sentiments towards his wife suggest: "He began to feel that she was a disagreeable attachment" (x 85).

The non-everyday, then, dissimulates rather than defies the everyday, and in so doing makes it both more tolerable and more entrenched. The difference between what the novel presents as common and what it offers as exceptional seems to be nothing more than a difference between an overt everydayness and a covert one. The spectacular, the dramatic, the tragic, and the extraordinary do not seem to suspend the mediocrity of the quotidian or eliminate the drudgery of the everyday but, instead, deny it. In other words, the spectacular makes it possible to pretend that the everyday is neither insistent nor irreversible. It is true that the everyday is often traversed by the non-everyday, but such a movement hardly challenges or alters the profound structure of the quotidian. Change, as Lefebvre suggests, becomes an unsuspected vehicle for reproducing the pleonastic structure of everyday life: "In modern life, the repetitive imposes its monotony. It is the invariable constant of the variations it envelops. The days follow one after another and resemble one another, and yet—here lies the contradiction at the heart of everydayness—everything changes. But change is programmed: obsolescence is planned. Production anticipates reproduction; production produces change in such a way as to superimpose the impression of speed onto that of monotony" ("Everyday" 10). Change and innovation occur, but they do so only as a vehicle for repetition and sameness.

While the foregoing analysis provides some insights into the formal logic of capitalism—i.e., the ways capitalism extends its rhythm to almost all spheres of vital activities—it nonetheless poses a number of problems. To content oneself with observing that the new is a mere strategy of the old, that difference is another form of repetition, and that non-everydayness is a mere corollary of everydayness, is to fall once again into the problem of determinism. For an analysis of the over-organized character of sociality under capitalism to be both polemically and methodologically viable, it has to confront an important but hitherto unaddressed question: if everything were so carefully calculated, so tightly programmed, and so meticulously measured, does this mean that life stagnates endlessly, irrevocably, and unassailably within everydayness?

A modest attempt to tarry with this question can be found in Stanley Cohen and Laurie Taylor's *Escape Attempts: A Theory and Practice of Resistance to Everyday Life.* What is of particular interest for the authors are the different strategies that individuals resort to in order to shake off the sense of routine, regularity, predictability, and repetition imposed by everyday life:

> The route we take to work, the clothes we wear, the food we eat are visible reminders of an awful sense of monotony. For some people, such feelings may be so intense that they are led to search for alternative realities; they set out to change their whole world. But for most of us ... [w]hat we object to is the sense that we are sinking into a patterned way of existence in all these areas; that they no longer appear to us as fresh and novel. They are becoming routinized. They no longer help us constitute our identity. (25–26)

For Cohen and Taylor, individuals are constantly looking for ways of escape which can ease the weight of everyday life and make it more tolerable. But these escape attempts are often doomed because individuals cannot disengage themselves from the grip of their social destiny:

> Destiny is social destiny; there is no reality other than that to be found within the density of social life.... The search for identity which we have described is an impulse to deny time, to ignore the sweep of history. It must be limited as an ideology because the facticity of the external· world cannot be denied. We are not just born into some free floating balloon of identity—but into a specific time and place. To base a resistance plan against everyday life on the invulnerability of the individual self must fail because of the ways that self is located in time and history and rooted to specific sets of social relationships. (Cohen 222–24)

This line of analysis recalls Walter Benn Michaels' argument about the hegemony of the market. From the perspective of *The Gold Standard and the Logic of Naturalism*, the individual cannot think outside the perspective offered by society, which in the case of naturalism is tightly connected with the logic of capitalism. More specifically, Michaels conceives of the market as a totality that encompasses everything, including the structures of belief. Be that as it may, the naturalist novelist cannot be said to resist or endorse the culture of commodification because such a position assumes an objective stance that is simply unthinkable.

While attesting to the sweeping force of history, however, Cohen and Taylor seem to be unwilling to make the totalizing move Michaels advocates in his analysis of late nineteenth-century American society. They are reluctant to give in to the resigned view that all forms of resistance are ultimately thwarted. To give their argument a more optimistic spin, Cohen and Taylor—who incidentally are sociologists by training—turn to literature. Following Tony Tanner's analysis of certain trends in contemporary American literature, they point out an imposing sense of confrontation and restlessness at the core of American fiction.[19]   For Tanner, as for Cohen and Taylor, the American hero becomes restless when trapped within a paramount reality. At the same time, however, his or her desire to escape is often restrained by a dread of formlessness that may accompany this new and uncertain reality: "the desire to step out of this into some kind of free space is checked by a dread of what might happen in such a formless world, a world without the safety of social conventions" (Cohen 223).   The thrill of stepping out of the system, even momentarily, is almost inseparable from the fear of formlessness. Hawthorne's short story, "Wakefield," ingeniously captures this dilemma. The story revolves around a bizarre character, Wakefield, who leaves his house and wife in order to take up a secret residence in the next street. After an absence of two decades, Wakefield returns to his house in the same incomprehensible manner he deserted it. The story is of course not without a moral: "Amid the seeming confusion of our mysterious world, individuals are so nicely adjusted to a system, and systems to one another and to a whole, that, by stepping aside for a moment, a man exposes himself to a fearful risk of losing his place forever. Like Wakefield, he may become, as it were, the Outcast of the Universe" (Hawthorne 80).   This conclusion suggests that the possibility of freedom—of getting out of the system—is constantly undermined by the fear of stepping into a void. To guard against such an unsettling void, the characters find themselves compelled to come to terms with their existing reality. But this apparently regressive move does not necessarily make them acquiescent, nor does it put an end to their struggle: "They sometimes find openings, hidden apertures in the social fabric; more often they resort to inner space; to fantasy. But they do believe ... that somewhere between inertia and commitment lies a space of personal freedom" (Cohen 224). Regardless of its outcome, this sense of restlessness that the characters experience is significant in and of itself; it may not be an escape in the full import of the term, but it is an escape nonetheless: "An ending which confirms these fictional possibilities is one we find more consoling than our nihilistic one—even though it might rest on a mistaken sense of identity. We would prefer to see the self as a construct which only becomes alive by being wary, elusive, mobile, keeping some distance from social reality. 'I escape therefore I am,' is ultimately the only ontological message we can manage" (Cohen 224). Cohen and Taylor find these escape attempts valuable in a specific way; while they may not effectively transcend the rhythm imposed by one's reality, they nonetheless disrupt it.

I would like to suggest that there is something similar at work in Dreiser's novel, although here the ensuing sense of restlessness is more threatening and more consequential. In *Sister Carrie* one can identify tensions that are generated by the system itself. The novel, in fact, revolves around a system that is intimately connected with the logic of capitalism but this system is not a seamless one; it is permeated with fissures and moments of disfunctionality. Nowhere is the disruptive element more insistent than in the episode of the railway strike. Scanning the paper during his long unproductive days, Hurstwood comes across a job announcement with the railway company. Exasperated at the humiliating remarks he occasionally receives from Carrie, he decides to get a job on the trolley line. In order to interfere with the coalition of its workers, control wages, and break an approaching strike on the trolley line in Brooklyn, the employers decided to hire scabs. Judging from the "bygone period of success" (xli 377) he experienced in Chicago, Hurstwood saw the futility of the strike and the powerlessness of the workers in the face of corporate power: "Hurstwood read this, formulating to himself his own idea of what would be the outcome. He was a great believer in the strength of corporations. 'They can't win,' he said, concerning the men. 'They haven't any money. The police will protect companies. They got to. The public has to have its cars'" (xl 371). Hurstwood's decision to risk his life and get a job on the trolley is a commentary on the "unassailable power of the companies" (xl 372) in particular and capitalism in general. A more careful consideration of Dreiser's depiction of unspoken tensions during the strike, however, will suggest otherwise. The kind of unrest that the novel foregrounds is, in fact, more real than Hurstwood's commentary about the power of corporations may suggest. The strike is potentially harmful to the system:

> He [i.e., Hurstwood] made his way into the heart of the small group, eyed by policemen and the men already there. One of the officers addressed him.
>
> "What are you looking for?"
>
> "I want to see if I can get a place."
>
> "The offices are up those steps," said the bluecoat. His face was a very neutral thing to contemplate. In his heart of hearts, he sympathized with the strikers and hated this "scab." In his heart of hearts, also, he felt the dignity and use of the police force, which commanded order. Of its true social significance, he never once dreamed. His was not the mind for that. The two feelings blended in him—neutralized one another and him. He would have fought for this man as determinedly as for himself, and yet only so far as commanded. Strip him of his uniform, and he would have soon picked his side. (xl 374)

This passage is fraught with an ambivalence that reveals an order more unsettled than the foregoing analysis would lead one to believe. The officers who are supposed to protect the company have as much grudge against the system as those who fight it.

This episode bespeaks a tension that is even more insistent in the case of Sister Carrie. It seems as if the more Carrie tries to disengage herself from her reality, the more this reality imposes itself: "On the street sometimes she would see men working—Irishmen with picks, coal-heavers with great loads to shovel, Americans busy about some work which was mere matter of strength—and they touched her fancy" (xv 135). Although Carrie has apparently escaped the misery of city life, she is often reminded of its bitterness: "Toil, now that she was free of it, seemed even more a desolate thing that when she was part of it. She saw it through a mist of fancy—a pale somber half-light, which was the essence of poetic feeling.... She felt, though she seldom expressed them, sad thoughts upon this score. Her sympathies were ever with that under-world of toil from which she has so recently sprung, and which she best understood" (xv 135). These sporadic moments of hybridity point to a threat that is always looming in the novel. The system that the novel presents threatens to produce counter-effects. What we get in *Sister Carrie* is not only an account of the insatiability of a covetous character, the lure of the commodity, and the unassailable power of corporations, but also a grim portrait of exploitation, unemployment, poverty, and deprivations—all of which are reminders of the necessary contradictions of capitalism.   Bruce Brown has aptly captured the inherently unstable nature of capitalism: "satisfaction and dissatisfaction go hand in hand, contradiction—while not always on the surface—is implicit everywhere and may become explicit at almost any time with the articulation of immanent desires which, while capital tries to absorb and rob them of their explosive force, nonetheless remain powerful" (168).   This observation becomes even more significant in view of the underworld that the novel portrays.   With the downfall of Hurstwood, after Carrie deserts him, the reader is introduced to an aspect of the city which, although not missing, was not particularly threatening.   Impoverished, desolate, and degenerated, Hurstwood resorts to the street; he ends up among the homeless, the beggars, and the vagabonds:

> A study of these men in broad light proved them to be all of a type. They belonged to the class that sit on the park benches during the endurable days and sleep upon them during the summer nights. They frequent the Bowery and those down-at-the heels East Side streets where poor clothes and shrunken features are not singled out as curious. They are the men who are in the lodging-house sitting-rooms during bleak and bitter weather and who swarm about the cheaper shelters which only open at six in a number of the lower East Side streets. Miserable food, ill-timed and greedily eaten, had played havoc with bone and muscle. They were all pale, flabby, sunken-eyed, hollow-chested, with eyes that glinted and shone and lips that were a sickly red that glinted and shone and lips that were a sickly red by contrast.... They were of the class which simply floats and drifts, every wave of people washing up one, as breakers do driftwood upon a stormy shore. (xlvii 446)

Scenes like this draw our attention to an unsettling reality—in fact, a certain hybridity or tension—in the novel.   The world of the less privileged that Hurstwood slips into at the end of the novel is a powerful reminder of the underside of the opulent and promising world Carrie strives to achieve.[20]

CHAPTER FIVE

Reading the Symptom:
History without Teleology

What I propose in the following is an attempt to link, in a more systematic and more explicit way, the various theoretical discussions that appeared in the readings I have provided. Such an endeavor, I hope, will not only reiterate some of the key points around which my argument revolves, but also situate my findings within a perspective that is amenable to our understanding of drifts or tendencies in cultural systems in general. It is clear that this project is not primarily concerned with the aesthetic properties of naturalism, nor is it an attempt to define what naturalism is, nor is it a search for what Foucault metaphorically, but disparagingly, calls "the 'face' of the period" (*Archaeology* 9). Rather, it is an examination of the dynamic structure and contentious nature of the historical moment in question. Investigating the logico-historical conjuncture that underlies the period under consideration has led me to the conclusion that naturalism constitutes a system, but one that is more complex and less hegemonic than Walter Benn Michaels' *The Gold Standard and the Logic of Naturalism* leads one to believe. Naturalism, I argue, has a transgressive element at its core, the appreciation of which calls for a special attention to an aspect that has not been sufficiently considered, namely the interplay between continuity and discontinuity or, more pointedly, between the dominant and the emergent.

The interplay I wish to bring to focus is, of course, historically specific. To the extent that this study is concerned with naturalism, it is also necessarily concerned with capitalism. What is of particular interest here is not so much what naturalism tells us about capitalism, but rather what the novels tell us about naturalism as the symbolic articulation of the logic of capitalism. Throughout this project, capitalism does not figure as an analytical grid or an interpretative model but, instead, as a structuring principle from which historical determination has been insistently derived since the nineteenth century.[1] Indeed, the logic of capitalism provides the complex structuring whole or the socio-symbolic field within which naturalism operates and from which it cannot be disengaged. What this means, in part, is that capitalism cannot be reduced to a purely economic category, for to talk about capitalism is to talk about a totality that can be seen at work in the different spheres of social activities. But this is not all. To content oneself with this systemic analysis is to fail to recognize the unevenness of social formations. This is precisely the blind spot in Walter Benn Michaels' account of the period. For Michaels, naturalism—the structure of which is predicated on the logic of the market—is a total and unfailing system. The tensions and contradictions he finds operative in naturalism are nothing more than internal strategies that are called for by the structure of capitalism itself. As I have noted earlier, however, the theoretical evacuation of any consequential negativity makes Michaels' model deterministic and ultimately untenable.

Pointing out these shortcomings does not necessarily entail a repudiation of the concept of totality; rather it points to the need for an adequate theorization of this concept. Michaels' proposition to conceive of naturalism as a body of literature that exemplifies the logic of capitalism can be retained provided one conceives of capitalism as an open and creative system rather than a seamless and evenly-constituted one. I borrow the concept of the open system from Kostas Axelos who argues for the methodological requirement to account for the role of the a-systematic in the systematic: "Negativity is omnipresent. Nothing ever escapes its hold.... Given that every action is likely to turn against itself, negativity does not just operate in every power that asserts itself and in the process tends towards its 'destruction'; it constitutes and determines the movement of every *theory* and every *practice*" (29–37). Underlying the theory of the open system is the proposition that we must account for an irreducible rift between the constitutive structure of a given social organism and the circumstances, contingencies, or developments that complicate this structure and even call it into question. From this vantage point, a true revisionism has to provide an account of the totality within which naturalism operates, but at the same time it has to endow the negative with a more prominent and more consequential role. A non-totalizing conception of naturalism, and by extension of capitalism, needs to grasp not only the deep structure of the system, but also its unstable dynamics; not only the rivets of the system, but also its rifts. It has to pay a special attention to emergent impulses—that is, those elements that are operative within the system but not perfectly consonant with its logic.

Before further elaborating on this proposition, it might be useful to point out a few instances from the novels I have discussed in which the interplay between the systematic and the asystematic is particularly insistent. In *Sister Carrie*, for example, we find a rhythm that is hard to ignore, one which reproduces the compulsion to repeat at the heart of capitalism. This rhythm can be observed in the different aspects of everyday life. It is the same rhythm that causes need to retreat in front of programmed consumption; the same rhythm that makes the rocking chair a central motif in the novel; and the same rhythm that makes Carrie's desire for what she has pale in front of her desire for what she can have. But this rhythm is far from being endlessly and unfailingly repetitive. A careful consideration of apparently minor episodes in the novel will uncover a tendency towards negativity and intensification that interferes with the regularity of such a rhythmic effect. The contingent developments associated with Hurstwood's fall provide an instructive example. Following the incident that led Hurstwood to steal money from Fitzgerald and Moy is a climactic development that entangles the novel in a series of swift and precipitative movements:

He must get out of the city and that quickly.

"I wonder how the trains run?" he thought.

Instantly he pulled out his watch and looked. It was nearly half-past one.

At the first drug store he stopped, seeing a long-distance telephone booth inside....

"Give me 1643," he called to Central, after looking up the Michigan Central depot number. Soon he got the ticket agent.

"How do the trains leave here for Detroit?" he asked.

The man explained the hours.

"No more to-night?"

"Nothing with a sleeper. Yes there is, too," he added. "There is a mail train out of here at three o'clock."

"Alright," said Hurstwood. "What time does that get to Detroit?"

He was thinking if he could get there and cross the river to Canada, he

> could take his time about getting to Montreal. He was relieved to learn
> that it would reach there by noon.
>
> "Mayhew won't open the safe till nine," he thought. They can't get on
> my track before noon."
>
> Then he thought of Carrie. With what speed must he get her, if he got
> her at all. She would have to come along. He jumped into the nearest cab
> standing by.
>
> "To Ogden Place," he said sharply. "I'll give you a dollar more if you
> make good time...."
>
> Reaching the number, he hurried up the steps and did not spare the bell
> in waking the servant.
>
> "Is Mrs. Drouet in?" he asked.
>
> "Yes," said the astonished girl.
>
> "Tell her to dress and come to the door at once. Her husband is in the
> hospital, injured, and wants to see her." (xxvii 244–45)

Underlying this passage is not only a certain suspense, but also a
threat of being lost. The image of the fugitive Hurstwood is
reinforced by a number of concomitant flights—news, stories, rumors,
noise, blabbing, letters, telegraphs, and telephone messages. This flux
of information does not merely reproduce the rhythm that defines the
novel but also accelerates it in a way that borders on disruption and
disorder. Every new development brings with it the risk of
dysfunctionality; that is why, often enough, for Hurstwood "no news
was good news" (xxiv 214).

Even prior to the unfortunate events that led him to steal money
from Fitzgerald and Moy, Hurstwood is constantly afraid of a sudden
turn of events and fearful of scandals: "He could not complicate his
home life, because it might affect his relations with his employers.
They wanted no scandals. A man to hold this position, must have a
dignified manner, a clean record, a respectable home anchorage" (viii
83). Hurstwood's comfortable life is continuously threatened by
undesirable developments and unforeseeable events:

> He also thought of his managerial position. "If she raises a row now I'll
> lose this thing. They won't have me around if my name gets in the papers.
> My friends, too!" He grew more angry as he thought of the talk any action
> on her part would create. How would the papers talk about it? Every man he
> knew would be wondering. He would have to explain and deny and make a
> general remark of himself.... All at once the Chicago papers would arrive.
> The local papers would have accounts in them this very day.... Back at the
> hotel Hurstwood was anxious and yet fearful to see the morning papers. He

wanted to know how far the news of his criminal deed had spread. So he
went to secure and scan dailies.... Very little was given to his crime, but it
was there, several 'sticks' in all, among all the riffraff news. He wished,
half sadly, that he could undo it all.... He left the papers before going to the
room, thinking thus to keep them out of the hands of Carrie. (xxiv
213–xxix 262)

The uncontrollable spread of the news is reinforced by the danger of
being apprehended. Hurstwood is haunted by the risk of the publicity
of his robbery. His fear of the spread of news is a fear of the aleatory,
the uncertain, and the unexpected. The threat of disorder inherent in
this episode is particularly significant because it interferes with the
rhythmic effect that infuses the novel; it points to a system which
produces its demise as it reproduces itself. The tension he experiences
upon the realization that he is being followed by a private detective
further highlights this element of contingency: "What would happen
now? What could these people do? He began to trouble concerning
the extradition laws. He did not understand them absolutely. Perhaps
he could be arrested. Oh, if Carrie should find out! Montreal was too
warm for him. He began to be out of it" (xxix 260–61). As the
novel progresses, the possibility of losing control intensifies and the
fear of a sudden turn of events increases. Hurstwood's confrontation
with the detective further conveys this threat of losing control: "I
know just what you can do and what you can't. You can create a lot
of trouble if you want. I know that all right" (xxix 263).

These moments of intensity and impending negativity are even
more insistent in the case of *McTeague*. The episode of the desert, in
particular, points to an aspect that is not quite on a par with the sense
of pleonasm that pervades the novel and for which Trina's hoarding
drive—her saving for the sake of saving—is the best elucidation. At
first reading, one may note a formal linkage between the economic
logic that infuses the novel and the metaphor of space. The desert,
with its open vistas, its unlimited stretches of sand, its measureless
leagues, and its endless extensions can be said to reenact Trina's
insatiable desire for gold—in fact, it epitomizes the very tautology of
capitalism in its endless drive towards surplus-value. At the same time,
however, the episode of the desert points to curious irregularities in
the novel. The intensification of McTeague's experience introduces
certain deviations. Cutting through Death Valley entangles the novel
in a sudden and unpredictable precipitation of events: "There was no
rest, no going back, no pause, no stop. Hurry, hurry, hurry on" (xxi
427). The irregularities that mark McTeague's flight in the desert are

only the most pointed manifestation of an informing madness which can be said to constitute the novel's latent theme.   McTeague's volatile experience in Death Valley points to the proliferation of intensities or (to use Deleuzian terminology) of lines of escape that can be seen at work in Trina's hysterical passion for gold, in Zerkow's fits of hallucination about the gold plate that Maria's parents used to own, and, most curiously, in the frantic behavior of the mule under the influence of the loco-weed: "Marcus moved toward the mule and made as if to reach the bridle-rein. The mule squealed, threw up his head, and galloped to a little distance, rolling his eyes and flattening his ears.... By and by the mule stopped, blowing out his nostrils excitedly.... Marcus went forward a step at a time. He was almost within arms' length of the bridle when the mule shied from him abruptly and galloped away" (xxii 436–38). Moments like this can complicate our understanding of the logic or system that the novel foregrounds.   The mule's erratic behavior, much like McTeague's asystematic flight and Trina's hysterical fervor, is symptomatic of a certain paradox at work in the novel; it enacts the very tendency of the system—i.e., capitalism—toward runaway.

Before further exploring the theoretical implications of these moments of intensity, particularly with respect to what I have called the open system, I would like to discuss a recent attempt in naturalist criticism—Paul Civello's *American Literary Naturalism and its Twentieth-Century Transformations*—to address some of the questions I have raised. Civello's purpose is clearly not to redefine naturalism, but to broaden its scope by following the history of its transformation from the turn of the nineteenth century to the present. He takes issue with the conception of naturalism as a well defined movement and a static form. Naturalism, as he puts it, is "a narrative mode closely aligned with historical processes, one that is developed and transformed as it moves through time" (2). Naturalism is not confined to the turn of the century, nor is it limited to the four canonical figures we usually hold as exponents of this movement (i.e., Crane, London, Norris, and Dreiser). Naturalism continues to exist because it has been continuously altered or reinvented. What this proposition means in part is that terms such as "'naturalism,' 'modernism,' and 'postmodernism'—terms usually used to denote separate narrative forms—prove too exclusive, that, in fact, there is a 'modern' naturalism and a 'postmodern' naturalism" (2).

In order to chart the transformation of naturalism, Civello focuses on three authors, Norris, Hemingway, and DeLillo, whose works exemplify the spirit of naturalism, modernism, and postmodernism, respectively. In each of these instances, the construction of the narrative is guided by a scientific or philosophical construction of reality that is specific to its age. For example, the rift between the self and the material world that ensued from the Darwinian challenge to the Enlightenment conception of a divine and ordered universe has been reconfigured during the course of the twentieth century in accordance with epistemological changes. In the case of Norris, the self is portrayed as powerless in front of the destructive and indifferent forces of nature. *Vandover and the Brute*, for example, tells the story of a character who is caught in an indifferent world and reduced to an incomprehensibly degenerated brute. In Norris' later novels this strict determinism is infused with a search for meaning. *The Octopus* is a case in point. Although the characters face grim realities and overpowering forces, they are nonetheless able to discern a cosmic or natural order that defines their relationship to the material world. With Hemingway, this abstract order is internalized. In Hemingway's fiction, consciousness provides an ordering principle. In the absence of an ostensible order, characters create their personal order and construct their own meaning. With modernism, then, we move from a perspective that is governed by biological determinism to one that revolves around the intricacies of the mind and the complexities of the inner self.

The literary transformation Civello highlights is, in many ways, a recapitulation of Charles Walcutt's assessment of contemporary forms of naturalism in the first major study of the period, *American Literary Naturalism*. For Walcutt, "the early zeal and confidence of naturalism lost their force, as the twentieth century passed, because science constantly found new limitations to man's freedom. Freudian psychology showed the mind to be largely controlled by drives buried in the subconscious. Statistics, economics, and sociology multiplied evidences of environmental forces that overshadow the will" (294). However, Civello does not just rehearse this view; he takes it to its limit. The discussion of DeLillo's *End Zone* and *Libra*, in particular, enables him to set naturalism against itself. DeLillo, Civello argues, presents a world the complexity of which eludes our understanding simply because the relationship between subject and object can no longer be contained within a cause-effect paradigm. In DeLillo's naturalism, linear causality gives way to a world that is intersected by interconnecting systems, a world that is incomprehensible and at times even irrational. This development not only undermines Hemingway's formulation of a self that can create an orderly world, but also undoes the very foundation of nineteenth century naturalism, namely the individual's relationship to a larger cosmic or spiritual order.

Such as it is, then, the movement from Norris (the cosmic) to DeLillo (the systemic) through Hemingway (the personal) is a movement from determinism to indeterminacy. Underlying this shift, Civello argues, is a momentous historical development in the sciences. The development of naturalism reproduces a parallel epistemological shift in scientific theories from Newtonian to relativity physics, a shift that adumbrates an increasing distrust of certainty and a dissolution of stable entities. Seen from this perspective, the progressive de-structuration of naturalism that Civello lays out seems to infuse the study of the period with a new breath. At least, such an approach saves him from both the polemical and methodological problems that plague *The Gold Standard and the Logic of Naturalism*. In Michaels' project, as I have noted earlier, the emphasis on the specificity of naturalism is achieved at the expense of freezing the naturalist movement within an all-encompassing or total system. Unlike Michaels, Civello offers a conception of naturalism that accounts for the logic of its organization as well as the dynamics of its transformation. The deconstructive strain in Civello's book is particularly notable in his proposition to conceive of the history of naturalism as a gradual movement from a "closed system" to an "open system," from the classical scientific paradigm (i.e., the second law of thermodynamics) to a more complex and less linear model.

Such a proposition reflects the critical possibilities that new interdisciplinary trends in scholarship have opened up for literary critics, especially with regard to systems theory and chaos theory; at the same time, however, Civello's project is not without limitations. Although Civello pays special attention to change and transformation, he does not go far enough in this direction. For one thing, he fails to critically probe the relationship between evolutionism and classical naturalism; that is, he neither reconsiders nor challenges the basic premise that naturalism is the literary articulation of evolutionary theories (a premise which, as recent critics of the period have suggested, is sustainable but by no means absolute).[2] More important for our purpose, Civello takes issue with the rigid demarcations between various literary movements but falls short of questioning the autonomy—or better yet the hegemony—of these movements. Civello attempts to show the continuity and development of naturalism from the waning decades of the nineteenth century down to the postmodern era but does not put into question the internal unity of each of the three naturalisms he identifies. The challenge, it seems to me, is not only to chart the reinvention of naturalism in other literary periods and movements (which Civello does), but also to examine the various ways in which indeterminate impulses operate within these movements. Compared with some recent critical trends in French readings of naturalism (which stress the presence of the aleatory, the stochastic, and the fortuitous within what has often been conceived as strict determinism), the discussion of classical American naturalism by American critics is still hemmed in within the contours of an all too well defined period and an all too limited account of the movement. The work of Michel Serres on the interplay between entropy and negentropy in Zola's novels,[3] and more recently Patrick Brady's analysis of the implications of chaos and indeterminacy in an apparently ordered and determined naturalist world,[4] point to new and promising critical avenues which, if vigorously pursued in the context of American naturalism, may tap the unsuspected complexity of a movement that has not yet divulged all its secrets.

These shortcomings notwithstanding, Civello's work is useful insofar as it draws our attention, once again, to the problem of periodization. Even a cursory consideration of some of the authoritative accounts of naturalism will suggest that this movement has been narrowly defined.[5] Lee Clark Mitchell is a revealing example. In a prominent revisionist anthology that claims to respond to the "significant developments in the theories of history and criticism that have affected the writing of literary history today" (Elliott xvi), Mitchell points out two important historical moments he deems crucial for understanding naturalism. This *fin-de-siècle* movement was, in many ways, a response to new developments whereby "[s]eemingly overnight, an agrarian nation became an industrial society" (Mitchell, "Naturalism" 527). Coterminous with these momentous socio-economic changes is a philosophical development—the rise of social Darwinism as the official philosophy of the period. The literature that Dreiser, Norris, London, and Crane produced depended on "specifically historical influences that for a brief period encouraged an unusual philosophical view" (Mitchell, "Naturalism" 545). What is particularly troubling about this conception of the period is not so much the fact that naturalism is presented as a fascination with "arid concepts of social determinism" (Mitchell, "Naturalism" 527), but that the historical perspective Mitchell offers strikes the reader as mechanistic and, in many ways, reductive. Naturalism here appears as a circumscribed historical event marked by its sudden appearance, its brief history, and its timely effacement: "The particular constellation of influences at work on writers now thought of as naturalists disappeared with World War I....

That the movement was short-lived simply testifies to the unique conditions it required" (Mitchell, "Naturalism" 545). The rigidity of such an account raises serious questions about both the hegemony of the period and the sanctity of the *ism* that defines the movement in question.

These considerations allow us to grasp a second aspect of the problem. Tightly connected with the issue of periodization is the question of historical change. The turn of the nineteenth century has often been considered as a threshold ushering in a decisive and thorough shift. The most familiar accounts of this period of "trauma" and "change," as Alan Trachtenberg calls it (5), accentuate a shift from a society of production to a society of consumption: "one of the fundamental conflicts of twentieth-century America is between two cultures—an older culture, often loosely labelled Puritan-republican, producer-capitalist culture, and a newly emerging culture of abundance" (Susman xxvi). Variations of this narrative emphasize a transformation from a Protestant to a secular culture, from asceticism to hedonism, from penury to affluence, and from entrepreneurial to organized corporate capitalism. Embedded in this bold endeavor to periodize is an overly simplistic conception of history which pays little attention to the unevenness of social formations.

These shortcomings did not go unnoticed. A few critics and historians have recently started to question the conception of history as a concatenation of periods separated by rigid demarcations and organized around punctual transformations. For Mark Seltzer, "the move to 'periodize' the fall into consumer culture takes the form of a standard, and remarkably portable, story of a fall from production to consumption (or from industry to luxury, or from use to exchange, etc.) that at times seems as crude as the claim that people grew things in the first half of the nineteenth century and ate them in the second half" (*Bodies* 60). Likewise, in a self-critique, T. J. Jackson Lears points out the need to rethink our conception of periodization: "I do not mean to abandon my own and other historians' stress on the late nineteenth century as a period of crucial transformation. But I now believe that an understanding of that transformation requires a subtler conceptual framework than simply the notion of a shift from a Protestant 'producer culture' to a secular 'consumer culture'" ("Veblen" 77; n. 8). Accordingly, Lears sets out to question the integrity, eventfulness, and swiftness of the changes in question. In his view, the trends that came to be dominant at the turn of the century are only the manifestation of changes that had been underway for decades. The expanding market society at the end of the nineteenth century did not create but only solidified inchoate impulses and intensified existing trends. To that extent, the history of hedonism predates the society of consumption:

> We are just beginning to glimpse the ways that this expanding world of goods was represented in popular culture, but preliminary evidence suggests that it may be a mistake to argue a shift from the plodding nineteenth century to the carnivalesque twentieth century: the carnival may have been in town all the time.... The reorganization of cultural meaning between 1880 and 1920 was too complex to be captured in any linear scheme of progress or decline. What is particularly suspect is the idea, derived partly from Veblen, that the emergence of new ways of assessing meaning to goods meant the rise of self-indulgent materialism and hedonism. We have always had materialization with us, in the sense that people have always used material goods to make cultural meaning; the history of hedonism has yet to be written. (Lears, "Veblen" 76–97)

Lears' attempt to complicate our understanding of the dynamics of historical change induces us not only to rethink the question periodization, but also to take all the more seriously Foucault's suspicion towards the common supposition that history "may be articulated into great units—stages or phases—which contain within themselves their own principle of cohesion" (*Archaeology* 10). Given that historical change cannot be made to culminate at a single point, the idea of a radical break and an absolute beginning is utterly reductive: "The idea of a single break suddenly, at a given moment, dividing all discursive formations, interrupting them in a single moment and reconstituting them in accordance with the same rules—such an idea cannot be sustained" (Foucault, *Archaeology* 175). For Foucault, ruptures, thresholds, and breaks are viable only when considered as relative points of reference: "We must not imagine that rupture is a sort of great drift that carries with it all discursive formations at once. Rupture is not an undifferentiated interval—even a momentary one—between two manifest phases; it is not a kind of lapsus without duration that separates two periods, and which deploys two heterogeneous stages on either side of a split" (*Archaeology* 175). Because historical developments are not even, demarcations between different periods are hardly ever rigid, transitions are not necessarily complete, and transformations are never vectored. Historical formations cannot be adequately grasped outside an expanded framework that accommodates the conjunctural overlapping of disparate tendencies—what Raymond Williams calls "Dominant, Residual, and Emergent" (121). Dominant practices are always in concert, if not in tension, with passive survivals and vestiges from the past, on the one hand, and inchoate (trans)formations and anticipatory developments, on the other hand. In history, there is only movement, and if there are structures, these are not closed—their continuity is relative, their stability momentary, and their equilibrium provisional. Simply put, history is a matter of tendencies.

The cursory differentiation between the dominant and the emergent points to yet another pseudo-distinction between the real and the virtual. To say that historical formations are not fixed is to say that the present always carries within its fold the condition of its future developments. This is the thrust of Marx's regressive-progressive method which highlights the originality of the capitalist mode of production and emphasizes its structural difference from anterior modes of production. Capitalism is not a mere extension of prior socio-economic formations, nor is it the sum of previous historical phases. A theory of history conceived in terms of lineage, serialization, and evolutionism is inadequate simply because history, as Walter Benjamin reminds us, is not "additive" (*Illuminations* 264). For Marx, monetary economy has always existed in pre-capitalist societies, albeit in an "embryonic form" (*Capital* 154). As soon as two individuals come together in order to exchange their goods, the value form is present in germ: "it makes its appearance at an early date, though not in the same predominance and therefore characteristic manner as nowadays" (Marx, *Capital* 176). It seems only natural, then, that an account of the money form has to start with an analysis of the simple commodity form: "we have to show the origin of this money form, we have to trace the development of the expression of value contained in the value-relation of commodities from its simplest, almost imperceptible outline to the dazzling money-form. When this has been done, the mystery of money will immediately disappear.... The whole mystery of the form of value lies hidden in this simple form" (Marx, *Capital* 139). For Marx, as Henri Lefebvre explains, the real and the virtual are not antithetical but complementary, not mutually exclusive but co-extensive:

> The axis of Marx's thought is not the accomplished but the virtual, not facts
> or origins but emergence.... For Marx, the *social* can be adequately
> conceived (a) neither in terms of *idealities*, laws, values, norms, forms,
> powers that transcend the social, relations without support, (b) nor in terms
> of *realities*, things, products, relations mistaken for things, natural

substances or economic forces of material nature, noticeable effects and well determined causes. In order to seize the social, one has to resort to a third term which mediates the relationship between the ideal and the real. This third term is the abstract-concrete, the fictive-real. *It is the prototype of the analysis of the commodity*. It has to be conceived neither as a material thing related to another thing, namely money, nor as a purely abstract entity endowed with an existence that is analogous to that of a sign or comparable to mathematical operations. Marx's thought posits no "substantialism," formalism, or ontology that is more or less "materialist," but no fetishism of abstraction either.... Marx's conception of the social is neither "ideal" nor "real"—it lies in the intersection between the two. (*Pensée* 219–55)

In order to expand the scope of historical analysis it becomes necessary to juxtapose the real and the virtual—to attend not only to the operative but also to the nascent, to posit not just a field of actuality but also a field of potentiality—a coming-to-be, so to speak.

This is partly why the symptom acquires a special theoretical relevance in Marx's thought (as well as in this project). The symptom, as Zizek explains, is "a particular element which subverts its own universal foundation, a species subverting its own genus" (*Sublime* 21). The symptom is a paradoxical element that functions simultaneously as an internal constituent and a subversive component; it is that which is necessary for the system to achieve its moment of completion but also necessarily that which prevents its closure.[6] In Marx's preoccupation with the symptom one can see a vigorous attempt not only to decipher the hidden kernel of the commodity but also to cut through the thick of history itself. The force and continuing relevance of Marx's project does not lie in his prognosis of a post-bourgeois society—induced by the dialectic of class antagonism and leading *willy nilly* to the imposition of socialism—but in having "combined the desirability of socialism (and the intolerability of capitalism) with a demonstration of the ways in which socialism was *already* coming into being *within* capitalism, in which capitalism by some features of its logic was already creating socialism, and in which socialism is not staged as an ideal or Utopia but a tendential and emergent set of already existing structures" (Jameson, *Postmodernism* 206).

It is from this vantage point that the concept of emergence acquires an added significance. In order to arrive at a more refined understanding of the period under consideration, one has to pay attention not only to the operation of hard facts, but also the

incremental unfolding of inchoate developments and dormant
impulses. To talk about emergence is to account for tensions, to
identify discordances, and to bring out differences. A theory of
emergence makes it possible to look at the ways in which quiescent
tendencies and nascent forms start to acquire a historical necessity that
intimates their flux and spurs their inevitability. More specifically, a
theory of emergence posits the germination of new formations that
are incompatible with the dominant structures: "emergence designates
a place of confrontation but not as a closed field offering the
spectacle of a struggle among equals. Rather, as Nietzsche
demonstrates in his analysis of good and evil, it is a 'non-place,' a
pure distance, which indicates that the adversaries do not belong to a
common space.... The isolation of different points of emergence
does not conform to the successive configurations of an identical
meaning; rather, they result from substitutions, displacements,
disguised conquests, and systematic reversals" (Foucault, *Language*
150–51). Foucault's emphasis on emergence as a "non-place"
vividly recalls Lefebvre's emphasis on the "virtual" as a space which,
although always implied, is present only as a symptom. Emergence
does not imply the mysterious or sudden transformation of the
dominant structures, but the progressive manifestation of new surfaces
of appearance. The emergent does not designate a pure fact or a
mysterious transformation, but a development that stands *in limine*.
As Foucault points out, the "object does not await in limbo the order
that will free it and enable it to become embodied in a visible and
prolix objectivity; it does not preexist itself, held back by some
obstacle at the first edges of light" (*Archaeology* 45).

One should not conclude, however, that emergence is a matter of
pure contingency or absolute indeterminacy. For a theory of
emergence to be methodologically viable, it has to recognize that the
emergent draws much of its significance from the dominant. It is
axiomatic, as Derrida points out, that "a radicalization is always
indebted to that which it radicalizes" (*Spectres* 152). Even more,
emergence is subject to a certain logic. If everything were a matter of
discontinuity, interruption, and diffraction, then nothing can be held
with certainty to be emergent or differential. Emergence is not a
debacle but a development that is constituted within structural (though
not absolute) limits. To ignore this fundamental premise is to fall
prey to what may be termed, after Lefebvre, a "spectral analysis"
(*Droit* 109) which accentuates difference and heterogeneity but falls
short of effectively synthesizing the ensuing discontinuities within the
precincts of a projected totality. Pursuing difference and

heterogeneity beyond any conceivable totality, as Steven Best has rightly pointed out, "mystifies the fact that in capitalist society, there are not just differences and antinomy, but also strong tendencies towards reified sameness, conformity, and generality" (362).

It is precisely the possibility of holding in tension the total and the fragmentary, without necessarily being inconsistent, that Fredric Jameson finds most appealing in Althusser's structural causality:

> Unlike canonical post-structuralism, however, whose emblematic gesture is that by which Barthes, in *S/Z*, shatters a Balzac novella into a random operation of multiple codes, the Althusserian/Marxist conception of culture requires this multiplicity to be reunified, if not at the level of the work itself, then at the level of its process of production, which is not random but can be described as a coherent functional operation in its own right. The current post-structuralist celebration of discontinuity and heterogeneity is therefore only an initial moment in Althusserian exegesis, which then requires the fragments, the incommensurable levels, the heterogeneous impulses, of the text to be once again related, but in the mode of structural difference and determinate contradiction. (*Political* 57)

Althusser's structural causality is of renewed interest because it offers a theoretical perspective that emphasizes the structure of the whole without ignoring the relative autonomy of the different instances. For Althusser, the social totality "is constituted by a certain type of complexity, the unity of a structured whole containing what can be called levels or instances which are distinct and 'relatively autonomous,' and co-exist within this complex structural unity, articulated with one another according to specific determinations, fixed in the last instance by the level or instance of the economy" (*Reading* 97). By proposing to see in the different instances the very condition of the existence of the structure, Althusser endows the regional instances with an autonomy and an efficacy of their own, while at the same time recognizing the structure of the whole. The different instances operate within a system of interrelated and interdependent practices determined in the last instance by the economic. It should not go unnoticed, however, that for Althusser "the lonely hour of the 'last instance' never comes" (*For Marx* 113), which is tantamount to saying that structural causality assumes what Althusser calls an "absent cause" for the structured whole. The principle of determination does not exist as such; what exists, instead, is the articulated structure of the instances:

despite appearances, Marx does not analyze any 'concrete society', not
even England which he mentions constantly in Volume One, but the
CAPITALIST MODE OF PRODUCTION and nothing else. This object is an
abstract one: which means that it is terribly real and that it never *exists* in
the pure state, since it only exists in capitalist societies. Simply speaking:
in order to be able to analyze these concrete capitalist societies (England,
France, Russia, etc.), it is essential to know that they are dominated by that
terribly concrete reality, the capitalist mode of production, which is
'invisible' (to the naked eye). 'Invisible', i.e. *abstract.* (Althusser, *Lenin*
77)[7]

The Althusserian effectivity, then, implies that social formations
cannot be reduced to a mere reflection of the economy. The unity of
the structured whole makes a theory of causal priority simply
irrelevant—the economic does not have an anterior function, nor does
it operate in a cause-effect paradigm. By insisting on a complex unity
structured around a hierarchy of determinations operative within
relatively autonomous instances, Althusser proposes an understanding
of social formations that goes beyond the limits of both transitive
causality, which reduces the whole to its parts, and expressive causality
(and behind it Hegelian idealism), which emphasizes the primacy of
the whole as an essence. A social formation cannot be reduced to a
pluralist organism in which everything causes everything else, nor can
it be equated with a totality in which the different instances operate as
a microcosm of the whole.[8]

In spite of its non-reductionist cast, the decentered unity Althusser
proposes is not void of theoretical problems. His reformulation of the
question of determination, in particular, is based on an assumption
that cannot be accepted uncritically. Structural causality assumes that
the instances are articulated in relations of domination and
subordination. Within this framework, the economic acquires an ever-
determining function: "in order to conceive of this 'dominance' of a
structure over the other structures in the unity of a conjuncture it is
necessary to refer the principle of determination 'in the last instance'
of the non-economic structures by the economic structure; and that
this 'determination in the last instance' is an absolute precondition for
the necessity and intelligibility of the displacements of the structures
in the hierarchy of effectivity, or of 'dominance' between the
structured levels of the whole" (Althusser, *Reading* 99). Althusser's
concept of determination in the last instance rests on a theory of
apriorism which privileges the mode of production as a transhistorical organizing category. The hierarchical bias one finds in

Althusser's project turns the economic into an absolute principle.
Laclau and Mouffe have aptly pointed out the limits of this position:
"If this ultimate determination were a truth valid *for every society*, the
relation between such determination and the conditions making it
possible would not develop through a contingent historical
articulation, but would constitute an a priori necessity.... The problem
is that if the 'economy' is determinant in the last instance *for every
type of society*, it must be defined independently of any specific type
of society" (98).   Even though Althusser and his followers have
attempted to solve this issue by forging a distinction between a
(constant) mode of production and a (variable) mode of domination,
this distinction is ambiguous at best, and in the final analysis does little
more than naturalize the category of the economic.[9] But this is hardly
surprising.   Viewed in the context of structural Marxism, the truth-
value that the economic acquires is, in many ways, a necessary
consequence of Althusser's scientific analysis of the modes of
production. For Althusser, as Robert Resch explains, "determination
in the last instance provides, for historical science, that minimal level
of theoretical coherence without which the very production of
knowledge is inconceivable" (56). Indeed, Althusser's Marxism rests
on an epistemological position which assumes the existence of a
certain objective discourse that can serve as an absolute standard
against which all claims of knowledge can be measured.

   To move beyond the limits imposed by this scientific and
epistemological perspective, one has to relativize Althusser's
theory—even if that means a reformulation of the concept of
determination in the last instance on grounds which Althusser himself
has systematically dismissed.[10] For the concept of economic
determination to be theoretically viable, it has to be considered as a
historically-specific claim rather than an absolute premise. If it were
otherwise, the economic simply takes over the historical.   This
nuanced position is precisely what informs Jean-Joseph Goux's
Symbolic Economies: "The fact that the mode of production and
exchange of the 'material means of subsistence' *fixes* in the last
instance the *moment* of the 'symbolic' logic which figures imposingly
during a given historical epoch ... does not necessarily mean that the
economic basis is an 'internal cause'" (*Freud* 44). In his theoretical
numismatics, Goux expresses a reluctance to ascribe to the economic a
role that extends beyond that of an "index," leaving the question
open as "to what extent it [is] also the determining factor" (*Symbolic*
34). While Althusser insists on the determination in the last instance
of non-economic by economic structures, Goux contents himself with

pointing out the eminence of the economic: "as long as the mode of consciousness depends on *symbolic charge* and on a syncretic and undivided conception of *value*, it would be impossible to establish social relations solely on the quantitative and rationalist 'economist' basis... Thus—and this point calls into question all reductions of a Marxiological cast—it would be impossible to write the history of economic relations without taking to account its solidarity with a stratified, discontinuous history of symbolization" (*Symbolic* 125). Implicit in this assertion is a proposition that conceives of the economic not as a strictly determinant factor but as a standard or gauge which can be used to reconstruct the general mode of symbolization within a given social formation.

Goux's symbology provides a theory of history that is intimately connected with an economic principle but not predicated on it: "It is not a matter, then, of ascribing to economic symbology an anterior or causal role. We can only note within the historical world of sociality correspondences and contradictions between its procedures and those that govern signifying metabolisms" (*Symbolic* 113). Although Goux insists on the need to prioritize the structure of the whole, he resists endowing the economic with more than a methodological pre-eminence; that is, the economic is privileged here, but only in an *ad hoc*, pragmatic way: "Notwithstanding Louis Althusser's caveat, which rejects this genesis on the grounds of excessively Hegelian implications, I felt that Marx's analysis held the lineaments of a general and elementary logic of exchange which exceeds the sphere of economic value for which it was initially produced" (*Symbolic* 3). If for Goux the field of political economy is "the most precious of the social sciences" (*Symbolic* 1), it is not because it has a determining value but because, on the one hand, Marx's anatomy of the bourgeois mode of production and his analysis of the historical organization of production provide the foundation for "a general theory of the production of the symbolic" (Goux, *Freud* 31), and on the other hand, because the economic category—by virtue of its apodictic value—provides the logical basis for understanding the structure and evolution of historical formations: "the regime of exchange specific to a social formation (its 'mode of symbolization') manifests itself in a more atomized way, as if the economic process offers a cross-section that is particularly revealing and coherent in a social reality of prodigious complexity" (Goux, "Catégories" 228). If the symbolic function is closely associated with the economic register, it is not because the symbolic depends on the economic, but because it is theoretically enunciated in the mode of production.

In Goux's formulations, then, the economic has to be conceived of as a "'measuring' point of view" (*Freud* 29) or a "reliable index" (*Symbolic* 34) and as a determining factor only as an exception. This exception, however, exists; it is the hallmark of the capitalist mode of production.[11] To say that under capitalism all institutions are subordinated to the economic is a fundamental proposition. At the same time, however—and herein lies the idiosyncracy of capitalism—the imposition of the economic has turned bourgeois society into a "non-transparent society" (Lefebvre, *Idéologie* 168). For Marx, the commodity is distinguished first and foremost by its mystery: "the products of human labor become commodities, sensuous things which are at the same time supra-sensible or social" (*Capital* 165). Such is the double-bind of the commodity—it is the substance that it is and more than what it is. This is so precisely because, under capitalism, the relationship between people takes the form of a relationship between things; the inert object hides, so to speak, the abstract social relationship that gives it its value. Because of this transfer of value—or "transubstantiation," as Marx calls it (*Capital* 203)—the commodity form cannot be the object of an empirical description or a superficial observation: "We may twist and turn a single commodity as we wish; it remains impossible to grasp it as a thing possessing value" (*Capital* 138). In order to apprehend the mystery of the commodity, Marx proposes to break away from the conception that locates value within the commodity itself. The relation of value that the commodity holds *vis-à-vis* all other products of labor is independent of its physical nature. To that extent, the apprehension of the commodity as a mere symbol that hides behind it either a substance or an essence omits the social determination that gives it both its meaning and value. The prodigious complexity that gives rise to this form of value can be adequately theorized only within a line of analysis that cedes to the "power of abstraction" (Marx, *Capital* 90).

The fact that one can analyze value in its pure economic manifestation, the fact that one can distinguish between material relations of production and other social relations, should not obfuscate the need to seize the system in its quintessence. Capitalism is not simply an economic system; rather it is a system of production of relations. For Marx, a wide-ranging critique of political economy necessitates an understanding not only of the secret of the commodity, but also its social ubiquity—not only its dissimulation, but also its dissemination.[12] Stated differently, Marxian exegesis revolves around two seminal propositions: the *invisibility* of the real character of the commodity and the *indivisibility* of the historical totality that the logic of the commodity engenders. This line of analysis calls into question the reductionist understanding, common in vulgar Marxism, of superstructural phenomena as a mere reflection of the economic base. If the architectural metaphor of levels is to be retained, the base and superstructure have to be conceived within a totality that proceeds at all levels of sociality. In other words, the economic is necessary but insufficient to account for the social totality. The imposition of capitalism implies the infusion of relations of exchange in virtually all spheres of vital activities: "The totality of the system of exchange ... is virtually posited with archaic forms of exchange. In order for exchange to constitute capitalism, it has to be generalized. It has also to transcend itself because social beings transcend the division of labor, the market, the commodity, money and its power" (Lefebvre, "Réflections" 22). The dominance of capitalism has to be conceived not as the dominance of an economic principle *tout court*, but as the economico-politicization of the lived totality; that is, the ability of capitalism to reproduce itself incessantly and indiscriminately in the different enclaves of the social totality, and to extend its logic into territories that are not strictly or purely economic. As Baudrillard explains, the economic works in extended structures and thrives upon an extensive deployment:

> capital has never really functioned on this imaginary distinction [between base and superstructure]; it is not that naive. Its power stems from its simultaneous development at every level.... Capital is content to extend its law in a single movement, inexorably occupying all spheres of vital activities without considering priorities. If it has put people to work, it has also ensconced them in culture, needs, language, functional idioms, information, communication, law, liberty, and sexuality... At the same time, it has clad them with myths that are simultaneously opposed and indifferent. The only law capital recognizes is indifference.... [T]o level, neutralize, square, indifferentiate—this is what it can do, this is how it proceeds according to its own law. (*Échange* 60–61)

Such is the dynamic character of capitalism: an urgency to generate an "overflowing contamination" (Derrida, *Spectres* 258), an ability to set in motion various operating levels, and an inclination to colonize other registers—in short, a tendency to reproduce itself as a complex but unified social whole. To talk about capitalism is to talk about the insidious deployment of a prodigious and polymorphous entity that subordinates and absorbs the totality of social praxis—a sumptuous machine that has a tendency to develop, propagate, abound, and exceed itself.¹³

However, to content oneself with an account of capitalism as a totality is to reproduce the same problems I have pointed out in Walter Benn Michaels' version of the market and, in doing so, ignore the dynamic character of history. I invoke Michaels again because the problems associated with his project transcend naturalist criticism proper; the most insistent pertains to the possibility of envisaging a system that is not totalitarian. Even in a project as far-reaching as that of the Frankfurt School—and more specifically Adorno and Horkheimer's neo-Weberian critique of the culture industry—this question has not been satisfactorily resolved. What Adorno and Horkheimer saw in modern industrial society is a "totality" (*Dialectic* 136) characterized above all by its ability to control individual consciousness, manipulate needs, promote obedience, and induce submission: "The might of industrial society is lodged in men's minds.... The industry as a whole has molded men as a type unfailingly reproduced in every product.... What is decisive today ... is the necessity inherent in the system not to leave the customer alone, not for a moment to allow him any suspicion that resistance is possible" (*Dialectic* 127–41). For Adorno and Horkheimer, the culture industry constitutes a seamless web in which all forms of resistance and all possibilities of change—being programmed by the system itself—are ultimately reified. This "administrative view" of culture, as Adorno calls it ("Culture" 127), however, poses more problems than it solves. For one thing, the type of domination described here is far from being historically specific. The crisis that plagues industrial and post-industrial societies has its origin in man's continuing attempt to control nature. As Rolf Wiggershaus points out, *Dialectic of Enlightenment* rests on the assumption that "the decisive event in the history of human culture was not the development of the modern period and of capitalism, but rather humanity's transition to domination over nature" (334). While Adorno and Horkheimer see this historical process as inevitable, in reality it is contingent.

But this is not all. Even if such a transhistorical premise is overlooked, the project of these two prominent members of the Frankfurt School remains vulnerable to criticism. There is something stultifying about the unrelenting insistence on the total domination of culture—its irreversible tendency to assemble, evaluate, and organize. The socio-economic system evoked in *Dialectic of Enlightenment*, much like the philosophical system adumbrated in *Negative Dialectics*,¹⁴ is totalitarian to say the least. Fredric Jameson has aptly captured the scandalous implications of this position: "the model of the 'total system' would seem slowly and inexorably to eliminate any possibility of the *negative* as such, and to reintegrate the place of an oppositional or even merely 'critical' practice and resistance back into the system as the latter's mere inversion" (*Political* 91).[15] In order to rid the concept of totality of its totalitarian bent, one has to recognize that an inexorable part of the system's logic is its tendency to develop contradictory tendencies which suggest the existence of limits to the capacity of society to be over-organized. This is the essence of the open system as Lefebvre theorizes it: "The fulfillment of the system implies a limit the attainment of which is impossible... Society stands out as an extremely complex whole, as an open totality.... How is it ever possible to seize a system or a sub-system without a critical distance, without an entry and an exit, without an opening?" (*Cybernanthrope* 122).[16] The emphasis on the openness of the system makes it possible to propose a more viable understanding of capitalism, namely that capitalism has not only a tendency to envelop the entirety of the social body, but also a proclivity to develop dysfunctionalities, create deficiencies, provoke deviations, and generate counter-processes.[17] Because of its inherent structural imbalance, capitalism constantly veers towards intensification.

This proposition has Deleuzian overtones. For Deleuze and Guattari, the strength of capitalism lies in the fact that its axiomatic is never saturated:

> capitalism, through its process of production, produces an awesome schizophrenic accumulation of energy or charge, against which it brings all its vast powers of repression to bear, but which nonetheless counteracts, constantly inhibits this inherent tendency while at the same time allowing it free rein; it continually seeks to avoid reaching its limit while simultaneously tending towards that limit.... Capitalism therefore liberates the flow of desire, but under the social conditions that define its limit and the possibility of its own dissolution, so that it is constantly opposing with all its exasperated strength the movement that drives it toward the limit. (*Anti-Oedipus* 34–140)

For Deleuze and Guattari, an unrestrained schizophrenic accumulation of energy is inconceivable because that would constitute the limit or absolute threshold of capitalism. A schizophrenic capitalism, in the full import of the term, can be posited only as an ideal and undesirable condition: "Schizophrenia is not the identity of capitalism, but on the contrary its difference, its divergence, and its death" (Deleuze, *Anti-Oedipus* 246). That is why capitalism functions not by fulfilling but countering and exorcising its limit. Capitalism is therefore caught between two investments; it exasperatingly oscillates between a "breakthrough" and a "breakdown" (Deleuze, *Anti-Oedipus* 278) or, more pointedly, between a schizophrenic pole and a paranoic pole.[18] Deleuze and Guattari's understanding of the dynamics of capitalism is inseparable, then, from the question of immanence. The capitalist tendency has no fixed or definitive limit because it reproduces its limit by constantly displacing it. The logic of capitalism is such that every deterritorialization adumbrates a new reterritorialization: "capitalism ... both does and does not have an exterior limit: it has an exterior limit that is schizophrenia, that is, the absolute decoding of flows, but it functions only by pushing back and exorcising this limit. And it also has, yet does not have, interior limits: it has interior limits under the specific conditions of capitalist production and circulation, that is, in capital itself, but it functions only by reproducing and widening these limits and on an always vaster scale" (Deleuze, *Anti-Oedipus* 250). In short, capitalism has an impassable limit.

Such an immanent axiomatic seems to invite the sort of deterministic reading for which there is certainly ample support in *Anti-Oedipus*.[19] In a typical moment, Deleuze and Guattari address this problem head on: "which is the revolutionary path? Is there one? To withdraw from the world market as Samir Amin advises Third World countries to do... To go still further, that is in the movement of the market, of decoding and deterritorialization?" (239). From the standpoint of the immanent axiomatic, the question here is rhetorical. The first alternative, as Deleuze and Guattari characterize it, is "a curious revival of the fascist 'economic' solution" (*Anti-Oedipus* 239). The second alternative—i.e., to further the deterritorialization of capitalism because the flow is not deterritorialized enough, and therefore not schizophrenic enough—is equally untenable because, in their view, schizophrenia is the "absolute limit" of society while capitalism is only its "relative limit" (*Anti-Oedipus* 176). The problem then persists. The notion that capitalism is at once expansive and totalizing, but fundamentally unbalanced and riven by its internal contradictions highlights the dynamic character of the system but does not emphasize its transformation. Deleuze and Guattari's schizoanalytical project does not pay sufficient attention to the movement of history; it presents capitalism as a space from which nothing can free itself and a space which nothing can penetrate—i.e., a system that has no inside and no outside. For the Deleuzian model to be theoretically viable, it has to conceive of immanence not so much as a deterministic logic but as a differential topology. The deployment of the system produces unpredictable conditions which call for a special attention not only to the reproduction of the system, but also the movement of its elements. As Lefebvre points out,

> [r]eproduction does not occur without undergoing changes. This excludes both the idea of an automatic reproductive process internal to the constituted mode of production (as system) and that of the immediate efficacy of a 'generative nucleus.' The contradictions themselves reproduce, and not without changes. Former relations may degenerate or dissolve... Others are constituted in such a way that there is *production* of social relations within the reproduction... These new relations emerge from within those which are dissolving: they first appear as the negation of the latter, as destroyers of the antecedents and conditions which hold them back. This is the specific behavior of the enlarged contradictions. (*Survival* 90-91)

What this means is that the continuity of the system does not reside in its identity but in the relation of its elements to their environment. Capitalism is an inherently unstable system which engenders a continuous interplay of its elements; this play of elements, however, is not without consequence—in attenuating its internal contradictions and replacing its elements, the system transforms itself. The system feeds on its own problems, but in the process it evolves and changes.[20]

It is this differential topology that I tried to explore in the context of naturalism. Such an endeavor requires a reformulation of the guiding question. What needs to be addressed is not what naturalism means but how it works. In other words, naturalism has to be seized as a historical tendency rather then a circumscribed historical moment. Only then can one recognize an irreducible transgressive element that works towards complicating the unfolding of the period in question. Indeed, a true revisionism of naturalism requires a special attention to the interplay between the dominant and the emergent, which the system—by virtue of its instable dynamics—calls for. To identify planes of emergence or moments of negativity—whether they take the form of indeterminacy in *Vandover and the Brute*, lines of escape in *McTeague*, or counter-rhythms in *Sister Carrie*—is not only to come to the conclusion that naturalism, and by extension capitalism, is an open system, but also to realize that uneven development is the basic law of social formations.

NOTES

Chapter One

1   Although these two studies stand out as compelling accounts of the period, they are not the only ones with considerable sophistication. Naturalism came to epitomize, among other things, a culture of surveillance (Mark Seltzer, *Henry James and the Art of Power*), a process of mechanization wrought in a masturbatory economy of production (Seltzer again, *Bodies and Machines*), the expression of a culture that is increasingly marked by mass consumption and theatricality (Rachel Bowlby, *Just Looking*), and a strategy for imagining and managing the threats of social change (Amy Kaplan, *The Social Construction of American Realism*).

2   Michaels' reading of naturalism has drawn considerable critical attention. For engaging discussions of the problems that *The Gold Standard* raises, see Fredric Jameson, *Postmodernism* 181–217, Cary Wolfe, "Antinomies of Liberalism," Amy Kaplan, "Naturalism with Difference" 583–86, Christopher Wilson, "Containing Multitudes" 470–76, Evan Carton, "American Literary Histories as a Social Practice" 128–32, and Kiyohiko Murayama, "Is *Sister Carrie* Really Not Anti-Capitalist at All?". See also, but to a lesser extent, Jennifer Fleissner, "The Work of Womanhood in American Naturalism" 80–83, Richard Lehan, "The Theoretical Limits of the New Historicism" 540–43, Gregory S. Jay, *America the Scrivener* 250–52, Donald Pizer, *The Theory and Practice of American Literary Naturalism* 203–06, and Leo Bersani, "Rejoinder to Walter Benn Michaels."

3   This is the critique that Christopher Wilson levels at Howard in "Containing Multitudes" 481–82. For other critical examinations of *Form and History*, see Amy Kaplan, "Naturalism with a Difference" 586–87, William Buckley, "Realism still Knocking on Academe's Door" 317–18, and Richard Lehan, "The City, the Self, and Narrative Discourse" 79–81.

4   For an engaging discussion of Foucault's rejection of the concept of ideology, see Michèle Barrett, *The Politics of Truth* 123–56, and Jorge Lorrain, *Ideology and Cultural Identity* 90–97.

5   Michael Spindler's *American Literature and Social Change* is a representative example of such a limited approach.

6   In *The Imaginary Institutions of Society*, Cornelius Castoriadis explains, in

useful terms, why reification is never fully achieved: "Reification, the essential tendency of capitalism, can never be wholly realized. If it were, if the system were actually able to change individuals into things moved only by economic 'forces', it would collapse not in the long run, but immediately. The struggle against reification is, just as much the tendency towards reification, the condition for the functioning of capitalism. A factory in which the workers were really cogs in the machine, blindly executing the orders of management, would come to stop in a quarter of an hour. Capitalism can function only by continuously drawing upon the genuinely *human* activity of those subject to it, while at the same time, trying to level and humanize them as much as possible. It can continue to function only to the extent that its profound tendency, which actually is reification, is not realized, to the extent that its norms are continually countered in their application" (16).

7   It is worth noting that Michaels fails precisely where Howard succeeds. While the model Michaels describes diffuses contradictions and conflicts, the version of history Howard proposes emphasizes unevenness and contingency. *Form and History* rests on the recognition of "the irrevocable openness of any historical moment and an apprehension of naturalism not as an exhibit in a gallery of literary types but as a dynamic solution to the problem of generating narrative out of the particular historical and cultural materials that offered themselves to these writers. This recognition is in some sense the discovery that our own history is contingent, that our world was not a foregone conclusion" (xi).

Chapter Two

1   For an overview of some of these trends in the context of naturalism, see James Colvert, "Stephen Crane and Postmodern Theory."

2   Intimately connected with Freud's theory of the "compulsion to repeat" (18:19) is his theory about the return of the repressed—i.e., the neurotic effects of an earlier psychic trauma upon later behavior. The correlation between the two will become clear when the figure of the father is examined.

3   On the relationship between the compulsion to repeat and the impulsion to remember, see Freud, "Remembering, Repeating and Working-through" (12:147–56).

4   Commenting on this passage in *Bodies and Machines*, Mark Seltzer points out a process of (auto)production which draws Vandover in an even closer relationship with the mother: "Vandover explicitly sees this 'death' of his art as an abortion, or as the 'death of a child of his,' and the agent of death or abortion, this midwife or witch-mother, is the very brute gestating within him.... The growth of the brute is also a return to the scene of birth—'he had become a little child again ... still near great white gates of life.' And if Vandover turns to his art as an attempt to 'deliver himself by his own exertions,' this attempt at self-delivery, in the novel's logic of generation, places Vandover in the places at once of mother, fetus, and obstetrician" (37). The connection Selzer draws between artistic production and biological reproduction is all the more compelling when read in

light of an interesting passage from Nietzsche's *Thus Spoke Zarathustra*: "Creation—that is the great redemption from suffering, and life's growing light. But that the creation may be, suffering is needed and much change. Indeed, there must be much bitter dying in your life, you creators. Thus are you advocates and justifiers of all impermanence. To be the child who is newly born, the creator must also want to be the mother who gives birth and the pangs of the birth-giver" (87).

5   On the relationship between idealization, inhibition, and passivity in the context of art, see Marion Milner's *On Not Being Able to Paint* 149–50.

6   See Derrida "From Restricted to General Economy" in *Writing and Difference* 251–77.

7   See in particular Adorno, "Culture and Administration."

8   See Deleuze, *Anti-Oedipus* 240–71.

9   See Hochman, "*Vandover and the Brute*: The Decisive Experience of Loss."

10 For Freud, one of the most defining aspects of repression is its exceedingly mobile character: "The process of repression is not to be regarded as an event which takes place *once*, the results of which are permanent, as when some living thing has been killed and from that time onward is dead; repression demands a persistent expenditure of force, and if this were to cease the success of the repression would be jeopardized, so that a fresh act of repression would be necessary" (14:151).

11 I use the term realist representation to designate representation in both realist and naturalist fiction. This is not to say, however, that the two are not distinguishable. For many critics, the naturalist conception of the real is a reaction to the realist notion of the real. In comparison with naturalism, realism, as T. J. Jackson Lears put it, in *No Place of Grace*, is "not realistic enough" (103). While realism tends to focus on the blander aspects of the prosperous middle class (high society), naturalism is more concerned with the lower ranks of society (low life). For others, however, naturalism is less a negation than it is a version or a variant of realism. Whether naturalism is situated within a dialogue to realism or in reaction to it is still a matter of argument. For an overview of the debate surrounding this problematic, see for instance June Howard, *Form and History* 10–14.

12 On this point, see Elizabeth Bruss, "The Game of Literature and Some Literary Games" 157–58, and Tzevtan Todorov's discussion of the concept of "obliquity" in "The Verbal Age."

13 Equally interesting is an observation in an anonymous review of Norris' *The Pit* which appeared upon the publication of the novel: "His books, in consequence, were remarkable rather than admirable, or, at least, more remarkable than admirable, and one sometimes gets from them the impression of reading a first draft manuscript instead of the printed page. They evince what it is customary to call fatal facility and seem to be written at high speed and left uncorrected. If this seeming is deceptive, and Mr. Norris did in reality give his books the careful revision without which the conscientious artist is never content, then there is a chance that his work would have been 'promising' to the end of a long life, as it was to the end of one pathetically short" ("*The Pit*" 32).

14 This is a concept that E. M. Forster has introduced in his *Aspects of the Novel* 73–78.
15 See Roland Barthes, "L'Éffet du réel," Philippe Hammon, "Un discours contraint," and more recently Lilian Furst, *All is True*.
16 This emphasis on irregularity becomes more poignant in light of Norris' insistence on the regularity that has marked Vandover's art throughout the novel: "His art was work with him now, hard, serious work. It was above all *work* that he needed to set himself right again, regular work, steady, earnest work, not the dilettante fancy of an amateur content with making pretty things.... He had long since abandoned his work at the paint-shop, but this time he returned there and asked for his old occupation. They laughed in his face. Was that the way he thought they did business? Not much; another man had his job, a much better man and one who was regular, who could be depended on" (xiv 221–xviii 338).
17 For an interesting perspective on naturalism as an open text, see Yves Chevrel, *Le Naturalisme* 140–47.

Chapter Three

1 Money, as Pierre Lévy puts it in *Qu'est-ce que le virtuel?*, "is not richness *per se*, but its virtuality" (124).
2 See Lacan, *l'Envers de la psychanalyse* 50–57.
3 See Lacan, *The Four Fundamental Concepts* 49–50.
4 Building on the hereditary theme, June Howard even points out an ideological dimension behind the naturalists' preoccupation with images of wolfish monstrosity: "one cannot appreciate naturalism's philosophical determinism without also recognizing the perspective from which those characters are viewed.... The terror of the brute includes, certainly, the fear of revolution and chaos, of the mob and the criminal, as invoked, for example, in *White Fang* by the prospect of being torn apart by the hungry wolf-pack or attacked by the murderous Jim Hall. It also includes the fear of becoming the outcast through the social degradation and psychological disintegration depicted in *Vandover and the Brute*; the brute can devour one from within, as it does Vandover" (95).
5 On this point see Derrida's "Economimesis" 87–93. I pursue the "tautological" implications of this auto-productive process in the next section.
6 In the same fashion, Wolfgang Fritz Hang observes that "capitalism is based on a systematic *quid pro quo*: all human goals, even life itself, matter only as means and pretexts ... in the functioning of the system. The standpoint of capital valorization as an end in itself, to which all human endeavors, longings, instincts, and hopes are just exploitable, means... This valorization standpoint which dominates absolutely in capitalist society, is diametrically opposed to what people are and want autonomously" (46).
7 Trina's passion here to consume and to be consumed by gold recalls the bed-scene where Norris' miser is seized by a consuming passion for her gold pieces. Still, what is more fascinating are the rich and immense possibilities that

realism gives its author. In the hands of Norris, the imaginative power of realism to convey the most complex images and concepts with a gracious economy and a rare simplicity reaches its peak. The juxtaposition of culinary and pecuniary desires, in fact, stands out not so much for its fictional strain but its realist quality—albeit a *recherché* realism. The prototype for both the curious bed-scene and the persistent images of gluttony is arguably a rendering of a real scene that Norris has witnessed during a visit to a South African mine a few years prior to the publication of *McTeague*: "the compound Kaffirs of the De Beers are human ... and they will steal diamonds if they can get the chance. The mine regulations, however, ... seem to have reduced the opportunities for theft to a minimum. The Kaffir who is taken on as a miner at the De Beers signs a contract whereby he allows himself to be kept practically a prisoner for the period covered by this contract—a month.... At the end of the month he has the option of renewing his contract or throwing it up. If he throws it up, he goes into what is called the 'detention house.' Here he is stripped to the skin and remains in that condition under constant surveillance for a week. Every act of his daily life is performed under the eye of the guards. Stealing diamonds by swallowing them is the most difficult and hazardous method a Kaffir miner can employ" (*Collected Writings* 225–26).

8   In their analysis of Henry James's "In the Cage," in *A Thousand Plateaus*, Deleuze and Guattari identify a similar dynamics which they call "objective intermination" (196).

9   See Lacan, *L'Envers de la psychanalyse* 206–07, and more pointedly "Radiophonie" 86–87.

10 Lacan's formulation revolves around Freud's theory of the castration complex. For Freud, the barrier against incest is a "historical acquisition" that has been established in persons by "organic inheritance" (7:222; n.3). Lacan does not question this proposition but extends it or, more specifically, linguisticizes it.

11 A similar observation can be pointed out in Vološinov's Marxist critique of Freudianism: "What we call the 'human psyche' and 'consciousness' reflects the dialectics of history to a much greater degree than the dialectics of nature. The nature that is present in them is nature already in economic and social refraction" (*Freudianism* 83).

12 To the extent that fantasy, as Lyotard explains, emanates straight out of that which is forbidden, it cannot be liberated: "fantasy contains within itself its own interdiction—it stages the tendency of desire to forbid" (*Dérive* 236).

13 This line of analysis finds its most ample articulation in the "Seminar on 'The Purloined Letter'" where Lacan addresses the problematic of the relationship between truth and the certainty of knowledge in relation to the compulsion to repeat (what Lacan refers to as inter-subjective repetition). In the Lacanian formulation, truth is always purloined. On the correspondence between the infinite and unnameable character of truth and the unattainability of *jouissance*, see Alain Badiou, *Conditions* 196–212.

14 The only point of access to *jouissance*, writes David-Ménard, "comes about through the possibility, programmed into the machine, of hallucination" (6).

15 One can even sense in Trina's waning confidence in the monetary sign a

precaution against the kind of devaluation her husband experiences. Although not implicated as cause and effect, the two developments, as French Warren has pointed out, are closely related. As McTeague loses his right to practice, Trina "becomes infatuated with the physical rather than symbolic value of her gold coins" (73).

16   In this sense, Leclaire is justified in insisting that "any object can in principle, release the object of desire" (*Psychanalyser* 79).

17   Such are, for instance, the limits of Lee Clark Mitchell's *Determined Fictions* which argues that "the 'mechanisms' of literary naturalism belong less to some physical 'universe of force' than to the grammatical pressures of distinctively verbal realms" (xv).

18   For the relation between language, stammering, and limits, see Deleuze, *Critique et clinique* 135–43.

19   On the dynamics of madness within writing—rhetorical madness, so to speak—see also Shoshana Felman, *La Folie et la chose littéraire* 125–37, 159–213.

20   See Derrida, *Spectres de Marx* 236–46.

21   See Baudrillard, *America* 63–64, 68–69, 123–24.

22   It is no accident that earlier in the century, the desert is one of the sites that fascinated Eugène Delacroix as both an exotic space and an esoteric motif. In the paintings of Delacroix one can discern not only an "object of aesthetic contemplation" but also a "system of abstract relations," to borrow Lévi-Strauss' terminology (25). What Delacroix has found appealing in the desert are the unlimited possibilities of reproduction. In the abundant and extended hills of sand of the desert of Algiers Delacroix (re)lives the experience of France's colonial expansion. The depiction of space (an aesthetico-ontological experience) is entangled with an economico-political experience (the colonial power of the imperial machine). Dolf Sternberger has eloquently captured the entanglement between the territorial expansion of capitalism in its imperial phase and the painter's experience of space: "Delacroix had gone on ahead, guided and prompted by the colonial expansion of France... [A]mid the limitless, fiery yellow desert sand ... he captured freedom itself, a hectic gaudy freedom, in his paintings or converted it into paintings, helping willy-nilly, as the illustrator of expansion, to curtail this freedom in the political reality. Freedom here was nothing but liberty of passion, ardor, savagery, heroism, as well as fanaticism and cruelty, jealousy and sensuality" (40).

23   The economic theme that runs through Norris' depiction of open and extended spaces becomes even more acute in *The Octopus*. Norris, in fact, revisits the same language he uses to describe the immensity of the desert in order to depict a gigantic and omnipotent force that symbolizes corporate power—the wheat: "there before him, mile after mile, illimitable, covering the earth from horizon to horizon, lay the Wheat.... Ah, yes, the Wheat—it was over this that the Railroad, the ranchers, the traitor false to his trust, all the members of an obscure conspiracy, were wrangling.... Indifferent, gigantic, restless, it moved in its appointed grooves.... There was nothing else to be seen but the limitless sea of wheat as far as the eye could reach, dry, rustling, crisp and harsh in the rare

breaths of hot wind out of the southeast" (v 299–vi 327–28).

Chapter Four

1   Rhythms, and more specifically the rhythms of society, have become the subject
    of increasing attention in the last few years. The two most elaborate studies of
    rhythms are probably Henri Lefebvre's *Éléments de rythmanalyse* and Michael
    Young's *The Metronomic Society*. For a modest attempt at examining the
    implication of rhythms in the context of naturalism proper, see Sylvie Collot,
    Les Lieux du désir 123–25.

2   The quotidian, as Herman Parret observes, "can neither be pronounced nor
    observed because it is lived without theory or distance" (20).

3   See Lefebvre, *Everyday Life* 53–54.

4   For a more elaborate discussion of the relationship between these two temporal
    modalities, see Lefebvre, *Fondements d'une sociologie de la quotidienneté*
    315–39.

5   This line of analysis complicates rather than refutes the biological reading of
    naturalism. A representative example of such a reading can be found in Richard
    Lehan's recent essay "The European Background": "it is unlikely that nature can
    long be suppressed: the rhythms of a day, of the seasons, the cycles of life
    (birth, sexuality, maturity, sickness, death) are all too strong to be distanced in
    our consciousness by forms of constructed reality" (70). My point here is not
    that natural cycles have disappeared, but that the type of temporality we usually
    associate with nature has become indistinguishable from, and even undermined
    by a more imposing linear temporality.

6   Everydayness, as Lefebvre put it, "is defined by the constraints and persuasions
    that maintain it" (*Vers le cybernanthrope* 160). This system of constraints
    means that individuals do not forge their everyday life but undergo it.

7   See Sartre, *Critique de la raison dialectique* 306–77.

8   This indifference is of utter importance because it exposes some of the key
    elements upon which the system thrives. The individuals who occupy these
    segmented urban spaces obey an organized rationality which subjects them to
    the dominant mode of production. Spaces are not only specialized just as
    operations are in the social and technical division of labor but are also
    exchangeable in accordance with the logic and language of the commodity. As
    Lefebvre points out in *The Production of Space*, "Repetitious spaces are the
    outcome of repetitive gestures (these of the workers) associated with instruments
    which are both duplicatable and designed to duplicate: machines, bull-dozers,
    concrete-mixers, cranes, pneumatic drills, and so on. Are these spaces
    interchangeable because they are homologous? Or are they homologous so that
    they can be exchanged, bought and sold, with the only difference between them
    being those assessable in money—i.e. quantifiable—terms (as volumes,
    distances, etc.)? At all events, repetition reigns supreme" (76). The conformity
    of the buildings Carrie observes (xxix 268–69) and the repetitiveness that
    characterizes the lives of the inhabitants (xxxi 280–81) confirm this

conclusion. The relationship between people is presented as a relationship between spaces.

9 On theatrical excess in *Sister Carrie*, see Rachel Bowlby, *Just Looking* 52–65, and Barbara Hochman, "The Portrait of the Artist as a Young Actress." On the city as a theater of consumerism, see Robert Shulman, "Dreiser and the Dynamics of American Capitalism."

10 See Lefebvre, *The Production of Space* 75–76.

11 See Lefebvre, *Le Droit à la ville* 71–72. Likewise, Franco Moretti's emphasis on the abstraction on which thrives advertising is useful here: "Advertising, therefore, is not so much the exhibit of 'a' commodity as of *commodity fetishism*: it boosts the product by making a fetish of it" (195).

12 See Dreiser, *Sister Carrie* 178–79, 132, 85, and 130–31, respectively.

13 Adorno and Horkheimer's critique of the subordination of the mind to the rules and values of what they call the culture industry is one of the earliest systematic analyses of this organized passivity (see in particular *Dialectic of Enlightenment* 120–67). In the concluding chapter, I will come back to the theoretical problems in their account of the hegemony of capitalism.

14 The sense of pseudo-change that fashion fosters points to a certain futility that is also central to everydayness as Blanchot conceives it: "the everyday is, paradoxically enough, that which we never experience for the first time but can only experience again, having perceived it through an illusion that is precisely constitutive of the everyday" (*Entretien* 358).

15 Although perceptive, Adorno's analysis is exceedingly negative, even when judged from the perspective of other members of the Frankfurt School. See for example Susan Buck-Morss' account of Walter Benjamin's analysis of the dynamics of fashion in *The Dialectics of Seeing* 97–99.

16 On flux and motion in the novel, see Robert Butler, "Movement in Dreiser's *Sister Carrie*," McAleer, "Flux Metaphor in *Sister Carrie*," and Fisher, "Acting, Reading, Fortune's Wheel."

17 See Donald Pizer, *Realism and Naturalism* 21–22.

18 For a discussion of the role and meaning of *fait-divers*—or what is known in the journalism jargon as "filler"—see Roland Barthes, "The Structure of the *Fait-Divers*" in *Critical Essays* 185–95.

19 See Tanner, *City of Words*, especially 11–31, 372–92.

20 Particularly useful here is Stallybrass and White's analysis of *la bohème* as the Other who constantly threatens to remap the body of the city. See *The Politics and Poetics of Transgression* 125–48.

Chapter Five

1 On the theoretical problems that accompany the failure to posit such a unified field—but at the same time one that goes beyond "a kind of ritual gesture of the schematic economic or class background sketch"—see Jameson, *Marxism and Form* 224–25.

2 Evolutionary theory in its traditional form is questioned by the very non-linear

theories Civello invokes. For an elaborate discussion of some of these non-linear theories, see for instance Varela, *The Embodied Mind*.

3   See Serres, *Feux et signaux de brume*.

4   See in particular Brady's "Chaos et naturalisme," "La Théorie du chaos et *L'Œuvre*," and "Mutilation, Fragmentation, and Creation."

5   For thoughtful exceptions, see for example Brian Lee, *American Fiction* 27–29, and Harold Kaplan, *Power and Order* x–xi.

6   See Žižek, *The Sublime Object of Ideology* 21–23.

7   Equally pertinent is Althusser's observation, in *Reading Capital*, that "[d]espite the massive 'obviousness' of the economic 'given' in the capitalist mode of production, and precisely because of the 'massive' character of this fetichized 'obviousness,' the only way to the essence of the economic is to construct its concept" (179).

8   See Althusser, *Reading Capital* 186–89.

9   See Baudrillard, *The Mirror of Production* 84–91.

10 See Althusser's argument as to why Marxism is not historicism in *Reading Capital* 119–44.

11 See Goux, *Les Monnayeurs du langage* 33–34.

12 See Vološinov, *Marxism and the Philosophy of Language* 9–24.

13 See Guattari, *L'Inconscient machinique* 7–19.

14 See in particular part two of *Negative Dialectics*, "Negative Dialectics: Concept and Categories" 134–207.

15 See also Jameson's discussion of the prison of the system in *Late Marxism* 25–34.

16 In *The Survival of Capitalism*, Lefebvre reiterates this same basic premise: "Those who believe in the system are making a mistake, for in fact no complete, achieved totality exists. However, there is certainly a 'whole', which has absorbed its historical conditions, reabsorbed its elements and succeeded in mastering some of the contradictions, though without arriving at the desired cohesion and homogeneity" (10). For a more elaborate discussion of the concept of totality, see Best, "Jameson, Totality, and the Postmodern Critique." For a discussion of the open system with a special emphasis on Deleuze, see Mengue, *Gilles Deleuze ou le système du multiple* 66–69.

17 See Bihr, *L'Économie fétiche* 35–44.

18 See Deleuze, *Anti-Oedipus* 259–60.

19 As Deleuze and Guattari put it, in *Anti-Oedipus*, the "death of a social machine has never been heralded by a disharmony or a dysfunction; on the contrary, social machines make a habit of feeding on the contradictions they give rise to, on the crises they provoke, on the anxieties they *engender*, and on the infernal operations they regenerate. Capitalism has learned this, and has ceased doubting itself... No one has ever died from contradictions. And the more it breaks down, the more it schizophrenizes, the better it works, the American way" (151).

20 Particularly useful in conceiving of the system's dynamics is Ilya Prigogine and Isabelle Stengers' concept of dissipative structures: "We now know that far from equilibrium, new types of structures may originate spontaneously. In far-from-equilibrium conditions we may have transformation from disorder, from thermal

chaos, into order. New dynamic states of matter may originate, states that reflect the interaction of a given system with its surroundings. We have called these new structures *dissipative structures* to emphasize the constitutive role of dissipative processes in their formation.... It is remarkable that near-bifurcations systems present large fluctuations of evolution, and the famous law of large numbers in its usual sense breaks down. A small fluctuation may start an entire new evolution that will drastically change the whole behavior of the microscopic system. The analogy with social phenomena, even with history, is inescapable. Far from opposing 'chance' and 'necessity,' we now see both aspects as essential in the description of non-linear systems far from equilibrium" (12–14).

BIBLIOGRAPHY

Adorno, Theodor W. "Culture and Administration." Trans. Wes Blomster. *Telos* 37 (1978): 93–111.
——. *Minima Moralia: Reflections from Damaged Life*. Trans. E. F. N. Jephcott. London: NLB, 1974.
——. *Negative Dialectics*. Trans. E. B. Ashton. New York: Seabury P, 1973.
Adorno, Theodor W., and Max Horkheimer. *Dialectic of Enlightenment*. Trans. J. Cumming. New York: Continuum, 1982.
Althusser, Louis. *Éléments d'autocritique*. Paris: Librairie Hachette, 1974.
——. *For Marx*. Trans. Ben Brewster. New York: Pantheon, 1969.
——. *Lenin and Philosophy and Other Essays*. Trans. Ben Brewster. New York: Monthly Review P, 1971.
Althusser, Louis, and Étienne Balibar. *Reading Capital*. Trans. Ben Brewster. London: NLB, 1970.
Axelos, Kostas. *Systématique ouverte*. Paris: Minuit, 1984.
Badiou, Alain. *Conditions*. Paris: Seuil, 1992.
Bakhtin, Mikhail M. *The Dialogic Imagination: Four Essays*. Trans. Caryl Emerson and Michael Holquist. Ed. Michael Holquist. Austin: U of Texas P, 1981.
Barthes, Roland. *Critical Essays*. Trans. Richard Howard. Evanston: Northwestern UP, 1972.
——. "L'Effet de réel." *Communications* 11 (1968): 84–89.
——. *Mythologies*. Paris: Seuil, 1957.
Baudrillard, Jean. *America*. Trans. Chris Turner. London: Verso, 1988.
——. *L'Échange symbolique et la mort*. Paris: Gallimard, 1976.
——. *For a Critique of the Political Economy of the Sign*. Trans. Charles Levin. St. Louis: Telos P, 1981.

——. *The Mirror of Production*. Trans. Mark Poster. St. Louis: Telos P, 1975.

——. *Le Système des objets*. Paris: Gallimard, 1968.

——. *La Transparence du mal: Essai sur les phénomènes extêmes*. Paris: Galilée, 1990.

Barrett, Michèle. *The Politics of Truth: From Marx to Foucault*. Stanford: Stanford UP, 1991.

Bell, Daniel. *The Cultural Contradictions of Capitalism*. New York: Basic, 1976.

Benjamin, Walter. *Charles Baudelaire: A Lyric Poet in the Era of High Capitalism*. Trans. Harry Zohn. London: NLB, 1973.

——. *Illuminations*. Ed. Hannah Arendt. Trans. Harry Zohn. New York: Harcourt, 1968.

Bergler, Edmund. *The Psychology of Gambling*. New York: Hill and Wang, 1957.

Berthier, Philippe. *Stendhal et la sainte famille*. Genève: Librairie Droz, 1983.

Bersani, Leo. "Rejoinder to Walter Benn Michaels." *Critical Inquiry* 8.1 (1981): 158–64.

Best, Steven. "Jameson, Totality, and the Poststructuralist Critique." *Postmodernism/Jameson/Critique*. Ed. Douglas Kellner. Washington, DC: Maisonneuve P, 1989. 333–68.

Bihr, Alain. *L'Économie fétiche: Fragment d'une theorie de la praxis capitaliste*. Paris: Le Sycomore, 1979.

Blanchot, Maurice. *L'Amitié*. Paris: Gallimard, 1971.

——. *L'Entretien infini*. Paris: Gallimard, 1969.

——. *The Writing of the Disaster*. Trans. Ann Smock. Lincoln: U of Nebraska P, 1986.

Bowlby, Rachel. *Just Looking: Consumer Culture in Dreiser, Gissing and Zola*. New York: Methuen, 1985.

Brady, Patrick. "Chaos et naturalisme." *Les Cahiers naturalistes* 67 (1993): 201–09.

——. "Mutilation, Fragmentation, Creation: Zola's Ideology of Order." *Emile Zola and the Arts*. Eds. Jean-Max Guieu and Alison Hilton. Washington, DC: Georgetown UP, 1988. 115–22.

——. "La Théorie du chaos et *L'Œuvre*: Peinture, structure, thématique." *Les Cahiers naturalistes* 66 (1992): 105–12.

Brenner, Reuven, and Gabrielle A. Brenner. *Gambling and Speculation: A Theory, History, and Future of Some Human Decisions*. Cambridge: Cambridge UP, 1990.

Brown, Bruce. *Marx, Freud, and the Critique of Everyday Life: Toward a Permanent Cultural Revolution*. New York: Monthly

Review P, 1973.

Brown, E. K. *Rhythm in the Novel.* Lincoln: U of Nebraska P, 1978.

Bruss, Elizabeth W. "The Game of Literature and Some Literary Games." *New Literary History* 9.1 (1977): 153–72.

Buckley, William K. "Realism Still Knocking on Academe's Door." *Studies in the Novel* 18.3 (1986): 314–19.

Buck-Morss, Susan. *The Dialectics of Seeing: Walter Benjamin and the Arcades Project.* Cambridge: MIT Press, 1989.

Butler, Judith. "Contingent Foundations: Feminism and the Question of 'Postmodernism'." *Feminists Theorize the Political.* Eds. Judith Butler and Joan W. Scott. New York: Routledge, 1992. 3–21.

Butler, Robert James. "Movement in Dreiser's *Sister Carrie.*" *The Dreiser Newsletter* 11.1 (1980): 1–12.

Caillois, Roger. *Man, Play, and Games.* Trans. Meyer Barash. New York: The Free Press of Glencoe, 1961.

Cain, William E. "Presence and Power in *McTeague.*" *American Realism: New Essays.* Ed. Eric Sundquist. Baltimore: John Hopkins UP, 1982. 199–214.

Caron, James E. "Grotesque Naturalism: The Significance of the Comic in *McTeague.*" *Texas Studies in Literature and Language* 31.2 (1989): 288–317.

Carton, Evan. "American Literary Histories as a Social Practice." *Raritan* 8.3 (1989): 99–133.

Cassuto, Leonard. "'Keeping Company' with the Old Folks: Unravelling the Edges of *McTeague's* Deterministic Fabric." *American Literary Realism* 25.2 (1993): 46–55.

Castoriadis, Cornelius. *The Imaginary Institutions of Society.* Trans. Kathleen Blamey. Cambridge: MIT Press, 1987.

——. "Time and Creation." *Chronotypes: The Construction of Time.* Eds. John Bender and David E. Wellbery. Stanford: Stanford UP, 1991. 38–64.

Chevrel, Yves. *Le Naturalisme.* Paris: PUF, 1982.

Civello, Paul. *American Literary Naturalism and its Twentieth-Century Transformations: Frank Norris, Ernest Hemingway, and Don DeLillo.* Athens: U of Georgia P, 1994.

Cohen, Stanley, and Laurie Taylor. *Escape Attempts: The Theory and Practice of Resistance to Everyday Life.* London: Allen Lane, 1976.

Collot, Sylvie. *Les Lieux du désir: Topologie amoureuse de Zola.* Paris: Hachette, 1992.

Colvert, James. "Stephen Crane and Postmodern Theory."

American Literary Realism 18.1 (1995): 4–22.

Conder, John J. *Naturalism in American Fiction: The Classical Phase.* Lexington: U of Kentucky P, 1984.

Cullick, Jonathan S. "Configurations of Events in the Narrative Structure of *McTeague.*" *American Literary Realism* 27.3 (1995): 37–47.

David-Ménard, Monique. *Hysteria from Freud to Lacan: Body and Language in Psychoanalysis.* Trans. Catherine Porter. Ithaca: Cornell UP, 1989.

Debord, Guy. *Society of the Spectacle.* Detroit: Black, 1977.

Deleuze, Gilles. *Critique et clinique.* Paris: Minuit, 1993.

——. *Foucault.* Trans. and ed. Seán Hand. Minneapolis: U of Minnesota P, 1988.

——. *Masochism: An Interpretation of Coldness and Cruelty.* Trans. Jean McNeil. New York: Braziller, 1971.

——. *Proust et les signes.* 4th rev. ed. Paris: PUF, 1976.

Deleuze, Gilles, and Félix Guattari. *Anti-Oedipus: Capitalism and Schizophrenia.* Trans. Robert Hurley, Mark Seem, and Helen R. Lane. Minneapolis: U of Minnesota P, 1983.

——. *A Thousand Plateaus: Capitalism and Schizophrenia.* Trans. Brian Massumi. Minneapolis: U of Minnesota P, 1987.

Derrida, Jacques. "Economimesis." *Mimesis: Des articulations.* Paris: Flammarion, 1975. 55–93.

——. "How to Avoid Speaking: Denials." Trans. Ken Frieden. *Languages of the Unsayable: The Play of Negativity in Literature and Literary Theory.* Ed. Sanford Budick and Wolfgang Iser. New York: Columbia UP, 1989. 3–70

——. *Spectres de Marx: L'État de la dette, le travail du deuil et la nouvelle internationale.* Paris: Galilée, 1993.

——. *Writing and Difference.* Trans. Alan Bass. Chicago: U of Chicago P, 1978.

Dreiser, Theodore. *The Financier.* New York: New American Library, 1967.

——. *Sister Carrie.* Ed. Lee Clark Mitchell. Oxford: Oxford UP, 1991.

——. *Theodore Dreiser: A Selection of Uncollected Prose.* Ed. Donald Pizer. Detroit: Wayne State UP, 1977.

Elliott, Emory, ed. *Columbia Literary History of the United States.* New York: Columbia, 1988.

Felman, Shoshana. *La Folie et la chose littéraire.* Paris: Seuil, 1978.

Fisher, Philip. "Acting, Reading, Fortune's Wheel: *Sister Carrie* and the Life History of Objects." *American Realism: New Essays.*

Ed. Eric Sundquist. Baltimore: John Hopkins UP, 1982. 259–77.

Fleissner, Jennifer. "The Work of Womanhood in American Naturalism." *Differences* 8.1 (1996): 57–93.

Forster, E. M. *Aspects of the Novel*. New York: Harcourt, 1927.

Foucault, Michel. *The Archaeology of Knowledge and the Discourse on Language*. Trans. A. M. Sheridan Smith. New York: Pantheon, 1972.

——. *Language, Counter-Memory, Practice: Selected Essays and Interviews, 1972–1977*. Ed. Donald F. Bouchard. Ithaca: Cornell UP, 1977.

——. *Power/Knowledge: Selected Interviews and Other Writings, 1972–1977*. Ed. Colin Gordon. New York: Pantheon, 1980.

——. "The Subject and Power." *Critical Inquiry* 8.4 (1982): 777–95.

Fox, Richard Wightman, and T. J. Jackson Lears, eds. *The Culture of Consumption: Critical Essays in American History, 1880–1980*. New York: Pantheon, 1983.

Freedman, William. "Oral Passivity and Oral Sadism in Norris's *McTeague*." *Literature and Psychology* 30.2 (1980): 52–61.

French, Warren. *Frank Norris*. New York: Twayne, 1962.

Freud, Sigmund. *The Standard Edition of the Complete Psychological Works of Sigmund Freud*. Trans. James Strachey. 24 vols. London: Hogarth P, 1953–1974.

Furst, Lilian R. *All is True: The Claims and Strategies of Realist Fiction*. Durham: Duke UP, 1995.

Gardner, Joseph H. "Dickens, Romance, and *McTeague*: A Study in Mutual Interpretation." *Essays in Literature* 1.1 (1974): 69–82.

Gilder, George. *Wealth and Poverty*. New York: Basic, 1981.

Gilman, Sander L. *Disease and Representation: Images of Illness from Madness to Aids*. Ithaca: Cornell UP, 1988.

Goux, Jean-Joseph. "Catégories de l'échange: Idéalité, symbolicité, réalité." *Encyclopedie philosophique universelle*. Paris: PUF, 1989. 227–33.

——. *Freud, Marx: Économie et symbolique*. Paris: Seuil, 1973.

——. "General Economics and Postmodern Capitalism." Trans. Kathryn Ascheim and Rhonda Garelick. *Yale French Studies* 78 (1990): 206–24.

——. *Les Monnayeurs du langage*. Paris: Galilée, 1984.

——. *Symbolic Economies: After Marx and Freud*. Trans. Jennifer Curtiss Cage. Ithaca: Cornell UP, 1990.

Graham, Don. *The Fiction of Frank Norris: The Aesthetic Context*. Columbia: U of Missouri P, 1978.

Guattari, Félix. *L'Inconscient machinique: Essais de schizo-analyze*. Paris: Recherches, 1979.

Hamon, Philippe. "Un Discours contraint." *Poétique* 16 (1973): 411–45.

Haug, Wolfgang Fritz. *Critique of Commodity Aesthetics: Appearance, Sexuality and Advertising in Capitalist Society*. Trans. Robert Bock. Cambridge: Polity P, 1986.

Hawthorne, Nathaniel. *The Complete Short Stories of Nathaniel Hawthorne*. Garden City, NY: Hanover House, 1959.

Hochman, Barbara. "A Portrait of the Artist as a Young Actress: The Rewards of Representation in *Sister Carrie*." *New Essays on Sister Carrie*. Ed. Donald Pizer. Cambridge: Cambridge UP, 1991. 43–64.

——. "*Vandover and the Brute*: The Decisive Experience of Loss." *Western American Literature* 19.1 (1984): 3–15.

Hofstadter, Richard. *The Age of Reform*. New York: Knopf, 1955.

——. *Social Darwinism in American Thought*. Rev. ed. Boston: Beacon P, 1955.

Howard, June. *Form and History in American Literary Naturalism*. Chapel Hill: U of North Carolina P, 1985.

Howe, Irving. "Naturalism and Taste." *A Critic's Notebook*. Ed. Nicholas Howe. New York: Harcourt Brace, 1994. 216–28.

Huizinga, Johan. *Homo Ludens: A Study of the Play-Element in Culture*. Boston: Beacon P, 1950.

Hutchinson, Peter. *Games Authors Play*. London: Methuen, 1983.

Jameson, Fredric. *Late Marxism: Adorno, or, the Persistence of the Dialectic*. London: Verso, 1990.

——. *Marxism and Form: Twentieth-Century Dialectical Theories of Literature*. Princeton: Princeton UP, 1971.

——. *The Political Unconscious: Narrative as a Socially Symbolic Act*. Ithaca: Cornell UP, 1981.

——. *Postmodernism, or, The Cultural Logic of Late Capitalism*. Durham: Duke UP, 1992.

——. "Seriality in Modern Literature." *Bucknell Review* 18.1 (1970): 63–80.

Jay, Gregory S. *America The Scrivener: Deconstruction and the Subject of Literary History*. Ithaca: Cornell UP, 1990.

Kaplan, Amy. "Naturalism with a Difference." *American Quarterly* 40.4 (1988): 582–89.

——. *The Social Construction of American Realism*. Chicago: U of Chicago P, 1988.

Kaplan, Harold. *Power and Order: Henry James and the Naturalist*

Tradition in American Fiction. Chicago: U of Chicago P, 1981.

Kristeva, Julia. *Tales of Love.* Trans. Leon S. Roudiez. New York: Columbia UP, 1987.

Lacan, Jacques. *Écrits: A Selection.* Trans. Alan Sheridan. New York: Norton, 1977.

——. "Radiophonie." *Scilicet* 2–3 (1970): 55–99.

——. *The Seminar of Jacques Lacan, Book 2: The Ego in Freud's Theory and in the Technique of Psychoanalysis, 1954–1955.* Trans. Sylvana Tomaselli. Ed. Jacques-Alain Miller. New York: Norton, 1988.

——. *Le Séminaire de Jacques Lacan, livre 20: Encore, 1972–1973.* Ed. Jacques-Alain Miller. Paris: Seuil, 1975.

——. *Le Séminaire de Jacques Lacan, livre 17: L'Envers de la psychanalyse, 1969–1970.* Ed. Jacques-Alain Miller. Paris: Seuil, 1991.

——. *The Seminar of Jacques Lacan, Book 11: The Four Fundamental Concepts of Psychoanalysis.* Trans. Alan Sheridan. New York: Norton, 1977.

——. *Le Séminaire de Jacques Lacan, livre 8: Le Transfert, 1960–1961.* Ed. Jacques-Alain Miller. Paris: Seuil, 1991.

——. "Seminar on 'The Purloined Letter'." Trans. Jeffery Mehlman. *Yale French Studies* 48 (1972): 38–72.

Laclau, Ernesto, and Chantal Mouffe. *Hegemony and Socialist Strategy: Towards a Radical Democratic Politics.* London: Verso, 1985.

Lears, T. J. Jackson. "Beyond Veblen: Rethinking Consumer Culture in America." *Consuming Visions: Accumulation and Display of Goods in America, 1880–1920.* Ed. Simon Bronner. New York: Norton, 1989. 73–97.

——. *No Place of Grace: Antimodernism and the Transformation of American Culture, 1880–1920.* New York: Pantheon, 1981.

Leclaire, Serge. *Psychanalyser: Un essai sur l'ordre de l'inconscient et la pratique de la lettre.* Paris: Seuil, 1968.

——. *Rompre les charmes: Recueil pour des enchantés de la psychanalyse.* Paris: InterÉditions, 1981.

Lee, Brian. *American Fiction, 1865–1940.* London: Longman, 1987.

Lefebvre, Henri. *Le Droit à la ville.* Paris: Anthropos, 1968.

——. *Éléments de rythmanalyse: Introduction à la connaissance des rythmes.* Paris: Éditions Syllepse, 1992.

——. "The Everyday and Everydayness." Trans. Christine Levich. *Yale French Studies* 73 (1987): 7–11.

——. *Everyday Life in the Modern World.* Trans. Sacha Rabinovitch. London: Allen Lane The Penguin P, 1971.

——. *Fondements d'une sociologie de la quotidienneté.* Paris: L'Arche, 1961. Vol 2 of *Critique de la vie quotidienne.* 3 vols. 1947–81.

——. *L'Idéologie structuraliste.* Paris: Anthropos, 1971.

——. *Une Pensée devenue monde: Faut-il abandonner Marx?* Paris: Fayard, 1980.

——. *Pour connaître Karl Marx.* 3rd ed. Paris: Bordas, 1985.

——. *The Production of Space.* Trans. Donald Nicholson-Smith. Oxford: Blackwell, 1991.

——. "Réflections sur le structuralisme et l'histoire." *Cahiers internationaux de sociologie* 35 (1963): 3–24.

——. *The Survival of Capitalism: Reproduction of the Relations of Production.* Trans. Frank Bryant. London: Allison & Busby, 1976.

——. "Toward a Leftist Cultural Politics: Remarks Occasioned by the Centenary of Marx's Death." Trans. David Reifman. *Marxism and the Interpretation of Culture.* Ed. Cary Nelson. Urbana: U of Illinois P, 1988. 75–88.

——. *Vers le cybernanthrope.* Paris: Denoël/Gonthier, 1971.

Lefebvre, Henri, and Catherine Régulier. "Le Projet rythmanalytique." *Communications* 41 (1985): 191–99.

Lehan, Richard. "The City, The Self, and the Modes of Narrative Discourse." *New Essays on Sister Carrie.* Ed. Donald Pizer. Cambridge: Cambridge UP, 1991. 65–85.

——. "The European Background." *The Cambridge Companion to American Realism and Naturalism: Howells to London.* Ed. Donald Pizer. Cambridge: Cambridge UP, 1996. 47–73.

——. "The Theoretical Limits of the New Historicism." *New Literary History* 21.3 (1990): 533–53.

Lévi-Strauss, Claude. *Structural Anthropology.* Trans. Claire Jacobson and Brooke Grundfest Schoepf. Vol. 1. New York: Basic, 1963. 2 vols. 1963–76.

Lévy, Pierre. *Qu'est ce que le virtuel?* Paris: Éditions la Découverte, 1995.

Lorrain, Jorge. *Ideology and Culture: Modernity and the Third World Presence.* Cambridge: Polity P, 1994.

Lyotard, Jean François. *Dérive à partir de Marx et Freud.* Paris: Union Générale d'Éditions, 1973.

——. *Discours, figure.* Paris: Éditions Klincksieck, 1971.

Macy, John. "Frank Norris, *Vandover and the Brute*: Some Notes on

His Later Works." *Critical Essays on Frank Norris*. Ed. Don Graham. Boston: G. K. Hall, 1980. 35–38.

Marx, Karl. *Capital: A Critique of Political Economy*. Vol 1. Trans. Ben Fowkes. New York: Vintage, 1977. 2 vols.

——. *A Contribution to the Critique of Political Economy*. Trans. N. I. Stone. Chicago: Kerr, 1911.

——. *The Economic and Philosophic Manuscripts of 1844*. Trans. Martin Milligan. Ed. Dirk J. Struik. New York: International Publishers, 1982.

——. *Grundrisse: Foundations of the Critique of Political Economy*. Trans. Martin Nicolaus. Baltimore: Penguin, 1973.

McAleer, John J. "Flux Metaphor in *Sister Carrie*." *The Dreiser Newsletter* 15.1 (1984): 1–9.

Mengue, Philippe. *Gilles Deleuze ou le système du multiple*. Paris: Éditions Kimé, 1994.

Michaels, Walter Benn. *The Gold Standard and the Logic of Naturalism: American Literature at the Turn of the Century*. Berkeley: U of California P, 1987.

——. "Race into Culture: A Critical Genealogy of Cultural Identity." *Critical Inquiry* 18 (1992): 655–85.

Milner, Marion. *On Not Being Able to Paint*. 2nd ed. New York: International Universities P, 1957.

Mitchell, Lee Clark. *Determined Fictions: American Literary Naturalism*. New York: Columbia UP, 1989.

——. "Naturalism and the Language of Determinism." *Columbia Literary History of the United States*. Ed. Emory Elliott. New York: Columbia, 1988. 524–45.

Moers, Ellen, "The Finesse of Dreiser." *Sister Carrie: An Authoritative Text, Background, and Sources Criticism*. Ed. Donald Pizer. 2nd ed. New York: Norton, 1991. 517–23.

Moretti, Franco. *Signs Taken for Wonders: Essays in the Sociology of Literary Forms*. Trans. Susan Fischer, David Forgacs, and David Miller. London: Verso, 1983.

Morrow, Nancy. *Dreadful Games: The Play of Desire in the Nineteenth-Century Novel*. Kent: Kent State UP, 1988.

Murayama, Kiyohiko. "Is *Sister Carrie* Really Not Anti-Capitalist at All?: Dreiser's Criticism of Capitalism." *Dreiser Studies* 26.1 (1995): 3–10.

Nietzsche, Friedrich. *Thus Spoke Zarathustra: A Book for All and None*. Trans. Walter Kaufmann. New York: Penguin, 1978.

Norris, Frank. *Collected Writings Hitherto Unpublished in Book Form*. Garden City, NY: Doubleday, Doran & Company, 1928.

Vol 10 of *The Complete Edition of Frank Norris*. 10 vols. 1928.
——. *The Literary Criticism of Frank Norris*. Ed. Donald Pizer. New York: Russel & Russel, 1976
——. *McTeague: A Story of San Francisco*. Ed. Kevin Starr. New York: Penguin, 1982.
——. *The Octopus: A Story of California*. New York: Batman, 1971.
——. *The Pit*. Columbus: Charles E. Merrill Publishing Company, 1970.
——. *Vandover and The Brute*. Lincoln: U of Nebraska P, 1978.
Orvell, Miles. *The Real Thing: Imitation and Authenticity in American Culture, 1880–1940*. Chapel Hill: U of North Carolina P, 1989.
"*The Pit*: A Dispassionate Examination of Frank Norris's Posthumous Novel." *Critical Essays on Frank Norris*. Ed. Don Graham. Boston: G. K. Hall, 1980. 32–34.
Parret, Herman. *Le Sublime du quotidien*. Paris: Hadès-Benjamins, 1988.
Pizer, Donald. "Introduction." *The Cambridge Companion to American Realism and Naturalism: Howells to London*. Ed. Donald Pizer. Cambridge: Cambridge UP, 1996. 1–18.
——. *The Novels of Frank Norris*. New York: Haskell, 1973.
——. *Realism and Naturalism in Nineteenth-Century American Literature*. Rev. ed. Carbondale: Southern Illinois UP, 1984.
——. *The Theory and Practice of American Literary Naturalism: Selected Essays and Reviews*. Carbondale: Southern Illinois UP, 1993.
Prigogine, Ilya, and Isabelle Stengers. *Order out of Chaos: Man's New Dialogue with Nature*. London: New Science Library, 1984.
Resch, Robert Paul. *Althusser and the Renewal of Marxist Social Theory*. Berkeley: U of California P, 1992.
Safouan, Moustafa. *Pleasure and Being*. Trans. Martin Thom. New York: St. Martin's P, 1983.
Sartre, Jean Paul. *Critique de la raison dialectique*. Paris: Gallimard, 1960.
Seltzer, Mark. *Bodies and Machines*. New York: Routledge, 1992.
——. *Henry James and the Art of Power*. Ithaca: Cornell UP, 1984.
Sephiha, H.-Vidal. "Introduction à l'étude de l'intensif." *Langages* 18 (1970): 104–20.
Serres, Michel. "Estime." *Politiques de la philosophie*. Ed. Dominique Grisoni. Paris: Bernard Grasset, 1976. 99–120.
——. *Feux et signaux de brume: Zola*. Paris: Bernard Grasset, 1975.
——. *The Parasite*. Trans. Lawrence R. Schehr. Baltimore: Johns

Hopkins UP, 1982.

Shulman, Robert. "Dreiser and the Dynamics of American Capitalism." *Sister Carrie: An Authoritative Text, Background, and Sources Criticism.* Ed. Donald Pizer. 2nd ed. New York: Norton, 1991. 560–75.

Smith, Allan Lloyd. "Frank Norris: The Crisis of Representation." *American Literary Realism* 27.2 (1995): 75–83.

Spindler, Michael. *American Literature and Social Change: William Dean Howells to Arthur Miller.* Bloomington: Indiana UP, 1983.

Stallybrass, Peter, and Allon White. *The Politics and Poetics of Transgression.* Ithaca: Cornell UP, 1986.

Sternberger, Dolf. *Panorama of the Nineteenth Century.* Trans. Joachim Neugroschel. New York: Urizen books, 1977.

Susman, Warren I. *Culture as History: The Transformation of American Society in the Twentieth Century.* New York: Pantheon, 1984.

Tanner, Tony. *City of Words: American Fiction 1950–1970.* New York: Harper & Row, 1971.

Todorov, Tzvetan. "The Verbal Age." Trans. Patricia Martin Gibby. *Critical Inquiry* 4.2 (1977): 351–71.

Trachtenberg, Alan. *The Incorporation of America: Culture and Society in the Gilded Age.* New York: Hill, 1982.

Varela, Francisco J., Evan Thompson, and Eleanor Rosch. *The Embodied Mind: Cognitive Science and Human Experience.* Cambridge: MIT Press, 1991.

Veblen, Thorstein. *Theory of the Leisure Class: An Economic Study of Institutions.* New York: Modern library, 1918.

Verma, S. N. *Frank Norris: A Literary Legend.* New Delhi: Vikas Publishing House, 1986.

Vološinov, V. Nikolaevic. *Freudianism: A Marxist Critique.* Trans. I. R. Titunik. Ed. Neal Bruss. New York: Academic P, 1976.

——. *Marxism and the Philosophy of Language.* Trans. Ladislav Matejka and I. R. Titunik. London: Harvard UP, 1986.

Walcutt, Charles Child. *American Literary Naturalism: A Divided Stream.* Minneapolis: U of Minnesota P, 1956.

Weber, Sherry M. "Individuation as Praxis." *Critical Interruptions: New Left Perspectives on Herbert Marcuse.* Ed. Paul Breines. New York: Herder and Herder, 1970. 22–59.

Wiggershaus, Rolf. *The Frankfurt School: Its History, Theories, and Political Significance.* Trans. Michael Robertson. Cambridge: MIT Press, 1994.

Williams, Raymond. *Marxism and Literature.* Oxford: Oxford UP,

1977.

Wilson, Christopher. "Containing Multitudes: Realism, Historicism, American Studies." *American Quarterly* 41:3 (1989): 466–97.

Winnicott, D. W. *Playing and Reality.* London: Routledge, 1991.

Wolfe, Cary. "Antinomies of Liberalism: The Politics of 'Belief' and the Project of Americanist Criticism." *Discovering Difference: New Essays on American Culture.* Ed. Chris K. Lohmann. Bloomington: Indiana UP, 1993. 126–51.

Young, Michael. *The Metronomic Society: Natural Rhythms and Human Timetables.* Cambridge: Harvard UP, 1988.

Žižek, Slavoj. *The Sublime Object of Ideology.* London: Verso, 1989.

——. *Tarrying with the Negative: Kant, Hegel, and the Critique of Ideology.* Durham: Duke UP, 1993.

MODERN AMERICAN LITERATURE
New Approaches

Yoshinobu Hakutani, General Editor

The books in this series deal with many of the major writers known as American realists, modernists, and post-modernists from 1880 to the present. This category of writers will also include less known ethnic and minority writers, a majority of whom are African American, some are Native American, Mexican American, Japanese American, Chinese American, and others. The series might also include studies on well-known contemporary writers, such as James Dickey, Allen Ginsberg, Gary Snyder, John Barth, John Updike, and Joyce Carol Oates. In general, the series will reflect new critical approaches such as deconstructionism, new historicism, psychoanalytical criticism, gender criticism/feminism, and cultural criticism.

For additional information about this series or for the submission of manuscripts, please contact:

Peter Lang Publishing
Acquisitions Department
516 N. Charles St., 2nd Floor
Baltimore, MD 21201